THE REFERENCE SHELF   VOLUME 45 NUMBER 6

CRISIS IN
URBAN HOUSING

EDITED BY
GRANT S. McCLELLAN

Editor, Current Magazine

THE H. W. WILSON COMPANY
NEW YORK   1974

THE REFERENCE SHELF

The books in this series contain reprints of articles, excerpts from books, and addresses on current issues and social trends in the United States and other countries. There are six separately bound numbers in each volume, all of which are generally published in the same calendar year. One number is a collection of recent speeches; each of the others is devoted to a single subject and gives background information and discussion from various points of view, concluding with a comprehensive bibliography. Books in the series may be purchased individually or on subscription.

Library of Congress Cataloging in Publication Data

McClellan, Grant S   comp.
  Crisis in urban housing.

  (The Reference shelf, v. 45, no. 6)
  Bibliography: p.
 1. Housing--United States. I. Title. II. Series.
HD7293.M18   301.5'4'0973   73-22126
ISBN 0-8242-0509-X

PREFACE

That a housing crisis faces America is widely admitted. The dimensions of the crisis are also widely understood. But no clear conception of the crisis is apparent to the vast majority of the people who live in our overcrowded cities and slums or in dilapidated homes of our countrysides. A somewhat clearer idea is, however, emerging after the two decades since World War II when housing officials, social scientists, and our political leaders turned their attention to the housing problems of the nation.

Now it is more and more realized that America faces not only a housing crisis, but a crisis involving our urban life itself. We are fast becoming an urban civilization (concentrated in limited areas of our vast continental domain), but we are not sure what this urban society is or will become. Are we destined to live in cities with suburbs? Are the suburbs to become the typical living areas of tomorrow? Will the concentrations of population constitute cities as we have known them, or become vast, sprawling extensions of what history has called cities?

This compilation necessarily deals with these larger aspects of the housing crisis. For the term *housing* has in recent years come to mean far more than the mere matter of building a house, per se, or even an apartment complex of many dwellings. Housing of multitudes, in fact of millions, faces us now, not only in terms of housing a family, of housing many families. We are now confronted with problems of great magnitude in terms of population density, in terms of livelihood for our congested population (where it is congested), in terms of transportation, in terms of racial and ethnic adjustments, in terms of governing city and suburban sprawl, in terms of . . . the problems go on and on.

3

Against this larger background, this compilation deals first with the dimensions of the housing crisis in the narrower sense. Thus Section I spells out the "crisis" in terms of living conditions, government problems, housing costs. Section II deals with the government policies that have evolved or are proposed to deal with the housing crisis. Section III covers several programs, some of them futuristic, suggesting what is being (or may be) done to solve housing problems. And Section IV is devoted to the general question of housing within the wider context of the ever-expanding urbanization of the country.

The editor wishes to thank the authors and the publishers of the selections which follow for permission to reprint them in this compilation.

GRANT S. McCLELLAN

December 1973

A NOTE TO THE READER

The reader's attention is directed to other Reference Shelf compilations dealing with related aspects of the problems covered in this volume: *The City in Crisis,* edited by Irwin Isenberg (Volume 40, Number 1), published in 1968; *Problems of Mass Transportation,* edited by Diana Reische (Volume 42, Number 5), published in 1970; *Land Use in the United States,* edited by Grant S. McClellan (Volume 43, Number 2), published in 1971.

CONTENTS

III. NEW HOUSING PROGRAMS

IV. HOUSING IN THE URBAN FUTURE

I. THE DIMENSIONS OF THE CRISIS

EDITOR'S INTRODUCTION

As noted in the Preface to this compilation, the housing crisis is inextricably bound up with the larger crisis of our urban civilization. The broader aspects of that crisis are dealt with in Section IV below. Here factors relating more directly to housing are explored. Opening the section is an article covering many facets of our housing problems by Joyce Pazianos, a housing specialist in the AFL-CIO Department of Urban Affairs.

The plight of America's slums is dealt with in the next two articles. Writing of what he terms "urban wastelands," Dial Torgerson of the Los Angeles *Times* staff, touches on the conditions of most of our larger cities. His article is based on reports from other Los Angeles *Times* staff members throughout the nation. Next, Pierre De Vise, project director of the Chicago Regional Hospital Study, explains the housing crisis in America's third largest city.

The problem of crime, all too well known to be related to city slum conditions, is, moreover intimately related to the type of housing erected in some cases in an effort to provide better housing for former slum-area residents. Jack Rosenthal, a reporter for the New York *Times*, gives details of a study showing that high-rise apartment dwellings generate high crime rates. His story is based on a study conducted by New York University's Institute of Planning and Housing.

The next two articles turn to housing for low-income groups and for blue-collar workers. The former relates to public housing, which is in deep trouble, not least because it has long been categorized as housing for "second-class citizens." J. S. Fuerst, assistant director of the Graduate

Program in Urban Studies at Chicago's Loyola University, explores various issues regarding public housing and suggests some improvements both in building and management of such units. George Sternlieb of the Urban Studies Center at Rutgers University deals with housing for blue-collar workers in an article entitled "Death of the American Dream House." He points out that in the last generation, workingmen of America have moved from being renters to owners. But many problems arise: Who builds such housing? How? Why? And where?

The last article of this section deals specifically with housing costs for individual homes or apartments. B. Bruce-Briggs, a member of the staff of the Hudson Institute maintains that the effects of inflation and rising family incomes over the past decade must be taken into account in assessing the cost factor as part of the housing crisis. He insists that most Americans, with the exception of the upper-middle class, are getting better housing at lower cost than at any time in the history of the United States.

THE MANY FACETS OF THE CRISIS [1]

The crisis in US housing has passed beyond a mere matter of the number of available units; it has become a social and economic crisis as well as a numbers problem.

Prospects for the future are dim. Homeownership may soon be considered a luxury available to only a small segment of our society. Four fifths of US households can no longer afford a conventional single-family house, according to estimates by George Romney, [former] secretary of housing and urban development [HUD]. At the same time, rents rise higher and higher, so that adequate-sized rental units are less likely to be a financially favorable alternative to home ownership.

[1] From "Housing: Clear Needs, Dim Prospects," by Joyce Pazianos, a housing specialist in the AFL-CIO Department of Urban Affairs. *American Federationist.* 79:1-8. Ag. '72. Reprinted by permission.

In 1968, when Congress pledged the nation to 26 million units of housing, including 6 million for low- and moderate-income families, it was both an acknowledgement of this country's housing problems and a commitment to solve them. Yet four years later the housing crisis is more severe, enveloping middle-income families as well as low- and moderate-income households. Workers frequently find themselves caught in the middle with incomes that are slightly too high to enable them to get federal assistance but too low to obtain housing in the private market.

The basic problem is that only a limited supply of adequate housing is available at a reasonable cost and in a suitable living environment. The cost of new housing continues to rise, while the supply of existing housing diminishes. Low- and moderate-income households find fewer and fewer opportunities for decent housing in the central city, but continue to be restricted in the suburbs. Middle-class households presently enjoy greater options, but rising costs threaten to eliminate many of these choices.

Underlying this dilemma are a number of factors, including exorbitant financing charges and rising land costs. Poor planning in the past has created an environmental crisis which now threatens to slow housing production markedly. Meanwhile, housing opportunities within existing stock decline as abandonment and foreclosures result in vacant housing and upset the normal flow of housing movement. The benefits of federal housing programs, the only source of housing for millions of families, are diluted by those developers, builders and financial institutions governed by financial rather than social motives.

The middle-income housing problem is essentially one of rising costs that threaten to affect both the ability to obtain housing and to maintain it. The lower-income family, on the other hand, faces a crisis which encompasses those same cost problems but also includes a variety of social and economic disabilities related to being poor.

In Department of Labor terms, a middle-income urban family of four would have an average annual budget of $10,971. The budget for lower-income families—$7,300—would be average for moderate-income families, but markedly higher than that enjoyed by low-income families where unemployment and female-headed households are common.

In terms of the family's money available for housing in those budgets, the Government indicates that the low-income family has up to $1,516 a year, or about $125 a month to allocate for housing, including utilities and maintenance, while the middle-income family has $2,600 a year or about $215 a month.

With the average manufacturing wage around $8,000 a year, most American workers are afflicted by one of the two crises in housing.

Housing Costs for Middle-Income Americans

For middle-income Americans, the national median sales price of a new single-family home jumped to $25,900, up 6.5 percent from the first quarter 1971 to the first quarter 1972. The median sales price of an existing home increased 7.5 percent from April 1971 to April 1972, with the median price of homes sold during that period at $26,450. The National Association of Home Builders estimates that for each $100 increase in the cost of housing, 14,000 families are priced out of the market.

The picture is no brighter in the rental market. From 1969 to 1970, the proportion of apartments renting for less than $150 monthly dropped from 32 to 13 percent; the proportion renting for more than $200 during this same period more than doubled, rising to 38 percent. Large working families have an additional problem: in 1969, 70 percent of all unsubsidized rental units with three or more bedrooms rented for $200 or more monthly.

It seems incredible, but these facts describe a period when home builders are pointing with pride to a record production year. More than 2.1 million units were started in 1971, including 1.3 million conventional units and 348,500 non-subsidized units insured by the Federal Housing Administration [FHA] and the Veterans Administration. Romney, the Home Builders and the Federal Home Loan Bank Board have all gone on record in projecting 2 million plus starts in 1972. Yet we are in the midst of a housing crisis.

An article in the May [1972] issue of *House and Home* magazine noted that HUD has issued new guidelines with respect to income and maximum mortgage amounts applicable to several of its housing programs. Under these guidelines, a $10,000 income homebuyer could qualify for no more than an $18,000 loan in the North and a $19,000 loan in the South. With the national median price of a new home in these areas at $28,950 and $26,130 respectively, the author concludes that the new guidelines "could have a chilling effect on the blue-collar market." If the $10,000 worker can only get an $18,000 or $19,000 loan, he needs an entire year's salary in reserve as a down payment to buy a "median" home.

In the middle-income crisis a significant factor in rising housing costs is undisputedly financing charges. Efforts to assure that an adequate supply of money is always available for an activity as socially important as housing continue to be thwarted. As a result, interest rates are kept high and frequently soar to prohibitive levels. During 1970, builders paid 12 to 15 percent interest rates on construction loans and homebuyers paid record high interest rates of 9 percent. A 1 percent increase in the interest rate will result in a 10 percent increase in monthly payments over the life of the mortgage.

In a paper presented to a congressional panel studying a variety of housing issues, Morton Schussheim, professor of city planning at the University of Pennsylvania, analyzed the effect of reducing various components of housing costs. Using the hypothetical example of a unit renting at $218 monthly, Schussheim compares the effect of lowering long-term financing costs, building costs, site costs and real estate taxes. At a 1 percent interest rate, rather than 7 percent, monthly payments are reduced 43 percent. Monthly payments become $125 as opposed to $218. Other reductions range from 17 percent—the result of a 25 percent reduction in building costs—to 6 percent, when site costs are lowered by 50 percent.

Schussheim's illustration supports the longtime AFL-CIO contention that attacks on labor costs should not be used to camouflage the real problems in providing reasonably priced housing. In reality, labor costs rank far down the list of causes of increased housing costs—well behind interest rates. Yet virtually every attempt to find an alternative to the financing problem has been resisted. Social responsibility has been ignored by lending institutions and housing has had to vie for credit with luxurious office buildings, speculative real estate ventures and even gambling casinos. A separate line of credit for family housing would contribute more than any other factor toward meeting US housing needs.

Settlement and Land Costs

Settlement costs also add substantially to the financial burden assumed by a would-be homeowner. Such costs vary widely across the country. A joint study by HUD and the Veterans Administration revealed that in 80 percent of the states, total settlement costs average over $1,500. The homebuyer's share of this cost is over $1,000 in three states—Maryland, New York and Alaska—and between $500 and $1,000 in 14 other states. In case studies of settlement costs in 12 counties, costs on a $20,000 home ranged from $369 in Ramsey County, Minnesota, to $824 in Essex County, New Jersey. The proportion of this cost paid by the buyer varied even more greatly, with a buyer paying about 30 percent in the Minnesota county compared to nearly 80 percent in the New Jersey county. Moreover, those costs technically paid by the seller are frequently passed on to the buyer in the price of the home.

Similarly, any solution to the problem of rising housing costs must deal with spiraling land costs. In its Third Annual Report on Housing Goals, the Nixon Administration admits that it has not developed policies to deal with this critical aspect of housing costs. Without a reversal of land costs, the single-family home will surely become a privilege of only the very wealthy. Land costs now represent over 20 percent of the total cost. During the 1960s, the average market price of a site for an FHA insured home rose at an annual rate of 7.2 percent, increasing 101.1 percent over the entire decade. Yet the size of the sites decreased.

Federal assistance programs often serve to inflate the price of land potentially available for unsubsidized residential construction. For example, under the Urban Renewal Program, the deteriorated, blighted condition of central city properties is ignored. No recognition is given to the fact that the large numbers of parcels that are either vacant or contain vacant, vandalized structures constitute an immense liability to a city forced to deal with the social problems and high incidence of crime that such properties foster. The government isn't required to pay inflated prices, but it often does.

As a result speculators are often permitted to obtain the market value of properties, with market value being defined as if the land were still in a prime location. Properties previously used for commercial purposes are purchased at higher commercial values, rather than the prices consistent with the residential use to which the land will be put. A recent example of the inflationary effect occurred in Washington, D.C., where the redevelopment agency paid $775,000 for a 1.2-acre parcel purchased 6 years earlier for $378,260. The example is not unusual.

Property taxes also encourage speculative land holding. Under the present system, assessments are based on present, versus potential use, and state laws tend to give preferential treatment to vacant or undeveloped land. Since taxes on such land remain relatively low, speculators have no incentive to put the land on the market, preferring to hold out for the right time and the right price. Efforts to accumulate large amounts of land are particularly hard hit by such practices. New community developments, looked to as part of the solution to the housing problem, may not prove able to provide reasonably priced housing if land costs are not curtailed.

A third situation detrimental to housing both in terms of number and cost of units produced is the inadequacy of utility systems, a legacy from years of helter-skelter home building when immediate profit took precedence over any concern for future development needs. Now, the shortage of sewage and energy facilities has begun to threaten home building in a number of communities. As such considerations slow or reduce production, they can also be expected to increase the cost of the more limited number of units built. In April . . . [1972], the Home Builders reported that over fifty communities had sewer moratoriums in effect. Such actions also contribute to rising land costs, making land with sewer connections already available more dear. The costs, of course, are passed on to the homebuyer or renter.

Gas moratoria are less widespread today, but will significantly affect the cost of housing built within the next ten years. A builder who does not properly evaluate the energy system he installs in a home built today may be passing on the major expense of conversion to the homeowner. The use of systems other than gas can result in increased cost for the homebuyer estimated in the range of $400 to $700.

Spurred by national environmental legislation, states and localities are enacting ordinances and laws that are already affecting housing starts. Throughout the country, local governments have held up rezoning decisions pending the development of land use plans and the conduct of environmental studies. Such studies are required under the National Environmental Policies Act of 1970 in connection with federally assisted projects likely to adversely affect the environment. While these requirements will do much to assure that housing is built in a suitable environment, they are also likely to lengthen the development period and add substantially to the cost.

The combination of these factors, plus a multitude of lesser problems, translates into the middle-income housing crisis. The seriousness of the problem is only beginning to be felt. Housing opportunities for middle-income households will become much more limited and families will increasingly "settle" for housing of a size and type that differs markedly from what they consider ideal. . . .

A mutual problem for both middle- and low- and moderate-income households is the sharp decline in housing opportunities within the existing stock. Some 600,000 units are removed each year due to demolition and natural disasters, while other units stand vacant due to abandonment, foreclosure and "steering," the practice pursued by realtors whereby whites are "steered" to white neighborhoods and blacks to black neighborhoods. These realities help to explain the growing inapplicability of the "filtering" theory, which assumes that decent housing becomes available as families vacate homes to move to new or improved housing.

Housing Abandonment

Instead of filtering, we have abandonment and foreclosure and steering. Abandonment, in the concentrated, contagious form that prevails today, is a fairly new phenomenon. Housing is abandoned when the owner no longer finds it profitable to continue to operate his property. This most commonly occurs when operating and maintenance costs begin to approach or even surpass the rents that can be charged tenants. So maintenance is postponed, the housing deteriorates and vacancies rise. Finally, the landlord walks away from his property, the tenants vacate the units and the empty building becomes a target for vandals and a blighting influence affecting the entire neighborhood. Lengthy foreclosures and receivership periods prevent public officials from gaining access to the property at a time when it is still in good enough condition to serve as a housing resource. Structurally sound buildings as well as substandard units are lost in the process.

Abandonment has been further aggravated in New York City by rent control, with an estimated 100,000 units standing vacant and another 15,000 to 20,000 abandoned annually. In Philadelphia, between 20,000 to 30,000 units have been abandoned. St. Louis has 10,000 abandoned units, with entire neighborhoods transformed into ghost towns. In Chicago, where vacancy rates are at an all time low of less than 2 percent, 5,000 units stand abandoned.

The Problem of Foreclosure

The problem of foreclosure is somewhat less severe at present. However, the rising number of defaults should be a clear warning that this process, like abandonment, could result in a significant underutilization of existing housing stock. At different times in the past, foreclosure rates have equaled and sometimes surpassed present rates. Yet the nature of the problem is much more serious today. . . .

At the end of 1971, HUD held title to approximately 36,000 units. Surprisingly, subsidized units constituted only a small portion of the foreclosed housing. The 235 program [subsidized-interest home-ownership program authorized by the National Housing Act], for example, had a foreclosure rate of less than 3 percent, as opposed to the 8 percent rate originally projected when the program was created. By the end of . . . [1972], the inventory of foreclosed units . . . [was] expected to rise to nearly 70,000 units.

The Effect of Steering

The effect of steering is much more difficult to measure. In all probability, the number of existing units that remain vacant because of this practice are insignificant when compared to the number of units affected by abandonment and foreclosure. But steering and the dual market it creates must be considered if approaches to the housing crisis are to be realistic. When realtors direct only white families to housing available in white neighborhoods and only black families to black neighborhoods, two separate housing markets are established and the availability of housing in one market is no help to the needs of the other market. Unscrupulous real estate agents promote the notion that neighborhood standards will decline if minority families are permitted to live in a white neighborhood. The argument is made without any consideration of the income level of the person desiring to rent or buy; as a result, middle-income blacks are denied housing they can afford. Nor are lending institutions completely free of blame. The availability of conventional mortgages to whites only, while blacks are directed toward FHA financing allows the seller to exercise his option to refuse to accept FHA financing. Vacancy becomes preferable to integration. The AFL-CIO and others have consistently condemned such self-interested efforts to perpetuate segregated housing patterns.

The Low- and Moderate-Income Housing Crisis

The low- and moderate-income housing crisis has reached a much more critical stage than the dilemma presently faced by middle-income families. Federal assistance programs, conceived as solutions, have often become an extension of the problem, with the effects being felt by households that find themselves virtually excluded from the conventional market, yet unable to have their needs met by subsidized housing. HUD estimates that 40 percent of all households in America—25 million in all—could presently qualify for federally subsidized housing. Only 2 million are presently being housed in such units.

The persons hardest hit by the crisis are the poverty stricken, the worker, the elderly, the minorities and the large families. These households are forced to depend on federal subsidy programs which suffer from a lack of funding and often appear to cater more to the interests of bankers than housing consumers.

The National Council of Senior Citizens illustrates the plight of its constituency this way: at 1970 funding levels for elderly housing and 1968 development cost, it would take approximately 180 years to meet the housing needs of senior citizens. Some 6 million elderly persons presently live in substandard housing. Minority households are in a comparable situation. The Kaiser Commission, in which the AFL-CIO participated, estimated that by 1978, one of four nonwhite families would require housing assistance.

Large families face an even tougher problem, finding a house that has adequate space at a reasonable cost. The rental units in HUD's Section 236 subsidy program [subsidized-interest apartment projects authorized by the National Housing Act] average only 2.1 bedrooms. A recent article in the Washington *Post* described the plight of a family of nine forced to live in a tent because public housing units in the county could not accommodate a family of that size.

The low- and moderate-income housing crisis goes much beyond income and costs. The millions of Americans living in substandard housing—probably closer to 11 million persons than the 6 million quoted by the Government, according to Joe Fried, author of *Housing Crisis: USA*—are not immune from the fever of "rising expectations." Having long been promised a "decent home in a suitable living environment," these citizens are now demanding that housing be more than just shelter. Federally subsidized housing now carries a one-year warranty against structural defects, encouraging builders to exercise more care and public housing tenants are gradually having demands met for facilities and amenities that will make life more pleasant—recreation rooms, day care centers, air conditioning and the like.

Nor have residents of substandard housing forgotten the promise that the housing provided should be in a "suitable living environment," which means away from neighborhoods with high crime rates, irregular trash collection, overcrowded schools and vacant and vandalized houses. Cries of equal services for all areas of a city are common today and when such cries go unheeded, housing in highly under-serviced areas is removed from the housing supply for all practical purposes.

Tasks for Federal Programs

Federal programs and the builders and developers participating in such programs must acknowledge and respond to these rising expectations and they must do this at a time when normal development costs are rising. While federal housing programs have rightly been hailed for setting new production records, the success appears to be a somewhat fragile one. Low-income housing has definitely not been low-cost housing. The optimistic goals of providing home-ownership opportunities and reduced rentals through interest subsidies have been tempered by high interest rates and administrative mismanagement.

Each of the federal housing programs has encountered the same problems and the conclusions reached are generally the same. Federally assisted housing is an expensive proposition, requiring a much greater national commitment than has been evidenced. Funds are limited and funding patterns are more irregular than consistent. The magnitude of the task and the complexity of program procedures are conducive to mismanagement and abuses. Finally, the problem of where to locate low-income housing has not been solved, with attempts to scatter low-income units in more affluent areas meeting strong resistance.

Federally assisted housing is subject to all of the forces that contribute to rising costs in the conventional housing market. The impact of such forces, however, have tended to be greater because of development-cost limitations built into the federal programs. It has become increasingly difficult for inner-city builders to develop multifamily projects that meet with FHA approval for economic feasibility. The result is to sacrifice quality: good design is out of the question, site locations are governed by finding cheap land and amenities like day care centers are forgotten.

Construction costs are not the only problem. Long-term financing obligations incurred by the Federal Government are beginning to force a major reevaluation of the use of interest subsidies to provide low- and moderate-income housing. . . . These programs operate on the assumption that the Government will pick up the tab regardless of the interest rate. Thus the nation would face a commitment in the interest of socially important housing goals which could amount to over $200 billion over the long term. An evaluation of less costly alternatives such as direct low-interest loans is certainly in order.

Another aspect of development costs that deserves greater scrutiny is the portion of federal assistance funds that go to parties other than the housing consumer. Bernard J. Frieden of the Massachusetts Institute of Technology estimates that between one fourth and one half of housing subsidies go for administrative expenses and investment tax benefits. "The most efficient" programs in terms of the subsidy going primarily for the consumer's needs "are the much maligned public housing program, public housing leasing of existing units and rent supplements in new housing," according to Frieden. A General Accounting Office study noted a variety of ways in which participants in 236 projects misused the program to line their own pockets: architectural fees often ran 200 percent greater per unit than in comparable conventional projects.

One of the more serious problems encountered by the federal housing assistance programs is the fact that operating costs have skyrocketed. Public housing authorities have been particularly hard hit, with intensified security requirements and extensive tenant services needed and changes required to comply with air pollution standards. A congressional committee was told of a public housing project in Washington, D.C., whose operating costs went from $127,000 in 1970 to $233,000 in 1972. In this case, the principal causes of the increase were maintenance requirements of the heating system, the elevator equipment and the air conditioning. Legislated rent reductions in 1969 and 1970 also added to the problems of public housing authorities. . . .

Maintenance costs in the case of homeownership programs have represented a different type of problem. In 1968, the AFL-CIO warned: "Homeownership should never become a life-long burden nor a cause of bitterness and despair. And where a family has very limited funds for emergencies or extraordinary costs, the unforeseen expenses of homeownership could be crushing." In a survey conducted in Detroit in 1970, 11.5 percent of the 124 mortgages in default were attributed to maintenance costs being too high. Meanwhile, funding levels for these housing programs have risen only very cautiously. . . .

Housing producers have also had to learn to live with the complex bureaucracy and innumerable procedures that have evolved to administer the housing programs. Designed to assist and control program participants, the organizational structure and complex requirements have in fact created a great many opportunities for mismanagement and abuse. The decentralized system of HUD area and insuring offices has permitted a close working relationship between federal officials, developers, realtors and lending institutions; at the same time it has created an interdependency conducive to favoritism, bribery and fraudulent practices. . . .

The Problem of Zoning

The most serious problem is where low- and moderate-income housing should be located. Zoning ordinances have long been used to control the type of housing built in a community and in turn the type of household likely to occupy that housing. In countless American towns, zoning for single-family homes is the norm. In several towns in Westchester County, New York, minimum lot sizes for single-family homes go up to four acres. Such zoning eliminates the possibility of homeownership opportunities or multifamily development that could be priced so as to be accessible to low- and moderate-income families. This practice operates to exclude housing for a great many working families. In Mahwah, New Jersey, minimum lots—one acre in size—sell for between $15,000 and $20,000. As a result, 90 percent of the workers in the Ford Motor Company plant have to travel as far as one hundred miles to get to their jobs from towns where housing is more reasonably priced.

Such practices by suburban communities have resulted in a containment policy toward low-income persons, confining them to the cities. Federal housing policies had condoned this one-sided decision until low-income persons complained in the courts. In two historic cases—the Shannon case in Philadelphia and the Gautreaux case in Chicago—the courts prohibited the use of federally assisted housing in areas of minority concentration unless comparable housing opportunities were available throughout the area.

Meanwhile, HUD had been developing regulations to deal with this problem as well as to provide other criteria for evaluating federally assisted housing projects. These guidelines, published as "project selection criteria" would have prohibited virtually all new construction activity in the cities until the suburbs accepted their responsibility for low- and moderate-income housing. Fortunately, HUD responded to the flood of complaints from public interest groups and civil rights organizations by modifying the criteria. Area offices were instructed to interpret the regulations "liberally," permitting the construction of low- and moderate-income housing in urban renewal and model cities areas.

While the root may be racial prejudice that has not been erased by fair housing laws, the arguments against such housing are often disguised in discussions over the impact of low-income housing on community facilities and services.

The most familiar complaint [is] that schools will be over-crowded. . . .

This confusion about where to locate low-income housing has been encouraged by the Nixon Administration's failure to take a positive stand on the issues of racial and economic integration in housing. While President Nixon himself has spoken out against federal actions to encourage economic integration, the administrative requirements of many of the HUD housing programs are strong proponents of such integration. This conflict within national policies has created an atmosphere in which community groups have bestowed upon themselves the privilege of changing their minds in midstream. . . .

Needed: A Comprehensive Housing Program

A comprehensive housing program must honestly assess housing needs and include specific strategies for dealing with each of the issues contributing to the crisis—first and foremost the cost and availability of mortgage money and land, but also the cost of maintaining and operating housing, the abandonment and foreclosure problems, and the unfair housing practices that continue to persist.

Present approaches to the problem—such as regional housing plans, new communities, state housing finance agencies—should be part of the comprehensive housing program. At the same time, serious consideration should be given to new approaches—such as requiring lending institutions to devote a certain percent of their reserves to socially important projects such as housing; adequately tested and evaluated housing allowances; low-interest, direct government loans at the federal or state level; or metropolitan housing authorities that channel all federal housing assistance funds. On a much larger scale, a quasigovernmental "TVA" of housing might provide a fresh, more inclusive approach to the problem; such a socially motivated body would consider all aspects of housing and the related environment from planning to financing to development.

A comprehensive housing program would be expensive. But we have reached a point where a commitment to more than numbers is absolutely necessary. How and when we provide housing for low-, moderate- and middle-income families is critical. Assurances that housing will be available at a reasonable cost are essential. Few would contend that decent housing should become a luxury enjoyed by only the wealthy—yet there is no evidence that the nation is living up to the goal of a "decent home in a suitable living environment" for every American.

AMERICA'S URBAN WASTELANDS [2]

Billions have been spent on federal programs to aid the slums. In the worst, a decade later, the effects would have been roughly the same had the money been dropped in small bills from the Goodyear blimp.

Existing programs of the Department of Housing and Urban Development were halted . . . [in January 1973] by a moratorium imposed by President Nixon. The entire structure of aid to the cities is being changed.

James T. Lynn, new secretary of housing and urban development, wants to turn the responsibility for the cities over to the state and local governments. "It is time," he says, "to dispel the myth that there is somebody in Washington, D.C., who knows better than the people themselves what is needed in their cities."

Just what is needed in the cities? A tour of some of the worst slums would suggest that whatever has been tried has been less than successful. [While reporters for the Los Angeles *Times*] found some hope, they often found islands of hopeless lives and physical devastation—the worst of the slums, those called wastelands. There, the disintegration of society has reached the point of self-destruction. . . .

[2] From "Urban Wastelands—Isles of Hopelessness," by Dial Torgerson, staff member Los Angeles *Times*. p 1, 16-17. Jl. 15, '73. Copyright, 1973, Los Angeles *Times*. Reprinted by permission. The article is based on reports by Los Angeles *Times* staff writers throughout the country.

Wastelands of Abandonment

Abandonment is the curse of the wastelands. It forces slumdwellers into a compaction of even greater density. The official population of the slum dwindles, but people with no place else to go, and unable to leave, crowd into ever tinier quarters, hidden from sight and ineligible to become even a statistic.

Abandonment has left gaping holes in the slums of America. Driving through a slum is like touring a European city in 1945, after the bombing. The lots are paved with broken bricks, the bricks agleam with shattered bottles, and garbage, strewn across the top, festers in the sun.

New York Mayor John Lindsay calls Brownsville—a sprawling slum in mid-Brooklyn—"bombsville." It has five hundred abandoned buildings, 432 vacant lots and hundreds of empty stores, some awaiting a long-distant urban renewal, some merely dead-ended to oblivion.

More than three hundred buildings have been abandoned in Chicago's Woodlawn in the past five years, most of them apartment houses. A third are still standing. It is difficult to find a block in the area without a hulk or two on it.

Are all the nation's slums headed for the slow oblivion of the worst wastelands?

There seems little that can be done for places like the South Bronx, Brownsville, and the worst of the Shaw-Cardozo area of Washington. By every indicator of blight, these areas are districts in a state of terminal decay.

But there is hope on the urban scene. In places where homeownership has remained high, and there are community agencies working to save the neighborhoods, blight has been slowed and improvements noted.

A Slum With a Chance

Bedford-Stuyvesant is a slum with a chance. It is a 653-block area of Brooklyn with 450,000 residents, 90 percent of them black and Puerto Rican—a community the size of Cincinnati, with the second largest black population in the country (Chicago's South Side is first).

Bed-Stuy, as its residents call it, is no longer self-destructing. The major distinguishing factor between Bed-Stuy and nearby Brownsville is that a great many more Bed-Stuy people own their own homes. There is a large block of residents with a share in the future.

In 1966 [the late] Senator Robert F. Kennedy (Democrat, New York) toured the area, then brought about the creation of the Bedford-Stuyvesant Restoration Corporation, a community-based group, and the Development and Services Corporation, an entity headed by prominent New York businessmen.

Combining the community's manpower and the white business community's financial know-how, the two groups have set up programs which are as varied and interlocking as the forces which combined to turn Bed-Stuy into a slum in the first place.

Homeowners who had been forced to turn row houses into rooming houses to pay two or three mortgages, at speculators' rates of up to 15 percent, were provided with loans arranged through the organizations. A total of 840 mortgages totaling $15.8 million have been written. Monthly payments have been reduced—from $354 to $182 for example —at lower interest rates.

Tenant-aid programs help tenants whose landlords refuse to make needed repairs, assist those conducting rent strikes, help residents seeking to buy properties as cooperatives, relocate those from homes too blighted to repair and train local workmen to restore the fronts of row houses.

The restoration agency also established community service centers which perform services from getting abandoned cars towed away to sponsoring health tests.

A Ford Foundation report on conditions necessary for success in curing slum ills found that the Bed-Stuy experience shows the need for:

1—A local institution "with credibility and authority in its community as well as with governmental agencies and financial institutions"

2—Property available and suitable for rehabilitation

3—The same kind of professional, technical assistance available on the open market for conventional developer-entrepreneurs

4—A broad spectrum of financing, from grants to mortgages

5—Finally, an anchor or node for development, a strength on which to build, such as a stable, working-class population.

In the wasteland slums, typically, homeownership is small and the populace largely unemployed and itinerant and that anchor is missing.

Take, for instance, Yeatman, the blighted home of 50,000 persons—about 95 percent of them black—on the north side of St. Louis. Of the 16,200 occupied units there, 10,800 were occupied by renters.

A survey of a key area of Yeatman found 72 percent of the housing stock deteriorated.

Los Angeles and San Francisco, with larger percentages of homeownership, have no slums comparable to those of the East. Even in areas of absentee landlords, slums in the West lack the doomsday quality of those of the East because the density is less.

Every depressed, central-city area with high rate of blight, crime and unemployment has been the scene of vast expenditures of government funds.

America's Worst Slum

But the problems remain, and the new, lower-echelon bureaucracy envisioned by HUD will find them waiting—in, for instance, the crowded, steaming streets of the South Bronx.

It is probably the worst slum in New York, and, just possibly, the worst in the United States. It covers four square miles just north of Manhattan. By every yardstick of distress, it is the "urb" least likely to succeed.

It has 136 kid gangs, with 10,000 members; 20,000 addicts (on Fox Street, for instance, police say 50 percent of the residents are on hard drugs); 40 percent of the population gets welfare; it has the highest crime rate of all New York. . . .

Men stand, unsmiling, in knots outside liquor stores— "waiting for their pusher," a local policeman explains—and prostitutes patrol in front of shops gaudy with cheap goods or heavy with the smell of frying grease.

" See that apartment?" An off-duty New York patrolman who works the side streets of the South Bronx points to a six-story apartment. "It was rehabilitated and reopened a year ago, like new inside. Junkies moved in, everyone else moved out, and vandals came in and stripped it."

The concrete blocks placed over the doors and windows to replace shattered wood and glass have themselves been smashed, and squatters furtively slip deeper into ruined interiors which smell of urine and feces.

People live here scarcely better than men did in caves at the dawn of civilization, or, perhaps, as they may in its twilight. People dying a little each day, on heroin, exist in ruins like the doomed troglodyte survivors of some science fiction holocaust.

Between structures still standing are vacant lots covered with rubble, where structures were vandalized, burned, then destroyed as dangerous. The sound of walking is a crunch. Broken bottles spread a glittering layer of shards everywhere.

Violence is waiting to happen at every corner. An argument which would mean harsh words elsewhere means the letting of blood here. Police found one hired assassin who worked for $30 a victim. One storeowner was robbed or burglarized one hundred times in fifteen years. A liquor store sells its products through a slot in bulletproof glass.

The South Bronx is 65 percent Puerto Rican, 35 percent black. The population is dwindling, as buildings are abandoned, but those who remain suffer even greater overcrowding, meaning less space, more tension, less chance to get the garbage picked up, more rats, more cockroaches, more disease.

"*Sal si puedes*," they say in the South Bronx, "leave if you can." Those who can, have. The people who are there are there because there is no place else for them. And yet, amid the agony, life persists.

A young mother waves to the policeman who delivered her baby in her tiny apartment. Boys surround a passing car, halting it, one crawls beneath it, and emerges, smiling, a reddish pigeon from his loft safe in his hand. "This is Strawberry Ranger," he says.

And on a wall, where The Blade, Kendo and the Boys, Mr. Phibes and Lil Taft I have spraypainted their names, the graffiti says:

"The city must find its meaning in its people."

People in wastelands such as the South Bronx complain of malign neglect.

Bulldozer urban renewal was halted in the sixties as the poor found a political voice. "Urban renewal is Negro removal," the saying went. The clearing of entire districts by governmental agencies is rare, now.

But the residents of blighted blocks see gaps appearing in the house fronts, year by year, and realize that attrition is achieving the same ends as the dozer blade and the wrecking ball.

Because of abandonment and demolition, slum populations statistically dwindle as overcrowding grows. Those who stay because they can't leave see those who can, departing.

Chicago's East Woodlawn

Take Chicago's East Woodlawn, for instance; the census showed 60,030 residents in 1960, 35,300 in 1970. The most dramatic exodus was among people from twenty to forty-four. *Sal si puedes* applies in the black community, too.

The children of welfare flee when they are old enough to do so—if they can. Darwinism in reverse rules the slums. The least able remain, the fittest depart.

Angry spokesmen for the slum dwellers charge that society warehouses the poor in its wastelands, letting them prey upon one another, providing them just enough care to keep the ghetto functioning.

Those who stay behind see themselves the victims of a loss of city services they interpret as part of a conspiracy against them. Sam Smith, editor of a community paper in Washington, feels that the power structure is purposefully slow about doing anything in Shaw, letting the population dwindle and housing decline so the poor will somehow fade away.

Some areas obviously suffer not because of malign neglect but because efforts to do anything for the slums have resulted in a barely penetrable superstructure of bureaucracy.

It has sometimes taken twelve years from acquisition through financing, bureaucratic approvals and construction of a project in a slum area subject to city, state and federal red tape. New HUD director Lynn shows a thirty-inch-long diagram of approval steps for slum projects under grant-in-aid programs now suspended.

"It looks like an electronic diagram for Apollo 17," he said.

Chicago demographer Pierre de Vise has estimated that $35 million in public funds has been spent on Woodlawn in the past decade. Says de Vise: "Probably no other neighborhood in the nation has had as much money and manpower lavished on it in the past ten years."

Leon D. Finney, executive director of The Woodlawn Organization (TWO), a community group which has been fighting a battle to save Woodlawn since the early 1960s, said: "The war on poverty, the Model Cities Program, they have been gross failures. These programs have not alleviated conditions here."

Look at Woodlawn today, and consider what $35 million has accomplished:

"When I go down 63rd Street, from Stony Island, it brings tears to my eyes," said Wynetta Frazier, a vigorous young black woman who has lived in Woodlawn for a long time. "Sometimes I actually broke down and cried. It's home, but it's the most demoralizing thing in the world to see that destruction."

Two major arteries, 63rd and Stony Island, cross in East Woodlawn. It should be the center of a thriving commercial district. The Parkside Hotel stands at the corner, abandoned. The windows and doors are gone. Stores and taverns on the first floor have been long deserted. There is nothing inside the shell but debris.

A few years ago the sidewalks here were crowded. Now there are few pedestrians in the daytime, virtually none at night. Thieves emerge from the ruins to rob passersby, and women have been dragged into them by rapists. The owner of a 63rd Street restaurant sends a car to pick up one of his women employes, day or night. She lives two blocks away.

Along the side streets properties abandoned but not yet demolished are poised in a state of near collapse, with bricks, stone and timber scattered in a dangerous disarray. Fires are frequent. "Would you feel like keeping your place neat if you had buildings falling down on every side?" asks one angry homeowner.

Woodlawn is the home of the Blackstone Rangers, now called the Black P. Stone Nation, possibly the nation's best-known street gang. In 1967 the group was given an OEO grant for a job-training project to assist gang members. Some leaders went to Washington for President Nixon's inauguration in 1969.

At the height of their power in 1969 there were about three thousand members of the Rangers in Woodlawn. A rival group, the Eastside Disciples, had about one thousand members. But after a policeman was killed in a gunfight with Rangers in 1970, the law cracked down hard on the gang, breaking its power.

It doesn't mean Woodlawn is any safer. On Woodlawn Avenue there is an apartment building which seems doomed for abandonment. When the landlord went there twice to collect rent he was beaten up by the tenants. Now he is afraid to go back.

Yet Woodlawn lies in an excellent location: only eight miles (twenty minutes' train ride) from Chicago's downtown Loop, bounded on the east by the spacious lawns of Jackson Park, which fronts on Lake Michigan.

Home of Professors

To the west is West Woodlawn, a black working-class area where many more of the housing units are owner-occupied, there are fewer abandonments, and the quality of life is infinitely better. A middle-to-upper-income integrated area lies south; and to the north, across a grassy mall, is the University of Chicago and Hyde Park.

In Hyde Park, college professors and professional people live on pleasant streets, trying to forget how easily those responsible for Woodlawn's high crime rate can cross the grassy mall of the Midway Plaisance.

TWO, the old-line neighborhood group, still fights for Woodlawn. City Hall is said to be getting to be slightly more responsive to the area's needs. A Model Cities grant is helping clean up some of the garbage.

And fires are growing less frequent. Everything which can burn easily has already burned, and in many hulks only ashes remain. "Let's face it," said Wynetta Frazier, who sometimes cries, looking at 63rd Street, "the community has died."

If the adults feel frustrated, what does it do to the kids? Listen to a veteran teacher in a high school in a ghetto area of Washington:

> The kids feel the reason they are ignorant is the fault of the teachers. They feel that if they had good schools and good teachers they would be brilliant.
>
> They constantly tell me that they don't learn anything. They feel insulted by so much of the teaching, and don't realize they are incapable of so many things.
>
> The worst thing is that they are so unsophisticated in the ways of the world—as distinct from the ghetto street. I had one boy who was seventeen and had never been more than a mile away from school in any direction. He had never seen the Capitol or any of the monuments.

One of the worst verities of the slums is that the land of the poor is also the land of the young. Statistically, it is the young who commit the most crimes, the most vandalism. Police can see the crime rate soar when school is out and young people wander the hot, glass-littered streets, looking for something to do.

The Curse of Interlocking Disasters

In each city, the experts point to the same basic problem: there is no one answer to the curse of the slums. Junkies' thievery and kids' vandalism can destroy good housing on a bad street. The best hospital can only treat crisis problems, not prevent the illnesses brought about by poverty, malnutrition, and frustration.

Attempts to attract industry to the very worst slums, where jobs are most desperately needed, has proven nearly impossible.

The problems of the Brownsvilles, the Cardozos, the Yeatmans must be considered as a total package. And this grim package of interlocking disasters must, somehow, be considered in the context of their relation to the big cities, the suburbs, and the nation as a whole.

As previous governmental techniques are phased out or reappraised, and new ones conceived, the people in the wastelands of America feel little hope. Quincy, a Cardozo alcoholic, viewed the future this way: "If you had problems like mine, you'd want to stay drunk all the time.". . .

How Does a Neighborhood Deteriorate?

How does a viable neighborhood become a wasteland, vacant lots heaped with garbage?

The process of abandonment is much the same in every inner city. It follows a similar course in Detroit, Brownsville or Cardozo:

1. *The first step.* The arrival of the minority—black or, perhaps, Puerto Rican—who have the color or language difference to mark what white homeowners consider an incursion. The new arrivals are frequently themselves middle class.

Often the newcomers are employed, upwardly mobile blacks, seeking to escape the worst slums. A study of the Bagley section of Detroit found that black families in the first wave had median incomes $1,000 a year greater than the median incomes for Bagley whites.

2. *White flight.* The exodus of whites from a neighborhood, says an official of the Department of Housing and Urban Development, is the "front end" of the process that leads to abandonment. Whites tend to disregard the caliber of the newcomers, considering their presence as an indication the neighborhood is about to become a slum.

Panic selling has often been noted, but research indicates the change from white to black may be mostly based on failure of white families to replace the whites departing in the usual 20 percent turnover normal in all US neighborhoods.

3. *Vacancies mount.* Historically, whites, with their suburbs, have had more options open to them than blacks for a place of residence. Soon the number of vacancies left by whites in the changing neighborhoods exceeded the number of striving blacks wishing to move in.

4. *Landlords compromise.* Trying to keep units filled
and cash flow up, landlords become less particular about
renters. They accept welfare families, those with large numbers of children and those of lower-income level and [less]
job stability.

Since buildings in the changing neighborhoods tend to
be older, the normal wear and tear of large numbers of
children adds to maintenance costs at a time when income
to the owner is slipping. Maintenance that was adequate for
smaller families won't suffice any more.

5. *Deterioration.* Vandalism and damage mounts. The
better-off tenants move to units not yet so badly off. Even
less desirable tenants must be accepted. The first family of
junkies slips in, financing expensive habits by stealing from
their neighbors.

6. *Landlord's dilemma.* "The combination of less income
and higher costs begins to whipsaw the landlord," a HUD
expert said. "And his taxes never go down." First comes
psychological abandonment—the landlord no longer cares.
He may "dead-end" the property by paying no taxes, doing
no upkeep and collecting what he can in rents as long as
he can.

7. *Services decline.* In some cities, building inspectors
called to an apartment because of needed repairs can be
bribed; where the landlord is dead-ending, he may be ignored. (Courts are clogged and punishment for safety in-
fractions unlikely.)

As density increases, police are unable to cope with rising
crime, fire hazards mount and city garbage services adequate
for smaller families can't handle the refuse generated in
crowded tenements. When plumbing breaks, and the landlord won't fix it, halls and elevator shafts become latrines.

8. *Abandonment.* "The landlord starts asking himself if
it's really worth it," the expert said. "Finally, he just walks
away and lets the building go for taxes." Squatters may stay
behind, many of them junkies.

9. *Destruction*. Fires set accidentally or on purpose may gut the building, or teams of looters may smash walls to get at pipes and wiring, which can be sold for salvage. Pockets of abandoned buildings doom a whole block.

"The threshold for an avalanche can be as little as 5 percent abandonment in a neighborhood. The streetwise people move out as soon as they see it start. They know crime, fires, rats and all will follow," the HUD official said. Eventually the wreck is bulldozed.

Bigger apartments, fifty units and up, last longer, because they have professional management. Two-and-three-unit apartments, owner-occupied, resist abandonment to the limit of the owners' finances. The ten-to-thirty-unit apartments are the first to go.

THE WASTING OF CHICAGO [3]

The poor, the black, and the unemployed continue to gravitate to Chicago. Chicago remains home for 64 percent of the metropolitan area unemployed, 75 percent of families below the poverty level, 76 percent of the Spanish-speaking, 85 percent of the welfare recipients, and 90 percent of the blacks.

At the other end of the social scale, Chicago contains but 29 percent of all metropolitan area families earning over $25,000 a year, 29 percent of the college graduates, 26 percent of the corporation executives, and 25 percent of the white public school children. A comparison of the 1960 and 1970 Census reveals that during the 1960 decade Chicago lost half a million whites and gained a third of a million blacks; lost 220 factories, 760 stores, and 229,000 jobs but gained 90,000 welfare recipients; lost 140,000 private housing units but gained 19,000 public housing units. The losses represent drains of 12 percent of the housing, 14 percent of

[3] From article by Pierre de Vise, project director of the Chicago Regional Hospital Study. *Focus/Midwest*. v 9 no 58:7-9. '73. Reprinted with permission of FOCUS/Midwest, © 1973 FOCUS/Midwest Publishing Company, Inc. P.O. Box 3086. St. Louis, Mo. 63130.

the jobs, 17 percent of the stores, and 18 percent of the whites in terms of 1960 assets.

Chicago's losses have been the suburbs' gains. In these ten years, the suburbs gained 800,000 whites; 350,000 housing units; and 500,000 jobs. These trends go back to the 1950s, but they were much stronger in the last ten years. In 1950, 66 of every 100 metropolitan area residents lived in Chicago and 78 of every 100 jobs were located in Chicago. By 1960, the city's share of metropolitan population and jobs had slipped to 57 and 68 percent, respectively. As of 1970, Chicago accounted for but 48 percent of the metropolitan population and 52 percent of the jobs.

How has this massive exodus of people, jobs, and homes affected the sending areas in the city and the receiving areas in the suburbs? Has suburbanization proceeded too fast? Have all classes of people and property benefited from the process? How have the housing and real estate industries responded to these trends? And what do these trends portend for the future of metropolitan Chicago?

Family Income Versus Higher Costs

First, let us consider the adjustments of family income to higher costs of housing and transportation in the suburbs. More metropolitan area families own their homes—53 percent in 1970 *versus* 51 percent in 1960. Two-car ownership has doubled—from 300,000 to 600,000 families. Average home value has gone up $100 since 1960, from $24,200 to $24,300. Average monthly rent increased 12 percent, from $104 to $116. Average family income grew by 24 percent, from $9,560 to $11,840 (all dollar figures are expressed in constant 1970 values). A greater proportion of women (45 *versus* 39 percent) and boys (41 *versus* 39 percent) but a smaller proportion of older persons (28 *versus* 35 percent) are now in the labor force.

Because the new homes and work places are more dispersed and are less accessible by public transportation, the average work trip is longer—6 *versus* 5 miles one way—and automobile commuters have increased by one third. A majority of Chicago residents now drive to work (53 percent in 1970; up from 45 percent in 1960), while the overwhelming majority of suburbanites now commute by car (80 percent now; up from 69 percent in 1960 in the case of Du Page residents).

The corresponding decline in commuting by public transportation saw the proportion of commuters going by bus fall from 19 to 14 percent (from 30 to 20 percent for Chicago residents), and that of railroad and subway commuters slide from 12 to 9 percent (from 13 to 10 percent for Chicago residents). Thus, the suburbanization of jobs has considerably aggravated the congestion of expressways and surface roads while contributing to the under-utilization of financially hard-pressed CTA [Chicago Transit Authority] and suburban bus and railroad companies.

The massive suburbanization of jobs has meant that fewer suburbanites now work in Chicago and that more Chicagoans work in the suburbs. Chicago, with 52 percent of the metropolitan jobs and 48 percent of the labor force, still has 8 percent more jobs than workers—but, of course, the city's jobs do not perfectly match the skills of its labor force, nor do the suburbs' jobs match the labor force. Suburban Cook County, which added 340,000 new jobs during the decade, has supplanted Chicago as the area's major importer of workers. With 29 percent of the metropolitan area's jobs and only 17 percent of its labor force, suburban Cook County now has 70 percent more jobs than local workers.

As a result of the shift of Chicago's industrial gravity center to suburban Cook County, there are more than twice as many reverse commuters from Chicago as in 1960: 18 percent of Chicago's labor force now works in the suburbs, compared to 7 percent ten years ago.

Correspondingly, suburban residents now rely less on Chicago work places and more on local industry. For example, only 36 percent of Park Forest's labor force now works in Chicago, compared with 56 percent in 1960, the bulk of the remaining labor force working in South Cook County. The proportion of Du Page County's labor force working in Chicago fell from 37 to 23 percent, with 49 percent now working in the county, compared with 42 percent in 1960.

Only in America: Central Cities for Poor

So interrelated and complex are the suburban shifts of people, jobs and stores, and the construction of new housing and expressways that it is difficult to separate cause-and-effect relations among these. Do jobs follow people to the suburbs or vice versa? Is the demand for housing in the suburbs the cause of suburban housing construction or does the supply of the latter create the demand? The same may be asked about expressways. New regional shopping centers are perhaps the most clearly dependent on existing consumer demand. Yet even they constitute magnets that have a multiplying effect on the demand for urban land within their service area.

Then there is the push-pull vector of forces—how suburbanization is affected by a combination of the repellent aspects of inner-city life and of the attractive aspects of suburban life. *North American cities are unique among the world's cities in having poor people living in the central city and rich people living in suburbs. In fact major urban strategies since World War II in Britain and France aim at inducing people and industry to move to the suburbs, an effort that so far has met little success.*

A team of British anthropologists accompanied by a crew from the BBC recently spent a month in Chicago's suburbs to find out what incentives we use to get people and industry to move from the city to the suburbs. They found out that we used two secret weapons.

In the central city, whites fear blacks and flee in terror, and in the suburbs we have private developers who build twice as much housing as we need to shelter refugees from the embattled city.

The housing industry responded to the challenge of Chicago's loss of half a million whites and gain of 300,000 blacks by building 110,000 new housing units, most of them on Chicago's white north side. Since Chicago had a net population loss of 200,000 people, it could not possibly use this massive infusion of new housing. Something had to give. What gave were the city's older black ghettos which contributed the bulk of the 140,000 units that were vacated, abandoned, and demolished during the decade. This housing was vacated by blacks drawn to the more attractive housing of racially changing areas emptied by whites who were attracted by the new housing proliferating on Chicago's white north side and the suburbs.

Even more housing was built in the suburbs: 344,000 units during the decade. Housing developers in the suburbs catered not only to the families with school-age children, the normally suburbanizing group, but also to single adults and childless couples traditionally oriented to the city. To accommodate the latter, there was a four-fold increase in suburban apartment construction since 1960—from 7,000 to 28,000 apartments a year. The two benchmarks in this trend are 1961, the first year that more apartments were built in the suburbs than in the city, and 1969, when more apartments than houses were built in the suburbs.

Altogether, developers put up 454,000 houses and apartments during the 1960s. This represents an increase of 23 percent in the metropolitan area's housing, or twice the 11.5 percent gain in population.

Chicago is paying for this prodigal housing construction with a current vacancy rate of 5 percent, and the abandonment and demolition of 15,000 housing units a year. A decade of overbuilding in the city and suburbs has left seven square miles of devastation on Chicago's west and south sides. Nor is housing construction slackening in the face of this catastrophic evidence of a housing surplus. The housing

industry established record construction levels in four of the
last five years. Last year's record of 63,000 new units was 50
percent above the high levels of ten years ago. . . .

The only restraint shown by suburban developers is that
they do not build for Chicago's blacks. Except for a handful
of ghetto developments in South Cook County, blacks remain shut out of suburban housing. The increasing separa-
tion between suburban work places and Chicago's black
ghettos creates a shortage of workers in the former and excessive unemployment in the latter. Unemployment rates
are between 1 and 2 percent in Northwest Cook and Du Page
counties and between 6 and 14 percent in Chicago's black
ghettos. As it is, 40,000 black workers make the daily trek
from Chicago to the suburbs, and many more would join
them if they had a car.

The Role of the Real Estate Industry

The real estate industry bears additional responsibility
for the despoliation of black ghettos on Chicago's west and
south sides. The inner city's blacks pay much more rent
than whites or Spanish-speaking people occupying similar
housing. These black communities suffered the loss of a
fourth of their housing in the 1960s, while similar inner-city
white and Spanish-speaking neighborhoods lost only 5 percent of their housing. Excessive property taxes based on discriminatory assessed valuations are a major factor in both
instances. The Cook County Assessor's valuation of property
in Woodlawn, for example, is above actual market value,
while in similar-aged housing construction on the north side,
his valuation is about a fourth of the market value. Property
taxes account for about 40 percent of gross rental income in
Woodlawn and only 15 percent of income on the north side.

Property tax discrimination is not intentional, based as
it is on the brick-and-mortar basis of assessing valuation.
But identical packages of brick-and-mortar are worth four
times more on the north side than in Woodlawn, wherein
lies the discriminatory effect.

The suspicion already exists in the minds of many that the government is taxing ghetto properties at confiscatory levels to clear and acquire the land without compensation to the owner, since urban renewal is no longer feasible. There is no better way for government to give the lie to this suspicion than by revising its assessment methods to conform to statutory requirements that ratios of assessed to market valuations be equalized. Since the real estate industry is best equipped to document this discrimination, and since property-owner and manager members in the black ghetto are victimized thereby, it should take the leadership in vigorously advocating this much-needed reform.

The Final Stage—Abandoned Housing

In stressing the primary responsibility of excessive housing construction in the outer city and suburbs, and of discriminatory taxation for the epidemic of housing abandonment in the black ghetto, it is not to minimize the importance of the self-destructive tendencies of tenants who are the final occupants of dying buildings. Housing abandonment is the ultimate stage of the collapsed housing markets of older black ghettos. At this stage, normal black households have moved to the plentiful vacancies of racially changing communities vacated by whites attracted by the even more plentiful new housing in outlying white communities. The only tenants that landlords can attract at this stage are the most destitute and least competent, many of whom are destructive and pathological. Rents are lowered, maintenance costs rise, and vacancies are quickly vandalized. In time all tenants leave because the buildings become too dangerous for even the most desperate. The empty buildings are soon wrecked or burned down by the neighborhood vandals.

Most of Chicago's ghettos that have been predominantly black for over thirty years contain neighborhoods that have reached this final stage. Communities like Kenwood-Oakland and Woodlawn have lost over a third of their housing since 1960, and currently have vacancy rates of 15 to 20 percent as part of this process.

The government apparently holds demolition and tax liens on the thousands of parcels so far cleared in this fashion. There seems to be no market and no buyers for this land. Very likely the land could not be given away in the present atmosphere of uncertainty over the future of the southeast side.

The future of the metropolitan area depends on the future of Chicago. The future of Chicago depends on the future of the southeast side. The future of the south side depends on the public accountability of the housing and real estate industry. From our present perspective, that is a grim prospect.

CRIME IN HIGH-RISE HOUSING[4]

A three-year study by a New York University research team has produced dramatic evidence of a major cause of the terror that afflicts public housing residents in many major cities: The higher the building, the higher the crime rate.

The most dangerous type of public housing of all, the study found, is the high-rise elevator building with floor upon floor of "double-loaded corridors" serving so many apartments, ranging along both sides of the hall, that residents can't tell neighbors from strangers.

The crime rate in such buildings is more than twice that in walk-up public housing. Nevertheless, the researchers conclude that even in such high-rise buildings crime—and the almost equally paralyzing fear of crime—can be curtailed.

Their primary solution lies in design, organizing a setting to maximize what Oscar Newman, an architect and the project director, calls "defensible space."

That is the title of a just-published book [October 1972] reporting the work of the $600,000 study. It was conducted

[4] From "Housing Study: High Rise—High Crime," by Jack Rosenthal, staff reporter. New York *Times*. p 41. O. 26, '72. © 1972 by The New York Times Company. Reprinted by permission.

by NYU's Institute of Planning and Housing and financed
by research grants from Federal and city agencies.

A major aspect of the research was analysis of 1969 crime
statistics that the New York City Housing Authority police
compiled for one hundred public housing projects.

In three-floor walk-up buildings, the study found, there
were 30 serious crimes, for every thousand families. In
buildings of six or seven floors, there were 41 serious crimes.
In high-rise buildings of thirteen to thirty floors there were
68.

What the researchers found even more striking were the
contrasts in the locations in which crimes were committed.

The rates differed little among the three types of housing
with respect to crimes committed inside individual apartments or on outside grounds. But there was a very different
result concerning crimes committed in interior public
spaces—elevators, lobbies, corridors, stairs and roofs.

While the total serious crime rate was twice as high in
tall buildings as in walk-ups, the rate of crime in public
spaces in the high-rises was seven times higher.

Why High-Rise Crime?

Why? The study offers the following answer:

In a high-rise, double-loaded-corridor apartment tower, the
only defensible space is the interior of the apartment itself; everything else is a "no man's land," neither public nor private.

Unlike the well-peopled and continually surveyed public
streets, these interior areas are sparsely used and impossible to
survey; they become a nether world of fear and crime.

By contrast, Mr. Newman said in an interview . . .

in the walk-up buildings, where few families share an entry, the
interior public space becomes an extension of the home. And so
does the street.

Kids can play outside and still be within calling distance of
the window. And as parents supervise their children at play, they
also monitor street life. Defensible space is extended. You begin
to get safe streets as well as safe buildings.

The contrast is evident from the sides of Stone Avenue in Brooklyn, as it intersects two kinds of public housing—the towers of Van Dyke Houses on one side, the low- and mid-rise buildings of Brownsville Houses on the other.

The two projects are almost identical in density, population, income, race and other characteristics except crime. In 1969, the study found, there were 432 reported criminal offenses in the tall Van Dyke project. There were 264 in the lower Brownsville project.

Attitude Toward Invasion

Brownsville residents and the police alike, Mr. Newman wrote in his book, regard the Brownsville project "as smaller and more stable than Van Dyke."

"All intruders, including the police and interviewers, feel more cautious about invading the privacy of residents at Brownsville," he said. "By contrast, their attitude toward the invasion of the interior corridors at Van Dyke is callous and indifferent."

Such differences between high- and low-rise public housing are evident regardless of neighborhood or city, Mr. Newman said. . . . The worse the neighborhood, the more dangerous high-rise public housing becomes by comparison with low-rise. And this is even more true in Newark, St. Louis and other cities than in New York, the study found.

The project called essentially for two solutions. One is to stop assigning families with children to high-rise buildings in large public housing projects.

Locating them in walk-up buildings would mean lower density—about fifty units an acre. But that, Mr. Newman contends in his book, would not be a problem anywhere but in New York.

He cites the enormous Pruitt-Igoe development of high-rise public housing in St. Louis, some of which has now been dynamited and most of which has been abandoned. There, density was only forty-eight units an acre.

Plan for the Elderly

And even in New York, he says, one solution would lie in concentrating elderly residents in high-rise buildings, familiar in walks-ups.

The second proposed solution calls for the design of "defensible space." The resident of a public housing tower, situated on a parklike superblock and with the entry facing inward, would be "much safer had he been able to go directly from street to front door," Mr. Newman writes.

Design improvements can even curtail crime in existing low-rise projects, Mr. Newman believes. He cites as evidence the modifications he has made, working with the [New York City] Housing Authority, of Clason Point Gardens in the Bronx.

This project houses four hundred families in two-story buildings. The modifications focused on giving them a stronger proprietary sense over the grounds and walkways. It was finished eight months ago . . . [in the spring of 1972].

"Eight months is not long enough to tell anything for sure," Mr. Newman said. . . . "But so far, compared with the same eight months last year, the total number of offenses is nearly six times lower."

THE CRISIS IN PUBLIC HOUSING [5]

Public housing, which presently numbers over a million units in this country, is in deep trouble. No doubt of it at all. Public housing is in trouble because from the beginning of the program thirty-five years ago the real estate and conservative communities, joined most of the time by the media, have categorized public housing as a mark of second-class citizenship and have been able to restrict it to the worst sites and worst conditions. Through their efforts, cost limitations have been imposed that made it poverty-oriented

[5] From "Survival Kit for Public Housing," by J. S. Fuerst, assistant director of the Graduate Program in Urban Studies at Chicago's Loyola University. *Commonweal.* 98:474-8. S. 7, '73. Copyright © 1973 Commonweal Publishing Co., Inc. Reprinted by permission.

and unworkable in our middle-class society, with structures identifiable only as penitentiaries, precemeteries, or massive conglomerations of the very poor.

The administrators of the public housing program have not greatly helped. Generally speaking, the programs have been administered by timid rather than bold men, men of modest talents rather than outstanding ones. Under such circumstances, the possibilities of circumventing the restrictive legislative provisions, bad press, or bad court decisions have not been great.

And such bad court decisions have not helped. Civil libertarians more interested in fighting to the last ditch for the mildest infraction of civil liberties than in any solution of the public programs they were thereby crippling, have plunged a knife deep into the housing programs. Local court decisions have prohibited evictions of bad tenants, have restricted even reasonable admission regulations of the housing authorities, and have prohibited the authorities (who are already excessively restricted by local communities) from building where they wanted.

Even social agencies haven't helped. Certainly they have been glad to use the public housing agencies as the repository for families whom they couldn't help and who had deplorable housing. As many families as the housing authorities took, there was always "another needy one." No self-restraint was used, not recognizing that a project has a very real "tipping point" for such families. Moreover the agencies did not pour in the social services because in all fairness they could not concentrate *their* limited resources on one segment of the community such as the projects. When all these difficulties were coupled with a national Administration that had no urge to build enough housing to serve low- and moderate-income families, this was bound to spell trouble.

Where are we now? We have about one million conventional public housing units in urban areas, most of which serve families who are not self-supporting and who receive the bulk of their income from either public assistance, pensions, unemployment, or veterans' compensation. Not only are most of these families receiving one or more forms of public assistance, but many of them are victims of serious social pathology for which no housing and probably few social agencies can legitimately provide effective help.

This then, in a broad general way, is the picture we are facing today in conventional public housing.

The Subsidized Housing Alternative

A few years ago the Johnson Administration, observing the plight of and apparently unwilling to believe that there was any real means of improving the existing programs, offered a new program in the form of tax subsidies to private industry to provide subsidized housing. During the past three to four years, about 500,000 units were built under these programs and provided some "people shelter" for the poor but enormous "tax shelters" for others.

But this subsidy program is also running into serious trouble. Despite the glowing prospects of a low-moderate income, low-rent program operated by private industry, there seem to be many pitfalls. In many cities even *these* projects cannot be placed in "good" areas because the local politicos are afraid to take a chance on apartments that may have the same tenant character as public housing. As a result many of these "236" projects [subsidized-interest apartment projects authorized by the National Housing Act] as well as "221-d3"s [projects financed under the extension of FHA mortgage insurance to the inner city authorized by the National Housing Act] were located in less desirable areas. This caused further difficulties in obtaining good tenants.

One of the primary difficulties in these projects is that vacancy losses, rent collection problems, and high maintenance costs are plaguing them much as they do public housing. Moreover, they experience very high local taxes relative to their rent, and many of them are on the verge of failure because their rents do not enable them to meet expenses. This is causing great concern among sponsors, and even among such organizations as the National Association of Home Builders because in the last few years these subsidy programs represented 28 percent of all housing constructed. Needless to say, while the shutting off of public housing caused no great havoc among businessmen and other investors, the stopping of subsidy programs shut off significant tax benefits for some important fat cats, causing screams of pain.

Can We Salvage Public Housing Programs?

Aside from the publicly subsidized, privately owned housing units, where does this leave the public housing program of one million units? In short, what can be done to salvage the existing programs? To prove that this question is neither theoretical nor frivolous we have only to look at St. Louis' Pruitt Igoe, which is being torn down at least in part, at boarded-up projects in Providence, Rhode Island, at Cabrini-Green and Robert Taylor in Chicago with 20 percent or so vacancies—and more to come. These conditions, coupled with the suggestion in many quarters that they be sold back to private enterprise, means that some actions have to be taken if the public housing program is not to be physically destroyed or returned to private hands. Seeing as we do the ever-growing number of abandoned low-rent apartments—15,000 a year in Chicago and perhaps 700,000 in the nation—and knowing how little standard housing is being made available, it may be taken for granted that some government housing is necessary. Certainly the housing that is presently in operation cannot afford to be scrapped. What actions are necessary to keep this stock going?

First, in our local housing authorities we must secure administrators and commissioners who are genuinely interested in and dedicated to public housing. . . . Anthony Downs, the executive vice president of Real Estate Research Corporation and a privately oriented housing economist,

[has] made the point that public housing has failed not because of the nature of the subsidy but because of its administration plus the fact that it has been directed toward solving problems which are outside its sphere of competence. Furthermore, said Downs, to be successful it must be operated by people truly dedicated to the principle of public housing. That this is not merely an empty observation is attested to by a 1969 article in the *Journal of Housing*, a publication of the National Association of Housing and Redevelopment Officials, in which it was indicated that more than half of the present commissioners of public housing did not believe in the possibility of public housing success. This must be changed.

Changing the Image of Public Housing

Now, once we have administrators and boards who are really interested in public housing, what can be done? Several changes must be made simultaneously. The first and most important is a change in public image. It must be beaten, pounded and drummed into the general public mind—specifically the would-be eligibles as well as the neighborhood residents of possible future public housing sites—that this program is for low- and moderate-income *workers*, for workers who cannot afford private, unsubsidized housing. This does not mean that welfare recipients or pension recipients or those on unemployment compensation cannot be admitted. On the other hand the program can not, as heretofore, be overwhelmed or dominated by these groups (particularly second- or third-generation public assistance recipients) so that these groups set the tone of the project. In short, public assistance recipients and broken families will form no greater proportion of public housing projects than they do of the low-moderate-income segment of the community.

Bad as the present housing market is, with large numbers of abandoned units and with many more characterized by bad maintenance and consequent deterioration, turnover still is high and getting higher in public housing. A recent Welfare Council survey of a number of Chicago public housing projects reported an attitude of many tenants that "they were there only as a last desperate resort and were waiting to find something else." Reasons are not hard to find.

What must be done in the housing authorities is to hold the available units that become vacant until good tenants can be found. In many badly located, badly built projects this presents a mammoth job but it can be done if there are radical changes in the projects themselves. In a few projects the needed changes may be less radical. At least in theory, newspapers, radio and television should be able to contribute significantly to improving the public housing image. Media that have been able to do such an effective job of selling soap, political candidates and the jingoism that passes for Americanism, should be able to sell a new point of view in public housing. This assumes, of course, that they will recognize that otherwise we are wasting $15-$20 billion worth of housing as the public housing program withers away, taking with it many worthwhile neighborhoods.

Now what must the authorities themselves do in the form of changes in planning, if public housing is to become adaptable?

—Change the name of many of the projects and break up the larger projects into separate operations, psychologically if not administratively.

—Improve the landscaping and play areas as well as the general view of the projects so as to make them look less poverty-oriented than they do at present.

—Convert some of the vacant apartments to community facilities such as arts and crafts centers, libraries, community meeting centers, day nurseries, class and study rooms, infant welfare clinics, etc.

—Simultaneously bring in more health, educational and recreational services and agencies as well as more commercial facilities.

—Sharply reduce the total density and curtail the number of children per apartment [A 1970 study by social planning associations in Chicago, conducted for the Chicago Housing Authority, and the Oscar Newman study in New York, *Defensible Space,* which was originally conducted for the New York City Housing Authority, indicate that crime is less in projects where there are fewer children and fewer persons per unit.] This could be done by converting some of the larger apartments to smaller ones, thus reducing the number of children per apartment.

—Finally, screen the tenancy and weed out as painlessly as possible the hard-core delinquent and antisocial families who have not been able to adjust to project living and who are making it difficult and unpleasant for others.

Dealing With Evicted Families

The first question that is asked, sometimes by social workers who need to feel that they have done something for their "untreatables," sometimes by those who *want* to see public housing fail, and sometimes by genuinely interested but inexperienced observers, is, "What happens to the evicted families?" Some of the families can be relocated in "halfway houses," rehabilitated old houses operated either by local authorities or subsidized groups, until they can better adjust to project living. In some cases where the family situation is intolerable, courts may be used to break up the family and place the children. In some cases the families may return to private housing.

While such return may seem retrogressive, it is only realistic to recognize that not all social pathology is curable. When the problem is one of the program itself surviving or sinking and there are no real alternatives, then evictions must be made. If the program collapses, as it has done in a number of places, *all* the families will have to find other places. It is far better to prevent this from happening by the bold step of evicting those few who are causing the collapse. When a patient has a gangrenous leg, there are times when surgery is necessary to save his life. The patient in this case is public housing itself.

Actually, the eviction of tenants who are seriously damaging the project should not be too difficult because they are frequently sufficiently openly disruptive or laggard in payment of rent so as to provide perfectly valid reasons. Justice Douglas said in stopping the Housing Authority of Durham from evicting a tenant who organized a tenants' union:

> This does not mean that a public housing authority is powerless to evict a tenant. A tenant may be evicted if it is shown that he is destroying the fixtures, defacing the walls, disturbing other tenants by boisterous conduct, as well as for a number of other reasons which impair the successful operation of the housing project.

Several examples of how to change the tenancy come to mind. Patrick Feeney, executive director of the local housing authority in Columbus, Ohio, describes how Langdon Courts housing project, which had considerable crime and social disorganization, was emptied of low-income tenants. Some were placed in other projects, some in leased housing, and some back in ordinary private housing, while the project was renovated into units for the elderly.

Another equally interesting example was a privately operated project in the "236" program [subsidized-interest apartment project authorized by National Housing Act] in Kankakee, Illinois, where the first local manager accepted tenants most of whom were black and most on welfare. The project became unmanageable, with great rent delinquency and considerable disruption. The owner-sponsor-manager recognized that if these conditions continued, failure was certain. Within a twelve-month period he emptied the project of all but 15 percent of the tenants. He replaced them mainly with low-income workers allowing about 30 percent welfare families. These latter families, however, he obtained on referral from the local public assistance agency after explaining to the welfare executives that it was imperative that the project have only those welfare families with good prognoses, who were likely to benefit from living in such a project. Likewise he believed that the project, located in a fringe neighborhood, should not have more than 30 percent black occupancy. When he was asked what happened to the original residents he said that "They went back where they came from in order to make room for other families who could benefit and progress in the housing."

All these suggestions require considerable cooperation of the housing authority with the welfare agencies, the courts, the black and Spanish-American communities, and of course the media, to see that they do not again press the authority to the wall. Only with such policies will housing authorities continue to survive and be able to provide housing for at least a few "hard-core families." The remaining hard-core families can only be served by a massive low-moderate-income program in which their numbers will be diluted. As Monsignor Vincent Cooke, the long-term administrator of the Catholic Charities of the Chicago Archdiocese, said, "Only if these families have many models to look up to is there any chance of good prognosis for them and their children."

Equal in importance to reducing the density and improving the quality of the tenancy through eviction is the raising of income levels so as to obtain a good cross section of the low-moderate-income group. The model to be kept in mind is the statistical profile of the low- and moderate-income group. In New York City, for example, the income levels have recently been raised to $9,000 for a family of four persons. However, the raising of income levels is of no consequence unless the admission policy keeps pace with the regulations. In Chicago and many other places, while the admission limit is only $6,000 for a family of four and up to $8,000 for larger families, the median income for the families admitted has been around $3,000, thus rendering useless the higher income limits.

A Role for the Media

All this requires widespread public information with massive help from newspapers, periodicals, TV, radio, and all other forms of the media to the effect that the new program is going to be different. This will not be easy to do with a public that has been accustomed to think of public housing as being only for the most seriously socially disadvantaged and mostly black families. The Chicago *Daily News* of October 15, 1972, at the time when new sites were being considered for public housing in the city, reported that letters were pouring in to the housing authority, 98 percent of which were from citizens protesting against any new public housing projects in their area. Another *Daily News* article reported that in suburban areas only 2 out of 103 areas were even willing to "talk" about public housing programs and those two were Flossmoor and Northbrook, two high-land-cost, upper-middle-class areas where the possibility of placing public housing projects was remote. Even Evanston, the home of Northwestern University and generally a very liberal suburb, seemed to be highly dubious about accepting public housing. This is, of course, not to be wondered at when the chairman of the Chicago Housing Authority [CHA] boasts about public housing's taking care of the "very neediest." Court decisions also spell out the necessity of making a place for "the poor." No suburb or city, middle- or lower-middle-class area, wants to radically change the character of its community. Partly as a result of these narrowed visions of local authorities and liberal groups, projects have been forced into such bad locations that upward-striving, low-moderate-income families, black or white, will not move in. Public housing was not meant for "unemployable hard-core poor" but for workers and for the low-moderate-income segment of the population who cannot afford existing private housing. Yet this intransigent attitude of the CHA is supported by many local liberal groups who are completely unable to see that the remaking of the image of public housing *in the city* is an indispensable

prerequisite to placing any public housing whatever in suburban areas.

Where the problem is not existing projects but the construction of new ones, the program is different. Here it is
of great importance to reassure the community in which
new projects are to be placed of the willingness of the authority to hold the lid on quotas: quotas of race, quotas of
low-income families, quotas of families receiving public assistance, quotas of broken families, and quotas of children.
In all cases the receiving community must be assured that
neither the community nor its schools will have their character materially altered. In this suggestion it is assumed that
new projects (and there will be some eventually from state
and local if not federal funds) will be built in areas hitherto
untouched by public housing

Building in Black Areas

This leaves open the great question of building in the
black areas, areas which are being abandoned today—Hough
in Cleveland, Bedford-Stuyvesant in Brooklyn, many sections of the Bronx, Lawndale and Woodlawn in Chicago.
Probably the most important factor in the new way of looking at public housing must be the building in black areas.
Heretofore this has been a "no no" because it has meant
displacement of black families with no new housing for
them, and the erection of new slums. Chicago more than
any other city has been a battleground where in 1948-55
many battles were fought to build in outlying vacant land,
city or suburban, in order to prevent black slum clearance
and black family displacement. Unfortunately the battle
was lost and black slum clearance took place. In short, the
pendulum had swung again. Because of the slum clearance
that occurred, and because of the great amount of abandonment and consequent demolition programs, there are now
vast areas in black-occupied communities that are vacant
and natural sites for building. Shortsighted attorneys and
courts have used 1948-55 liberal positions to say that hous-

ing cannot be built in these areas because of black displacement. They have coupled this with emphasis on the horrors of the existing gargantuan housing projects and have not recognized that it is possible to build low-rise and medium-rise housing projects which could be in enormous demand.

More farsighted social scientists, while recognizing clearly that integration must push ahead in outlying areas, also recognize the felt need in black areas for housing, integrated or not. And it is in these areas that much housing can be built. This is not to fall into previous errors of building exclusively in these areas, but it will help to break the bottlenecks being caused by such naive decisions in planning as the Gautreaux decision in Chicago which was echoed in Philadelphia and other courts and in some of the federal agencies. [These cases charged that the Chicago Housing Authority's site-selection policies violated the rights of blacks.—Ed.]

On the other hand, in order to make any change in image, as the occasional new project is built—and what with the federal holdback there are not likely to be more than a few—they can be at the outset "vest pocket" projects of 150-200 units, of much the same type as the present privately subsidized "236"s and "221-d3"s [projects financed under the extension of FHA mortgage insurance to the inner city authorized by the National Housing Act]. These are more likely to win community acceptance than anything larger. This also means an end to the principle of infinitesimal housing project units, known as scattered sites, four or five to a site, because such projects are not viable either management- or development-wise. They require much more management service per unit, and are impossible to provide social services for. They are, moreover, as Europeans—who have infinitely more experience in public and nonprofit housing—would tell us, economically impossible. Likewise, if they are to serve only the very poorest families, which is the only reason for making them so small, they become pockets of infection and incurable at that, because there is no dilution of the problem, no models, and the residents are easily identifiable.

There are those who say that public housing is finished, and that the future lies with publicly subsidized, privately owned programs. Certainly some of the existing "vest pocket" projects are living proof that this type of project, in units of 150-500, is viable. Nevertheless, closer looks are needed. Are these projects managing? If not, is it merely because of high property taxes? Are they really capable of handling at minimum expense to the taxpayer the program of serving the low-moderate-income family? Is it worth the large tax subsidy in the form of income tax exemptions presently being allowed? Is it worth the local tax exemptions which so many of them seem to require if they are to be viable? Could they not be managed as well or better by public operators, with less expense to the taxpayer? (Norman Watson, former deputy secretary of housing, indicated that the present subsidy allows to the sponsors about 17.5 percent return on their money even before cash flow.)

There are reasons for believing that many of the private operators will fail. What will happen will be most interesting. With the growth of state housing agencies, mostly to operate or supervise moderate-income housing but some to supervise low-rent housing, new familiarity exists. What could happen is that although the local public housing programs would like to take over the failing "236"s or "221-d3"s from FHA [the Federal Housing Administration], the state agency would be a much more likely possibility. It might well be that under the aegis of the state housing agency, the program could continue as a public moderate- to low-income program. It would not have the stigma attached to public housing now and might easily be a transitional form even for some present public housing operated by local authorities. It is certainly a possibility worth considering since it would also make placement of housing in greater metropolitan areas easier.

WHAT HOUSING FOR
BLUE-COLLAR WORKERS? [6]

The private house in America is the focal point of the myth/dream/reality of the good life for its middle classes as well as the aspirants to those anointed ranks. The automobile has lost much of its glamour: the boat, the trailer, the vacation to Europe are separately and together becoming powerful symbols, but their use—and excursions involving their use—begins with the house.

To current blue-collar workers, moreover, the private house is what the old postal savings system or employer-automatic wage deductions for the purchase of Liberty Bonds or Savings Bonds or War Bonds were to previous generations—a form of relatively painless savings. For all but the more affluent in our society, a house is not only a home, it is typically a major repository of capital investment and stored equity. As any imaginative architect will testify, houses are purchased to be sold, not to be lived in. Their ultimate sale represents the edge which makes Social Security and old age pensions endurable. Possession of a house makes a man a full citizen of the work group.

In this last generation, workingmen of America have moved from being renters to owners. The ramifications of this past shift are far from fully explored, but more important to understand now are the present facts and future realities of the housing stock for American workers. Who builds it? For whom? How? Why? And where?

The New Home Business

About 90 percent of all the new private one-family housing under $15,000 built in the United States in 1971, for example, was in the form of mobile home units. This type of configuration will yield approximately 450,000 out

[6] From "Death of the American Dream House," by George Sternlieb, author, professor of urban and regional planning, director of the Urban Studies Center at Rutgers University. *Society.* 9:39-42. F. '72. Copyright © 1972 by Transaction, Inc. All rights reserved. Reprinted by permission.

of the anticipated 1971 total of two million or so units. Another 400,000 units will be divided nearly evenly between single-family homes and multiple-family residences supported by government mortgage subsidies under the 235-236 Programs [subsidized-interest homeownership program and subsidized-interest apartment program authorized by the National Housing Act] which, depending upon income levels, may bring interest rates down to the 1 percent level. These particular programs are now the primary form of direct federal subsidization of the housing market. (Left out of this discussion are the interminable squabbles on government subsidization of private ownership through preferential tax treatment. Rarely considered are the changes in rents—and possible tax rates—if these nominal windfalls were rectified.)

During the 1930s simple Government guarantees of mortgages under the earlier FHA (Federal Housing Administration) programs were sufficient to inspire developers. In more recent years the inflated amounts of Government-guaranteed indentures, as a function of federal deficits, has increased the interest rate which these bear to the point of making the guarantees in themselves of little use in providing housing. States and municipalities have used the tax-exempt status of their securities with increasing abandon in stepping into the gap. Substantial amounts of housing have been generated under such programs. About a quarter of the states, for example, currently have housing authorities which are financing middle-class housing using tax-exempt securities—and their number is being added to. Again, however, the enormous amount of such tax-exempt securities—windfalls for the rich though they may appear to be—has created a market situation in which the interest rates required to market them is too substantial to permit housing for anything approximating the blue-collar group. In New York City, for example, the Mitchell-Lama Program, which involves tax-exempt fifty-year mortgages and local tax exemption up to the 85 percent mark, yields a housing unit renting currently for $90 per month per room. We will come back to why this should be, but for the moment let us accept the case, even though involving perhaps the national high spot in the providing of public housing, as all too characteristic of what has occurred under tax-exempt financing.

In the last decade, the Federal Government substantially exhausted the potential of even below-market interest rates, which under the 221-d3 Program [projects financed under the extension of FHA mortgage insurance to the inner city authorized by National Housing Act] for example, brought interest rates down to the 3 to 3.5 percent level. This too lost its charm and so the 235-236 Programs at the 1 percent level.

Even with these subsidies, however, the absolute costs of amortization involve cash-flow requirements of enormous magnitude. Even stretched out over more than lifetime expectancies (fifty years with Mitchell-Lama, the forty-eight years of New Jersey Housing Finance Agency and the like), together with steep rises in local taxation and operating costs, they increasingly leave the working classes out of the spectrum of housing groups that can be accommodated within the present state of the art. In Trenton, New Jersey, for example, four hundred units under the 236 Program were just completed at costs of $33,000 per unit. The rents with the full subsidy package approximate $200 a month for two-bedroom units. Since there is an income limit under the 235-236 Program of 135 percent of public-housing admission standards for people who will be subsidized by the program, the answer was to raise the local public-housing limits so that people with incomes of $10,000 and more are presently being housed by a program which was dedicated in its inception to the needs of blue-collar America.

There is a growing body of opinion which holds that the very intervention of governmental subsidy mechanisms into the housing market has served to engender additional increases in the housing costs which they were intended to resolve.

Residential construction costs in America over the last twenty years have never been forced to meet the test of the market. When housing starts to slow down, when land speculators begin to be worried about the inflated values of their holdings, when building-trade workers start shading their prices, the cry comes up that something must be done about housing and a new stimulant is added to the market. This is all in good cause and good conscience. The result, however, is that private conventional housing in much of the Northeast has substantially disappeared at anything under the $25,000 mark; indeed in many of the more affluent suburbs one would have to add another $10,000 to the cost.

In many cases the blue-collar worker finds himself too poor to compete in the unaided market and too rich or sometimes too poor to take advantage of the current forms of Government subsidy. There is little in the way of technological innovation which would seem to alter this picture. The answer presently being implemented, in any case, is the lessening of housing quality, size of structure and general lowering of standards; and all of these efforts succeed only at best in momentarily stabilizing prices.

The new private house may be the dream of blue-collar America; its reality, however, is drifting away.

The Suburban Squeeze Play

The question of where new housing is to be built is one of the most publicized elements in the current dilemma. It has been highlighted not only in terms of the provision of housing but also for securing a variety of public ends.

There has been a significant upgrading of land-use requirements in most suburbs. In the northern half of New Jersey, for example, more than half of all the vacant land zoned for residential purposes requires lots of one or more acres. And this, to any good, concerned citizen is *prima facie* evidence of the wickedness and sinfulness of the suburbanite.

To paraphrase Bertolt Brecht: the rich (and the middle-class and the blue-collar worker) may love the poor, but they hate living near them. This is particularly true when their skin color or languages may be different from the mainstream.

Without minimizing the role that prejudice undoubtedly plays in suburban freezeout, one should also not disregard the old-fashioned role of economics. The poor cost more. To use very rough numbers, if one assumes that local realty taxes (which are the main source of revenue for community expenditures) represent at most 25 percent of the rent dollar (and in public housing typically the payments in lieu of local tax are only 10 percent of the gross shelter rent) it becomes very evident that typical local revenues derived from poor families are inadequate to provide the schooling of even one child. This is without attention being paid to any of the other increments in cost generated by the addition of a family. And the same holds true for the blue-collar worker at typical incomes.

In some unique, highly affluent suburbs, liberal forces are at work to crack the suburban barrier. In Princeton, New Jersey, for example, there are presently under consideration more than five hundred units of public and low-income housing. The resistance to this addition comes not so much from the affluent of the community as it does from the lingering remnants of blue-collar workers and low-level municipal employees—from the policemen making $10,000 a year and paying 10 percent of it in local taxes, from the maintenance worker working in the local RCA plant and third generation in the community, owning a house and feeling it slipping from his fingers as local taxes increase at a 10-percent-a-year, compounded annually, rate.

The great bulk of government programs which intervene in the municipal sphere at best supply subsidies for capital grants; at worst they tend to involve the community, practically willy-nilly, in greater levels of operating cost. Until, and unless, there is some fiscal packaging of the local costs generated by the additions of moderate- and low-income families to the community, the political reality—"cracking zoning is suicide"—will hold. The recent California court decision, *Serrano et al. v. Ivy Baker Priest,* which declared that substantial dependence on local property taxes violated the equal protection clause of the Fourteenth Amendment, may have much more in the way of positive results in opening up the suburbs than all of the efforts at intervention based upon racial equity.

In the meantime, however, the blue-collar workers, particularly those who reside in the older suburbs, guard the walls as best they can from the middle-class aspirants who are fleeing the central city. Certainly this is in substantial part because of prejudice but even more through economic fear.

Racial factors cloak basic economic elements and keep us from coming to political grips with them at great general cost. And for proof that these fears within the parameters of present societal organization are not merely fantasies, the suburban blue collars have only to look at the plight of those of their fellows who remain in the central city.

Trapped in the City

There are many profundities that have been exchanged on the subject of the relatively poor interface between older ethnic minorities, particularly those in the blue-collar occupations/income levels and the black and Puerto Rican populations within central cities. Perhaps so obvious as to be beneath intellectualizing are the impacts of the basic economic elements.

Newark, as in so many other areas, is a clear-cut prototype. The current tax rate is approximately 8 percent of real value. The worker residing in the city—perhaps in one of its white enclaves—or for that matter, since skin color is irrelevant here, the new minority-group homebuyers find that the house, that may have been purchased a dozen years ago and which was looked forward to as the essential cushion for the Florida retirement or as the cash with which to make the down payment on a more desirably sited residence, is instead a dead end. The man that can afford a $1,600 tax bill on a modest $20,000 house doesn't want to live in Newark; the man who can only afford $20,000 for a house can't afford the tax bill. And in neither case is there a bank to grant a mortgage or an insurance company to give essential coverage. The blue-collar worker in Newark is joined by his equivalent on the police department or the fire department in a strong resentment against those who he feels have occasioned this impasse.

There is an interesting variation in owner attitudes towards the central city's problems. In a recent survey of Newark, absentee owners, typically of multiple tenancies, viewed their tenants as their prime problem. Resident owners, on the other hand, ranked taxes and tax increases as the premier difficulty and this is a response which is substantially independent of racc. Whether in the central city or in some of the older suburbs that are open for mixed occupancy, there are an increasing number of black homeowners typically recruited either from the ranks of the better paid blue-collar workers or equivalent income levels of white-collar and governmental operations. Their attitudes and responses, at least to our surveys, are much more in accord with the economic frame of reference, regardless of their skin color, than they are of any racial element.

The Myth of Homeownership

For the first time since the Second World War the level of multiple-tenancy housing starts will exceed that of private one-family houses. In part this is a tribute to the characteristics of our new household formation; the postwar baby boom is rapidly coming to fruition; the children of 1946, 1947, 1948, 1949 are forming the new households of 1971 and must be housed. Typically this takes on the form of the garden-apartment house or its equivalent. But these accommodations, in turn, at least according to folklore and for that matter much reality of the recent past, are viewed by consumers as essentially way stations on the life cycle, serving as a temporary abode until (with one-and-a-half children) the migration is made to the one-family tract development. There is increasing evidence that at least for the blue-collar workers in America and for all others of equivalent income this may no longer be a tenable mode.

As pointed out earlier, the well of housing subsidies is beginning to run dry; its effects no longer, at least in the higher-cost areas of the country, adequate in providing modest one-family developments in conventional settings. Again the response in earlier years has been to increase the level of subsidies in one form or another. The question may well be asked, given the political pressures that are so virile in housing, as to whether this process may not be repeated in the future.

ARE HOUSING COSTS REALLY RISING? [7]

The cost of housing construction has risen so much that people cannot afford as much housing as they formerly bought at lower income levels when construction costs were cheaper.

—Yale Brozen, *Barron's Weekly,* 25 January 1971

While the middle class may well be indifferent to the plight of the poor, it can no longer ignore the fact that they themselves are being priced out of the housing market.

Testifying before the House Banking and Currency Committee in early 1970, HUD [Department of Housing and Urban Development] Secretary George Romney stated that to afford the median-priced home then being offered for sale ($27,000) without unreasonably stretching its budget, a family needed an income of

[7] From "The Cost of Housing," by B. Bruce-Briggs, a member of the staff of the Hudson Institute. *Public Interest.* No. 32:34-42. Summer '73. Copyright © 1973 by National Affairs, Inc. Reprinted by permission of the author and of *The Public Interest.*

nearly $14,000. Yet fewer than one family in five had an income that high. It's a remarkable statistic and, despite modest decreases in financing costs since then, it is not much improved today.

The housing crisis is clearly spreading to the once comfortable middle class, and if land and construction costs continue to increase faster than personal incomes, the crises will surely intensify. In these circumstances, it seems likely that housing inevitably will command a substantially greater share of our natural resources.
—Thomas L. Ashley, *City*, Summer 1972

The two quotations above illustrate the widely held belief that more and more Americans are being priced out of the housing market. This belief is by no means limited to radical critics of the American economic system—Ashley is a ranking Democratic member of the House Banking Committee (the committee responsible for housing legislation), while Brozen has done work for the conservative American Enterprise Institute. The idea of housing becoming more dear is a commonplace in discussions of urban affairs. Happily, this notion is quite incorrect.

Of course, finding decent housing at a reasonable cost remains a major problem to poor Americans, particularly in big cities. And there are local areas where housing is getting more expensive, particularly in New York City.

It is unfortunate that the New York experience has so flavored the media's perception of housing issues. A city containing mostly rented, multifamily, rent-controlled housing built on limited land is hardly relevant to a nation of mostly single-family, owned, and uncontrolled housing built on nearly limitless land. Even the East Harlem tenements observed by Penn Central commuters are not typical of the prevailing "shanty-town" slums of most cities.

However it is easy to show that *nationally* housing is not getting more expensive; but since the belief in "escalating housing costs" is so widespread (indeed, nearly universal), it is necessary to make the demonstration in detail, employing a lot of dull numbers.

To begin with, housing, like almost everything else, has become more expensive in current dollars because of inflation. But has housing become more dear relative to income? According to the United States Census Bureau it has not:

TABLE 1. *Income and the Value of Houses, 1960-1970*

	MEDIAN FAMILY INCOME	MEDIAN VALUE OF HOUSES
1960	$5,620	$11,900
1970	9,867	17,000
(Gain 1960-1970)	(75%)	(43%)

Perhaps it may be doubted if the ratio of median family income to the median value of homes properly represents the relationship of *all* families to *all* homes. Actually, the distribution of incomes around the median has been nearly constant during the last generation. One way to check this relationship is to compare the median new-home cost with the distribution of income. The following table assumes the "two-to-one" rule common in the housing market—i.e., a family is able to afford a house worth twice its annual income. Thus, if the median home sells for $20,000, any family with an income above $10,000 "can afford it."

TABLE 2. *The "Two-to-One" Rule*

	MEDIAN VALUE OF HOUSES	PER CENT OF FAMILIES WHO CAN AFFORD MEDIAN HOUSE
1960	$11,900	46
1970	17,000	54

But many people question the accuracy of the Census. No doubt many homeowners reported the purchase price rather than the market value of their houses. Fortunately, we have some more detailed statistics on housing costs published by the FHA [Federal Housing Administration]. All these figures refer to *new* homes *sold* and indicate that new homes have been getting relatively cheaper:

TABLE 3. *New Homes Sold, 1963-1971**

	MEDIAN PRICE FHA MORTGAGED HOUSES	MEDIAN PRICE ALL TYPES OF FINANCING	MEDIAN FAMILY INCOME	RATIO OF FHA MEDIAN TO MEDIAN INCOME	RATIO OF ALL HOMES MEDIAN TO MEDIAN INCOME
1963	$15,500	$18,000	$ 6,265	2.49	2.89
1965	16,500	20,000	6,957	2.31	2.87
1968	19,200	24,700	8,032	2.25	2.86
1969	19,300	25,600	9,433	2.05	2.74
1970	19,200	23,400	9,867	1.95	2.37
1971	19,800	25,200	10,285	1.93	2.45

* *Statistical Abstract of the United States*

One could argue that median family income is a poor indicator of real resources. Social Security and state and local income taxes have greatly increased in the 1960s and, despite tax cuts, inflation has pushed families into higher federal income tax brackets. Happily, in the *Monthly Labor Review* the Bureau of Labor Statistics publishes an indicator of weekly "spendable income for a nonsupervisory worker with three dependents." "Spendable income" is not quite the same as "take-home" pay because it does not deduct local taxes, union dues, and medical insurance, but still it is a reasonable indicator of the disposable income of a blue-collar family.

TABLE 4. *"Spendable Income" and Housing Prices, 1960-1970*

	"SPENDABLE INCOME" WEEKLY	MEDIAN HOUSE PRICE
1960	$ 72.96	$11,900
1970	104.61	17,000
(Gain 1960-1970)	(43%)	(43%)

Some Breakdowns of Housing Costs

One often-mentioned cause of the alleged escalation of housing costs is that construction costs are "skyrocketing," particularly building-trades wages. The indicators of residential construction costs shown in Table 5 [below] would seem to give little support for this analysis:

TABLE 5. *Price and Cost Indices for Construction and Select-
ed Components of Construction, 1971 (1967 Base)**

Median Family Income	129**
All Consumer Prices	121
Price of New One-Family Houses Sold	123
Wholesale Prices of Construction Materials	119.5
Building Trades Union Wages	144
Boeckh Small Residential Structure Cost Index	133
Boeckh Apartments, Hotels & Office Buildings Cost Index	135

* *Statistical Abstract*
** Calculated from USBC, P-60; 85

Some wages and some materials have very high costs, but not all construction labor is highly paid, especially where it is ununionized. In 1970 the median income of all full-time male workers (including bosses) in the construction industry was $9,091, lower than all industry groups except agriculture, retail trade, and business services. (*Monthly Labor Review,* December 1972, p. 19.)

Little public attention has been given to the improved productivity of on-site labor, the gradual improvement of management skills, and the steady shift from on-site labor to off-site preassembly of major components. Certainly, there is a lot of graft and featherbedding in the industry, but most construction workers are highly skilled and highly productive.

Another alleged villain in the "housing crisis" is the rapidly escalating cost of land, said to be caused largely by exclusionary" zoning ordinances which "bar" poor people from the suburbs:

TABLE 6. *Site Value, 1960-1970**

	FHA MORTGAGED NEW HOMES	FHA MORTGAGED USED HOMES
1960	$2,404	$2,285
1965	3,137	2,955
1970	4,477	3,469
(Gain 1960-1970)	(86%)	(52%)

* *Statistical Abstract*

Since median family income went up 75 percent in the same decade, it might be argued that the higher gains for new home sites indicate that many people are being priced out. Actually, however, the cost of land is a tiny part of total housing costs. For example, take the breakdown of monthly cost for a then typical $16,000 home (Table 7 [below]) published by the (Kaiser) Commission on Urban Housing in 1968. Merely halving the cost of land would reduce the total cost by 1 percent, and would achieve some, but not proportionate, savings in land development costs.

TABLE 7. *Monthly Cost Breakdown for a $16,000 Home (1968)*

Land	$ 4	(2%)
Development	9	(5%)
Construction	29	(17%)
Interest	50	(29%)
Taxes	45	(26%)
Utilities	29	(17%)
Maintenance & Repair	8	(5%)
Total	$174	(100%)

When someone writes, "X percent of the public cannot afford a house," and cites the cost of new homes to support his position, he is ignoring the fact that most families buy *used* homes. The readily available data for used homes are less complete than for new houses, but they show the same lack of increase in relative cost.

TABLE 8. *Existing Homes Sold, 1960-1970**

	WITH FHA MORTGAGES		WITH VA MORTGAGES	
	SALES PRICE	RATIO TO MEDIAN FAMILY INCOME	SALES PRICE	RATIO TO MEDIAN FAMILY INCOME
1960	$13,227	2.36:1	$12,238	2.19:1
1965	15,114	2.18:1	16,371	2.35:1
1970	17,842	1.81:1	19,500	1.98:1

* *Statistical Abstract*

The gain in value of VA houses between 1960 and 1965 [see Table 8, page 73] suggests that World War II and Korea vets were getting more prosperous and buying better homes. After 1965 younger "cold war" and Vietnam veterans began to obtain VA mortgages.

But what of the $27,000 house cited by Ashley above? That figure is the *asking* price of a new house—a price rarely paid. But even here the trend has been favorable, as is shown in Table 9 [below].

Homeownership Costs and Trends

Another commonly available source of data is the consumer price indices (CPI) published by the Bureau of Labor Statistics. The "homeownership" price index rose 49

TABLE 9. *Asking Prices of New Houses, 1965-1971**

	MEDIAN INTENDED SALES PRICE, NEW HOUSES FOR SALE	RATIO TO MEDIAN FAMILY INCOME
1965	$21,300	3.06
1968	24,600	2.85
1969	27,000	2.86
1970	26,200	2.66
1971	25,900	2.52

* Statistical Abstract

percent during the period 1960-1970 compared with 43 percent for "spendable income" and 75 percent for median family income, so apparently while our middle family is better off, our "typical" blue-collar family fell back slightly. Yes, but more interesting things were happening in the cost of housing. Table 10 [page 75] employs an artificial indicator derived by dividing spendable income by the price index for homeownership:

TABLE 10. *"Spendable Income" and CPI-Homeownership, 1955-1972*

	"SPENDABLE INCOME"	CONSUMER PRICE INDEX— HOME- OWNERSHIP	WAGE/ HOME- OWNERSHIP RATIO
1955	$ 63.41	77.0	.82
1960	72.96	86.3	.84
1965	86.30	92.7	.93
1966	88.66	96.3	.92
1967	90.86	100.0	.91
1968	95.28	105.7	.90
1969	99.99	116.0	.86
1970	104.61	128.5	.81
1971	112.12	133.7	.84
1972	120.79	140.1	.86

Note that the relative position of the wage-earner improved steadily until 1965, then began to deteriorate until 1970, and has improved since. These changes are attributable not to the cost of a house but to fluctuations in other housing costs—mortgage interest rates, property taxes, insurance, and maintenance, which together make up well over half the cost of homeownership. The changes in these costs for the period 1960-1972 are presented in Table 11 [page 76].

The big items are interest rates and property taxes, both of which rose sharply in the late 1960s. These increases can be blamed not on inadequacies of the housing market, but rather on governmental policy. The high interest rates were caused by the deficit spending of the Johnson Administration's "guns and butter" programs and the Nixon Administration's initially ineffectual attempts to deal with the consequent inflation. Increased property taxes are the result of swelling local government costs, prompted largely by the unionization of municipal employees, but with some encouragement to spend by "the Feds" through various "matching grant" programs.

TABLE 11. *Consumer Price Indices (1967 Base)*

	MORTGAGE INTEREST RATES	PROPERTY TAXES	PROPERTY INSURANCE	MAINTENANCE AND REPAIRS
1960	95.3	N/A	76.9	84.6
1963	90.0	86.7	80.0	87.7
1965	89.7	91.5	89.8	91.3
1966	96.4	94.4	94.6	95.2
1967	100.0	100.0	100.0	100.0
1968	106.7	105.6	104.7	106.1
1969	120.0	111.9	109.3	115.0
1970	132.1	121.0	113.4	124.0
1971	120.4	131.1	119.9	133.7
1972	117.5	145.7	123.2	140.7
Gain 1960-1970	(39%)	(N/A)	(48%)	(47%)
Gain 1960-1965	(−6%)	(N/A)	(4%)	(8%)
Gain 1965-1970	(47%)	(32%)	(26%)	(36%)
Gain 1970-1972	(−11%)	(20%)	(9%)	(13%)

The final answer to the argument that people are being "priced out of the housing market" is that the number and percentage of homeowners increased during the decade of the 1960s. According to the Census, 64.2 percent of housing units (houses and apartments) were owner-occupied in 1970 versus 61.9 percent in 1960. (Also worth noting is that nonwhite homeownership gained from 38 percent to 42 percent during the same period.) The fact that this gain was trivial compared with the rapid growth in homeownership during the early postwar period may be attributable to the vast augmentation of newly-formed households as the postwar "baby boom" generation came of age, married, and settled down. Certainly this group does not appear to have been cramped for space—the percentage of married couples not living in their own household (mostly with his or her parents) dropped from 2.9 percent to 1.4 percent during the 1960s. Our national standard of housing has increased so much that we find it difficult to recall that once upon a time young couples had to postpone marriage until they could find a place to live. Another change taken for granted today is the near disappearance of rooming and boarding houses.

The Situation of Renters

Maybe this concentration on homeownership is misleading—what about the one third of the nation that rents? Generally, the renters are less prosperous than owners and, according to some lights, more deserving of public concern. Rental data are less complete than those for ownership, but show almost the same pattern, as can be seen from the Census data in Table 12:

TABLE 12. *Income and Rental Costs, 1960-1970*

	MEDIAN FAMILY INCOME	"SPENDABLE INCOME"	MEDIAN MONTHLY RENT
1960	$5,620	$ 72.96	$58
1970	9,867	104.61	90
Gain 1960-1970	(75%)	(44%)	(55%)

And using the crude rule that a family should be able to afford to rent a home for 20 percent of its income, we arrive at the figures in Table 13 [below]. Of course, use of these (or any other) rules of thumb shows that housing remains too expensive, particularly for the poor. The amount of housing units available at low cost or rent falls far short of the number of low-income families. Much needs to be done, but there is no evidence that the situation is deteriorating.

TABLE 13. *The 20 Percent Rule*

	MEDIAN YEARLY RENT	PER CENT OF FAMILIES WHO CAN AFFORD THE MEDIAN RENT
1960	$ 700	73.4
1970	1,180	75.6

And comparing "spendable income" with the consumer price index for rent, we come up with Table 14 [page 78]:

TABLE 14. *"Spendable Income" and CPI—Rent, 1950-1972*

	"SPENDABLE INCOME"	CONSUMER PRICE INDEX—RENT	RATIO OF WAGES TO RENT
1950	52.04	70.4	.74
1955	63.41	84.3	.75
1960	72.96	91.7	.79
1965	86.30	96.9	.89
1968	95.28	102.4	.93
1969	99.99	105.7	.94
1970	104.01	110.1	.95
1971	112.12	115.2	.97
1972	120.79	119.2	1.01

The cost of rent relative to wages has steadily dropped through the 1960s and into the early 1970s. And of course, today's rental housing, like owned housing, is on the average qualitatively better than it was in the past in terms of unit floor space, floor space and rooms per person, plumbing, and structural condition. Indeed, much of the worst housing is now being "thrown away"—i.e., abandoned.

The Sources of Misconception

All of these data may be wrong (the consumer price indices are suspicious), but it is striking that they all lead to the same conclusion—that American housing is *not* getting more expensive, except for the minority whose income is not keeping pace with national gains. The data cited above are available to anyone. Indeed, almost all of this information is published in the most widespread sources for social science information—the *Statistical Abstract of the United States* and the *Monthly Labor Review*. The few calculations I have made can be done by anyone who has mastered long division. Why then is it widely accepted that housing costs have been increasing during the past decade? On *this* question there are no readily available data, and I prefer not to speculate here on social, political, and ideological matters. Of course, we all tend to repeat what J. K. Galbraith calls "the conventional wisdom."

But perhaps more important is the rather narrow upper-middle-class perspective of most writers on urban affairs. At seminars and meetings I often ask the audience to estimate the median value of all rents in the Borough of Manhattan [in New York City]. The answers always range between $200 and $300 a month. According to the 1970 Census, Manhattan's median rent was $99—not far from the rents for the other boroughs of New York or for the rest of the nation. The upper-middle-class audience of our seminars and meetings only seeks space or knows people who occupy space in rather limited areas of the borough. Large areas of the city are *terra incognita* to this group on account of its class standards and racial biases. The upper-middle class has expanded rapidly in recent years and demand for its established residential areas has far outstripped supply. Swank inner-city areas (e.g., Manhattan's East Side), "bohemias" (e.g., Chicago's Old Town), and good inner suburbs (e.g., Boston's Brookline) are under heavy pressure. The availability of plenty of moderate-cost housing in lower-middle-class neighborhoods or "ticky-tacky" suburbs is irrelevant to the urban upper-middle classes. Happily, most other Americans are getting better housing at lower real cost than at any time in our history.

II. GOVERNMENT HOUSING POLICY

EDITOR'S INTRODUCTION

More than two decades ago (in 1949) Federal legislation promised to provide "every American with a decent home in a suitable living environment." That this has not been accomplished—rather that a crisis situation in housing has developed—is now obvious. The many housing programs, their successes and failures, undertaken in the intervening years since 1949 cannot be surveyed in this compilation, but Federal legislation of 1972-73 is dealt with. The following articles chiefly concern the present Nixon Administration views and proposals on housing.

At the very beginning of 1973, President Nixon, in keeping with his proposals for a "new federalism" and the curbing of Federal spending, halted several housing programs, announcing an eighteen-month moratorium of new commitments for subsidized housing; termination of community development programs, which were to be replaced in part by special revenue sharing; and impounding of 1973 funds for housing, community development, and rural development.

As a result of these actions, the Government's housing programs have remained in virtual limbo. But the Nixon Administration's viewpoints on housing and urban development have, nevertheless, become fairly well known. They are set forth below in an interview with James T. Lynn, Secretary of Housing and Urban Development.

The status of urban renewal policies, and a plea for continuation of urban renewal, is presented by Ralph Thayer, a member of the editorial board of the *Ripon Forum*. And next, the subject of direct housing allowances is canvassed by Joseph P. Fried, a journalist who reports on housing and urban affairs. The Nixon Administration's proposal for direct housing-allowance legislation is reported by Harry B. Ellis, business-financial correspondent of *The Christian Science Monitor*. An editorial from the New York *Times*, critical of such legislation, closes this section's discussion of past and current Federal housing policies.

The last three articles cover suggestions for future Government housing and urban development policies. Housing lessons for the future are set forth by M. Carter McFarland, formerly with the Department of Housing and Urban Development and now director of urban affairs and housing programs for the American Institute of Architects. Next, the need for regional government units to deal with housing and related urban-area problems is touched on by Martin Gallent, a member of the New York City Planning Commission. Last, a broader program for reshaping metropolitan America is given by Sol M. Linowitz, chairman of the National Urban Coalition.

VIEWS OF THE NIXON ADMINISTRATION [1]

Reprinted from *U.S. News & World Report*.

Q. Mr. Secretary, some experts are saying that the big cities, by and large, are outdated and hopeless. What should this country be doing about its cities?

A. I hear a lot of gloom and doom in this regard, but I don't think the situation is that bad, by any means. The challenges vary greatly from one city to another.

We have some cities with large problems of poverty in the inner city; areas that are terribly overcrowded, where housing is deteriorating very rapidly. There are still cities with major crime problems. But when you go through some other cities, you find problems of this kind being relatively minor.

[1] "What Can Be Done to Save the Big Cities," interview with James T. Lynn, secretary of housing and urban development. *U.S. News & World Report*. 74:51-4. Je. 18, '73.

For the larger city with its big problems, one of the best things we can do is to give the people in that city the right kind of support to find solutions.

Q. Does that mean more money for housing and community development, for example?

A. It certainly means providing funding assistance for community development. After all, the problem of the city is not just a housing problem, or a problem of jobs, or of health or transportation; it is a combination of all those problems and more.

What we are trying to do in the Better Communities Act which the President has proposed to Congress is to give the people back in the community the opportunity to work on their own problems and to assist them with funding. The President will also be proposing a Responsive Governments Act that would provide better funding to assist both states and local governments to improve the planning and management of their programs.

We want to put these communities into a position where they can get the facts on their own situation, see what the alternatives are, and manage and evaluate their programs properly.

One of the most encouraging things we've seen is that the cities themselves and states are spending more money on planning and management—more than matching the funds that have been provided in the last couple of years by the Federal Government—in order to beef up their own capacity. After all, running a local government today is a big business, requiring many kinds of skills to handle it well.

The Better Communities Act

Q. What is the basic philosophy of your Better Communities Act?

A. Our main thrust is to return the decision making on community development to the officials who are closest to the people and who are elected by those people.

Another very important aim is to divide our money among the communities on the basis of objective needs, not on the basis of which city is the best "grantsman" or happens to have a problem that can be met through a narrow program of categorical grants.

Q. How much money would the Act provide?

A. $2.3 billion a year in the initial years. That is more than has been appropriated in the fiscal year ending June 30, 1973, for the seven grant-in-aid programs that the Act would replace: Urban Renewal, Model Cities, Open Space, Public Facilities, Neighborhood Facilities, Rehabilitation Loans, and Water and Sewer Grants.

Q. How would the money be split up?

A. There are three elements in the formula: population, overcrowding and the number of people living in the community with incomes below the poverty level. The poverty factor would be given double weight.

Q. What would all this mean, for instance, to a city in as much difficulty as New York?

A. First, it will help the city of New York solve its problems, because it means substantially more funds to that city than it now receives under the seven categorical programs the Act would replace.

In the second place, it will help in this way: It will turn the attention of the interest groups—the people who care about New York, who want to keep it one of the great cities of the world—toward the city fathers of New York City. That should be a lot more cohesive than the present situation, where you have those people walking from one Federal office to another in Washington, D.C., with their hands out trying to get money. It will bring coordination to city planning that you can't get when people are out after a variety of different grants in Washington.

Q. Should the Federal Government do anything to reduce the concentrations of poor people and minorities in the inner cities?

A. That is an important problem in a number of cities. This creates terrible problems for the people who live under those conditions, and for city services.

The President has said that when it comes to dispersal based on housing patterns, we are not going to compel any community to accept any particular pattern of income levels. On the other hand, we do want to encourage each community to provide housing for people of various economic levels, and, where they want to do it, we want to give assistance if it's possible to do so.

Now, a very clear line has to be made between housing patterns that are based on differences of income and those that are based on racial discrimination. The law doesn't tolerate racial discrimination, and I'm not going to either. It's important to note that in the Better Communities Act there are sanctions to be imposed if there is discrimination.

Q. Would it be better to tackle these local problems on a metropolitan-area basis instead of having to depend on a lot of independent governing bodies in the cities and the suburbs?

A. We have to work with what we have now. If you're going to return the power closer to the people under the existing structure, you have to return it to the cities that presently exist and that have the authority to solve the problems. Putting some of the funds under the Better Communities Act in the hands of the governors should bring some meaningful efforts at coordination, however.

Q. How would the governors fit into the scheme?

A. This Act, for the first time, would provide substantial responsibility and authority in the field of community development to the states. In the beginning, about 8 percent—and eventually 21 percent—of the funds would go to the states. Half of this amount would have to be allocated by the state government to units of general local government within the standard metropolitan areas in amounts reflecting the basic-needs formula.

It would be up to the state to decide which problems and sections of each metropolitan area should get the funds, and the governor is going to have a great interest and great authority in tackling problems that cut across the local political boundaries. So we will get coordination such as we have never seen in the old grant-in-aid programs.

Of course, what's going to bring about real coordination is an increasing realization by the people in the outer cities —in the suburbs around the inner city—that their own destinies and the health of their communities rest on solving the problems of the inner city as well as their own neighborhood problems.

Q. What would happen to the other half of the money that would be given to the state officials to allocate?

A. The state can apportion the other half to any community in the state: rural towns, suburbs outside the standard metropolitan areas, or cities within metropolitan areas.

Q. Do you have evidence that the money the cities are now receiving for Urban Renewal, Model Cities, Open Space, Public Facilities and the like is being wasted?

A. The basic problem is that these programs too often artificially distort a city's priorities.

Take Urban Renewal: The program may cause a city to spend money buying a particular piece of real estate for development when it would have preferred to use the money for restoration of existing buildings or perhaps for better management of urban-renewal projects that were already under way.

One of the best examples is the story of the mayor who wanted to find out what Federal monies were coming into his community and what the results were. He found that he had received $56 million in Federal grants but—to his horror —he also discovered that he was spending $26 million of local money to get the $56 million. And it took a separate $200,000 Federal grant and one year of study to find this out. When he compared the things he was getting with that money with the things he thought were really important to his community, there were many distortions.

Action on Housing Programs

Q. Turning to housing programs, Mr. Lynn: Why did the President decide in January that the Government should stop approving new housing projects for Federal subsidies?

A. We felt these programs had been found wanting in very serious respects, considering the standpoint of our dual goals of housing the needy and getting the most benefit for the taxpayer's dollar.

Remember that we have built more subsidized housing in the last 4 years—1.5 million units—than had been built in the previous 34 years.

Some good housing has been produced by those programs, but we also found major faults.

First of all, somewhere between $65 billion and $85 billion of subsidies will be payable on those 1.5 million units over as long as the next thirty to forty years. We can't help but think there must be a better way of serving people for less money.

Second, we found all sorts of inequities in the program. For example, it doesn't seem right for one man to qualify for a subsidy to buy or rent a new home while another man who is making $50 a week more doesn't qualify and has to go on living in an old home.

We also discovered that the laws are operating in such a way as to jeopardize the financial responsibility of public-housing projects. People who can afford to do so are moving out, often leaving behind a more unstable element. As a result of severe statutory income limits, the projects find themselves with declining rents and rising expenses.

It seemed to us that we had to find solutions for problems of that sort.

Q. Is there growing support for the idea of giving low-income people direct cash allowances to help pay for their housing, instead of paying subsidies for construction or financing?

A. That is a view held by a number of very reputable people. The Department is conducting experiments that will involve about 20,000 families and $150 million to test various forms of housing allowances.

Proponents of the housing allowances say: "Let the person choose his house. Don't tie your Federal assistance so much to new construction. After all, the idea is to house people, not to build new housing for them. And, what's more, people will have more choice as to where they want to live."

The opponents claim that what will result is a fair amount of rent gouging. They say that as you put more money in the hands of people to pay for housing, the landlords will raise their rents.

Other people say there will be fraudulent practices—where the tenant will make a deal with the landlord, and they'll claim the rent is more than it actually is and split the difference.

It seems to me the only fair way to find out where the truth lies is to give the idea a try in various ways, and that's what we're doing.

Q. How long will it take to test the idea?

A. Several years.

Q. Does it worry you that housing costs and real-estate prices are going up sharply across the country?

A. It's of great concern to me. We've seen areas where housing costs have escalated tremendously.

What I don't know is: How much have rents and mortgage payments really gotten out of line with increases in wages? If you take a person making a certain amount ten years ago and compare what he's making today, can he buy more or less housing than he could then?

I suspect that with our lower-income people the rise in costs has had quite an effect. As to people in what I would call middle-income America, I'm not at all certain.

Q. Do you think people are getting better houses for the higher prices?

A. One builder said to me the other day:

It's hard to tell, Jim. How many houses do I put a twenty-five-gallon hot-water heater into any more? How many houses are there with a living room that is only 9 feet by 8 eight feet? How many houses do I build today that have gravel driveways? It's very hard to compare because, although we see higher-priced houses, the higher price at least in part reflects a different-quality house than was on the market ten years ago.

And another thing I have to add: A figure that stands out very starkly is that we have cut in half the number of substandard houses in the United States in the ten-year period from 1960 to 1970.

Suspending Model Cities Programs

Q. Will suspension of Model Cities programs and other grants-in-aid to the cities put some of them in a financial bind?

A. Let me put that in perspective, if I can.

As of June 30, 1973, we will still have $7.4 billion committed for grant-in-aid programs. That money has not yet been spent by the communities to whom we have made the commitments. It will be paid out in some cases over a one- or two-year period; in other cases over as much as a seven-year period.

The cities will be building more neighborhood facilities with this money in the next fiscal year than they are building in the current year, ending June 30, 1973. So there is momentum here that takes care of the transition until Congress approves the Better Communities Act.

Q. But will some cities be hard pressed as a result of the decision to suspend new commitments?

A. I wouldn't use the term "hard pressed." There will be some communities where there will be some reduction in activity in one program—Model Cities—during the course of the next fiscal year. HUD has determined that a number of communities really weren't doing a good job under that program and that they should be dropped from the program. Other Model Cities cities had their funding reduced because of poor performance.

Even so, the funds for all cities remaining in the program for the year beginning July 1, 1973, will still total about 70 percent of what they would have received under prior funding levels. Programs for two thirds of the cities will be funded at a level of 85 percent.

Q. What happens to a city that has plans for community development that weren't approved before the suspension? Is it going to be stopped dead in its tracks until Congress acts on your new proposal?

A. First, you have to consider what the situation would be under present law if there had not been a suspension of the old grant programs.

If local officials have a new project, they would have to go through a process that looks on a chart like an electronic diagram for Apollo 17, and it would take them at least fifteen months to get all of the necessary approvals and get the money and start breaking ground. That means they'd be well past July 1, 1974.

Under the Better Communities Act, effective July 1, 1974, these cities will have the money in hand—if Congress approves—so that if they've assessed their priorities and determined how they want to spend the funds under that new legislation, they can, with no red tape whatsoever, go ahead and immediately start spending for that purpose.

Extent of Federal Involvement

Q. The programs become a local responsibility, supported by Federal funds—

A. Absolutely. The Federal involvement will be (1) dis-
tributing the money according to the formula laid down in
the law; (2) receiving plans from the communities once a
year setting forth their priorities, objectives, how they in-
tend to spend the funds; and (3) receiving certification that
they are in compliance with the law. There is an audit function also.

Q. Are any guidelines laid down for the cities to follow?

A. First, the city or the county would prepare a proposed
plan. Then they would have to take their statement of proposed activities to the community and make it available for
review and comment for sixty days. It's only after those com-
ments are in that the local officials could finalize the plan.

What we do by this is to return the power to the people,
because we're giving the money to the elected officials near-
est the people and cutting out the red tape that has been
required for approval of plans in Washington. We'll also
get rid of the interminable delays we have seen in the past
and provide a very democratic way for people to have their
inputs into these programs.

Plenty of Room for Diversity

Q. What if the program the local people favor has little
or nothing to do with community development, or if they
wind up spending the money on things that are not related
to the plan they submit to you for review?

A. Keep in mind that money under the Better Communities Act must be spent for community-development purposes. However, the particular activities are decided by the
local officials.

I think it is time to dispel the myth that there is somebody in Washington, D.C., who knows better than the peo-

ple themselves what is needed for community development in their cities. There is plenty of room for diversity in what the communities may do.

After all, the problems and opportunities of communities in this country aren't the same. Our communities do have common aims and desires. They want happiness for their people, employment, a sound economic base, a decent environment. But every community is different, and the best means of accomplishing these objectives are different.

So I think we are going to see a wide diversity of what people consider their top priorities from city to city. That's the strength of what we're trying to do. When mistakes are made with a Federal program, you make a mistake for all fifty states of the union. But if we have a few communities that make mistakes, all right, they're still mistakes, but they affect only the people in those communities, and the officials who make these mistakes have to answer to the local voters.

Q. Then why the Federal review, if you're going to allow every town to do what it wants with the money?

A. The review gives us a chance to see what things are working and spread the good word to other communities: "Look, city *x* did this. It worked. It's effective. Why don't other people try that, too?"

Q. We've heard it said that your Better Communities Act will mean less money for the larger cities and more for smaller cities and relatively affluent suburbs. Is that true?

A. No, it's not true.

For example, New York is going to get substantially increased funding over the first three years. There are other large cities that will get more or less what they have been getting because of a provision in the bill that says that if a city's entitlement under the new formula would be substantially less than what it received in the past, the reduction will be made gradually over a transitional period. The changes would not begin to occur until the third year, and reductions at that time would be gradual.

Finally, remember that we are phasing in cities that have received little or no money in the past, and their allotments will be stepped up gradually over three years.

Our goal is to make assistance available objectively, on the basis of a formula that reflects the true needs of our nation's communities.

UNRENEWED URBAN RENEWAL [2]

The caricature of urban renewal as a monolithic "Federal bulldozer" slashing indiscriminately through stable city neighborhoods lingers despite advances in program management that have been evident in urban renewal projects for some time. In fact, while there will always be criticism of large-scale urban projects, urban renewal is one of the major tools that can be and is used to redevelop blighted areas of our cities. Its application has been improving vastly each year.

Unfortunately, as a result of questionable advice from the Department of Housing and Urban Development [HUD] pressured by the Office of Management and Budget [OMB], urban renewal is in serious danger of not receiving adequate funding to continue its progress. The Nixon Budget for Fiscal Year 1974 requested an appropriation of $137.5 *million* for urban renewal; compared to $1.45 *billion* appropriated in 1973.

An attack on urban renewal in this fashion is very confusing and reflects an almost complete misunderstanding by Federal officials as to how and for whom urban renewal works. The Office of Management and Budget claims that $5.7 *billion* of unexpended urban renewal grant authorizations are available in the "pipeline" to sustain urban renewal activities in FY [Fiscal Year] 1974. Even assuming that HUD has a clear idea of what funds are in the pipeline—and

[2] From article by Ralph Thayer, a member of the editorial board of *The Ripon Forum*. *Ripon Forum*. 9:6-7. S. '73. Reprinted by permission.

there is some indication that HUD does not know the amount with any degree of precision—such a statement contradicts the nature of renewal funding. The local urban renewal agency, upon receipt of project approval, borrows funds from private institutions to carry out the project and is reimbursed by HUD as the project is completed. Combining "progress grants" and proceeds from the sale of redevelopable land, the local agency repays its loans to private institutions.

Thus, to know how much is "in the pipeline" would require a very sophisticated fund tracking system which ascertains what portion of the authorization had been borrowed against at the local level, what part was already either committed or earmarked for local agency repayment, and what portion of the total had been programmed solely for mandated relocation payments, disaster relief, or early termination of certain programs. Assuming all these variables were known for over one thousand areas having urban renewal programs, it would then be necessary to know the precise project states in order to estimate whether the funds assumed to be sufficient for continuation were available. If HUD knows all these variables in addition to the first set, they might have some justification for program limitation; virtually no one suggests this information is presently on hand in HUD.

To give an idea of how serious the miscalculation is, a national survey of local urban renewal agencies indicates:

1. 51 percent of the "pipeline" $5.7 billion has already been borrowed against or is earmarked for mandatory relocation payments.

2. 49 percent (the remainder) is contracted for by HUD to pay for previously authorized and approved activities.

Assuming, as is reasonable, that local agencies have a survival stake in enunciating as strong a case as possible for higher funding and might therefore overstate the case, the question here could just as easily be posed this way: is it not appropriate for HUD to understate the case so as to justify the termination? This has occurred: HUD Secretary James T. Lynn contends that the mayors' survey of urban renewal shows about half the money "in the pipeline" is for future expenditures. This type of adversary nonreasoning leads nowhere.

Why End Urban Renewal?

The search for a middle ground is severely handicapped by HUD and OMB's failure to reveal why urban renewal is to be ended. To say that (nonspecified) "program failures" underlie the cut-off decision is to tar everyone with the same brush and to highlight how woefully inadequate is our ability to evaluate programs. The National Survey of Urban Renewal agencies points out the following:

> Given HUD's statement that $5.30 of the local private and public investment is generated for every dollar of Federal funds, and given Department of Labor multipliers, Federal withholding taxes from construction and materials' workers equal or exceed the Federal Government's original grant. *Construction workers alone pay for the Urban Renewal Program.*

Has this factor been considered? What other ones are involved? It is entirely likely that urban renewal is falling victim to forces only partially related to its activities and blamed for trouble areas not entirely of its doing.

For example, to state that a program is a failure is to imply that there exists a standard of accomplishment by which programs are measured. It would be enlightening to see an enunciation of what was expected and where the shortfall of urban renewal occurred. A program of this magnitude deserves better than a nonceremonial burial bereft of substance. One can only wonder what sort of leverage local officials will have trying to reinstate an urban renewal activity under the Better Communities Act when the previous program has been branded with the scarlet letter. Do we mean urban renewal failed or our total urban nonpolicy finally caught up with us?

It is well known that inflationary pressures in the build-ing-supplies arena have been very strong. Mentioned in President Nixon's Controls Message of June 13 [1973] was plywood; other items in short supply are all lumber, bricks, cement, and pipe. Perhaps, the wage pressures of contractors figured is also a factor. At any rate, there is a reasonable case for saying that the demise of urban renewal could dampen inflationary fires in the building arena—and this is a valid objective. Yet, urban renewal was responsible for stimulating a significant amount of innovative city construction; it was also a primary (often the only) force providing for the con-struction of low- and moderate-income housing. We now have the possibility that inner-city construction will be sac-rificed to keep the price down on new suburban sprawl. Those who build low-income housing in the cities know full well that spiraling land costs in the cities preclude anything but luxury residential units unless a land write-down mech-anism is used to partially offset initial costs.

Optimistically, the Administration expects to implement the Better Communities Act in July 1974. Without com-menting directly on this timetable, suffice it to say that the present confusion over subsidized housing activity has every likelihood of delaying this target considerably. Even prior to the erosion of executive control following Watergate, the block-grant idea had many serious hurdles. Thus, it is all too likely that this coming year will see sharply reduced ur-ban renewal activity which could distinctly hurt on-going projects.

Certainly it is possible to hope that local agencies will be able to "ride out the storm" and still be ready with a capable staff in place to handle renewal responsibilities under the Better Communities Act. There may even be some ulti-mately beneficial side effects of this funding hiatus: for ex-ample, given the expected drop in low- and moderate-in-come housing construction, pressures to open up suburban residential areas to equal opportunity housing might in-crease. This would be both beneficial and belated. But, to hypothesize this was an intended result and the cut in funds was therefore for our own good would be a bit farfetched. Could it be that urban renewal, by creating opportunities for lower-income housing in the city, has diverted the pressures for open suburbs and that this is its "failure?"

It is probable that the pressures for adequate (?) funding for urban renewal in 1974 will build up against a weakened Chief Executive to the point where a compromise allotment will be granted. Since the amount finally to be settled upon is apt to be far below stated needs, the burden of "fiscal heat dissipation" will fall on the shoulders of HUD officials at regional and area offices. To cope with this tenseness, a style of operation by local HUD officials that cultivates obduracy and nitpicking to camouflage a lack of funds or information on local-fund availability can be expected; in many areas it is already in operation.

There appears to be a distinct lack of courage exhibited in the back-door manner in which urban renewal was deleted. Whether this action masks an absence of substantive documentation available to justify the decision is a moot question. Given the amount of money previously spent, the number and quality of evaluation studies performed, and the long history of the program, urban renewal would be presumed to merit a more just hearing. That it did not, to all appearances, receive a full and fair public hearing is yet another indication that the Administration remains bored with the many problems of cities. Would that each citizen could afford to become bored with cities because he or she did not have to face stark urban reality on a daily basis.

A CRITIQUE OF HOUSING ALLOWANCES [3]

A new panacea is abroad in the land. It is the "housing allowance" and it is being trumpeted as the long-sought

[3] From "The Latest Panacea," by Joseph P. Fried, a reporter on housing and urban affairs for the New York *Times* and author of *Housing Crisis U.S.A. Nation.* 216:304-8. Mr. 5, '73. Copyright 1973 by the Nation Associates, Inc. Reprinted with permission.

answer to the nation's slum-housing problem. Senator George McGovern [Democrat, South Dakota], when he was campaigning for the presidency, urged that it be made a staple of the Federal Government's housing effort, and George Romney, ... [former] secretary of housing and urban development, has declared it an alternative to the present grab bag of scandal-ridden programs. Urban experts are grinding out statistic-laden treatises to advance its merits, and newspaper and magazine writers have begun implanting it in the public mind with all the scrupulous documentation of a medicine man limning the virtues of his latest elixir.

In short, as in 1937 (public housing), 1949 (urban renewal), 1965 (rent supplements), 1966 (model cities) and 1968 (mortgage-interest subsidies), we are to suppose that yet another bright new day is about to dawn in America's sometime battle against its widespread housing blight. Moreover, that day may well have been brought nearer by the Administration's ... announcement that it is suspending approval of virtually all new projects under present housing-subsidy programs, while a search is made for new and better methods—one of which, many believe, is the housing allowance.

It would work as follows: families otherwise unable to afford decent housing would be given an allowance sufficient to bridge the gap between what they could pay and the actual cost of such housing in their areas. The subsidy could be in cash or in "rent certificates" analogous to food stamps; either way, a low-income family could compete in the private housing market on an equal economic footing with families able to pay their own way.

In sharp contrast to existing devices, enwrapped in such befuddling intricacies as "land writedown," "housing authority bond retirement," "below-market interest rates" and "accelerated depreciation," the allowance approach has the charm of simplicity. The now chronic discontent with housing programs, and the surge of abuses and controversy that currently plague them, make obvious the appeal of a proposal that would simply hand a man the money he needed to get his family a decent place to live.

Unfortunately, the current federal housing scandals demonstrate that abuses and failures can occur not only in the "builder-subsidy" or "construction-oriented" programs but also in the minority of housing programs that already resemble an allowance approach.

A number of major questions must be answered before an allowance system can be safely adopted on a large scale. Government-sponsored experiments have recently been undertaken to answer these questions, but it will be at least five years before sufficient data are available to make a meaningful assessment of the most vital matters in doubt. Meanwhile, there is danger that impatience with present programs will lead to hasty adoption of allowances, thus replacing one set of abuses and inadequacies with another.

Annoyance with existing programs is understandable. The Housing and Urban Development Act of 1968 was passed for the stated purpose of wiping out, once and for all, the vast bulk of substandard housing in America. Hailed as a landmark piece of social legislation—a possible "Magna Carta to liberate our cities" was how Lyndon Johnson put it—the Act called for construction or rehabilitation by 1978 of 26 million houses and apartments, including 6 million units to be federally subsidized for low- and moderate-income families. The existing public housing program was sharply expanded and several new programs were created, including a system of mortgage-interest subsidies to home owners and to developers of apartment projects. In addition, the Federal Housing Administration's [FHA] mortgage-insurance program—which had benefited a generation of for the most part middle-income families and had played a major role in the creation of suburbia—was extended to the crumbling areas of the inner city, which previously had been excluded from its advantages through the process known as "red-lining." The Nixon Administration initially accepted the production goals; the output of federally subsidized housing soared tenfold, to more than half a million units a year, while the FHA insurance mantle was spread over the urban slums.

The Scandals of Subsidized Housing

But instead of the hoped-for millennium, scandal and controversy erupted. The sordid details have been displayed in congressional and grand jury investigations across the country: shoddy construction, serious financial instability, and charges of profiteering by land speculators, builders and other realty interests who took advantage of the subsidized-interest apartment program; grossly inflated mortgage values and slapdash renovations by speculators in the homeownership program and in the extension of FHA insurance to the inner cities; the indictment of nearly three dozen FHA employees in half a dozen cities on various collusion charges, with the head of the important insuring office that covers New York City already sentenced to ten years in prison for bribe taking, and the chief appraiser in the Newark office sentenced to eight years.

The overall cost has been staggering, socially as well as economically. The poor have been treated to yet another proof that the reality of government housing programs mocks the rhetoric with which they are launched. The abandonment of entire neighborhoods has been speeded up, while Uncle Sam has become the nation's biggest slumlord, and a losing one at that. Estimates are that the FHA will have to foreclose more than twenty thousand homes in Detroit and Philadelphia alone, with resulting losses that could run higher than $250 million. Given that sorry record—and notwithstanding that much good housing has also been produced under the beleaguered programs—the call for a new approach is understandable.

The housing allowance, its proponents say, could be such an approach, because a subsidy given straight to the consumer would largely eliminate "subsidy-skimming" real estate middlemen and the puffed-up public agencies that process traditional housing projects, thus sharply reducing costs and opportunities for profiteering. It is also argued that an allowance system would save still more money by making better use of existing housing, whereas present programs tend to emphasize expensive new construction. Some estimates are that, overall, the allowance approach could cut Washington's housing-subsidy expenses by as much as 50 percent.

The proposed method is offered as a remedy for still other bitterly resented aspects of existing programs. Instead of requiring subsidized families to move into "stigma-bearing" housing projects, allowances would assertedly offer these families the same freedom of choice that is available to nonsubsidized families. As a result, it is held, not only would subsidized families retain their dignity, but racial and economic integration would be promoted far more effectively than under present programs, and the rancorous battles that have erupted over where to locate subsidized projects would be avoided.

What Hopes for Housing Allowances?

In theory it all sounds persuasive. But in fact—given the uncertain state of our knowledge and the experiences of current scandals—the asserted advantages are at best hopeful suppositions.

An allowance system would certainly avoid many of the abuses of the subsidized-interest apartment program (the so-called Section 236 program, named for the portion of the National Housing Act that authorizes it). The shortcomings of this builder-oriented program have included poor construction and mismanagement in an alarming number of new projects, with profiteering by the developers, investors and others involved in "packaging" and constructing them. But an allowance system would be threatened by the *very same kind of abuses* that have afflicted the subsidized-interest homeownership program (Section 235) and the extension of

FHA mortgage insurance to the inner city (Sections 221d2 and 223e).

In both programs, the Government enhances the housing consumer's purchasing power without restricting him to a housing project, as under a formal housing allowance scheme. And in both it is this Government-augmented purchasing power that has been exploited by fast-buck real estate artists and the con men with schemes involving "paste-up" renovations of essentially decrepit structures, bloated mortgages and inflated selling prices.

In the case of Section 235 subsidized-interest homeownership, the similarity to a formal housing allowance is readily apparent, especially when this section has been used to finance the purchase of used rather than new housing. (Used housing is what families receiving an allowance would most often require, and where the most frequent abuses in the program have occurred.)

The subsidy under 235 makes up the difference between 20 percent of a family's income and the monthly mortgage payment; under a typical housing allowance proposal, it would make up the difference between a similar percentage of income and some average housing cost calculated for an area on the basis of Bureau of Labor Statistics figures. Under 235 the Government commits itself to providing the subsidy after the family has found the house it wants, and the FHA pays the funds directly to the bank; under a formal housing allowance, a money grant may be given or promised a family in advance of its search for a new home, and the family itself may get the subsidy to pass on to the bank and to other providers of housing services.

But aside from such differences in detail, the process is the same: the Government increases the housing consumer's purchasing power without forcing him into a traditional project. And one need not stretch one's imagination far to envision the same type of exploitation, with the collusion and ineptitude of Government employees involving building inspectors assigned to certify the soundness of housing rather than the FHA appraisers who are supposed to police 235.

In the case of inner-city mortgage insurance—in which the speculators' abuses may have been even more rampant than under 235—the parallel with a housing allowance is not as apparent because there is no money subsidy. Rather, the program makes homeownership possible for low-income families by arranging *circumstances* in their favor: small down payments (as little as $250) and high prospects that mortgage lenders will extend credit to such families (the program encourages this cordiality by transferring the lending risk from the bank to the Government).

But the result—a possibility of homeownership that would otherwise not exist—is no different than if the family had its purchasing power enlarged by cash. And if swindlers have so readily exploited a program based on the Government's mere agreement to underwrite the credit of the poor, who can doubt that they will be quick to exploit a program that puts cash right into the hands of the poor?

What Cost for Housing Allowances?

In short, the housing allowance, contrary to the hopes of its many enthusiastic supporters, is no cure for windfalls and profiteering. And if the allowance method were to become the dominant approach, with rental as well as purchased housing included, the total economic and social costs of the perpetuated abuses could well be as great as the total costs of the several kinds of present abuse. One need think only of the countless decrepit tenements that would suddenly be patched over with a few cans of paint to qualify as "renovated" for allowance-receiving families. (Anyone pointing this out may find himself called a "mouthpiece" of the high-powered homebuilders and investors who oppose adoption of an allowance system to replace the construction-oriented programs that benefit them so handsomely. But this charge cuts both ways. If the builders and tax-shelter-seeking investors find programs like Section 236 apartment development a boon, the rental slumlords and quick-buck rehabilitation sharpsters are equally keen for a widespread housing allowance.)

The other asserted advantages of a housing allowance are equally uncertain. There is, for example, the matter of overall cost effectiveness. Allowance proponents note that by 1978 present programs would require an annual federal expenditure of $7.5 billion on housing subsidies to benefit about 7 million low- and moderate-income families. By contrast, they maintain, allowances to that amount could assist twice as many families.

Such arguments are based on studies like those done by Frank de Leeuw of the Urban Institute. He has projected that an allowance program designed for some 13 million to 17 million families would cost from $7.4 billion to $9.5 billion a year. (That, as of 1969, is the number of families believed unable to afford adequate housing at a reasonable percentage of income.) His estimate is based in part on the following: $5.1 billion to $7 billion as the original cost of the allowance itself; $0.7 billion to $0.9 billion as the cost of administering the program (determining eligibility, verifying rents and inspecting the housing to assure that it is in decent condition), and $2 billion in higher housing costs caused by a large-scale allowance system itself.

But de Leeuw notes that, at best, his projection is only "a crude estimate," and many veterans of the battle for better housing agree. Remarking on the uncertainty as to just how high administrative costs would run, Albert A. Walsh, former housing and development administrator of New York City, says: "My own experience is that as soon as you have this kind of program, there's an immediate demand for the Government to see that the money is used for better maintenance—for expensive inspection programs requiring a tremendous bureaucracy to administer them."

That intensive monitoring, code enforcement and consumer education would be needed to avoid pouring Government dollars into tenement ratholes has been amply demonstrated not only by the misfortunes of Section 235 used-housing and inner-city mortgage insurance but by the shelter-allowance portion of the welfare program—as direct a housing allowance as anything has been to date. In recent years, according to one estimate, about $1.5 billion of the nation's annual welfare payments has been allocated to housing. Much of this has been nothing more than a subsidy for slums.

But perhaps the greatest uncertainty is the extent to which a large-scale allowance program would inflate the cost of existing low-income housing without improving its quality. De Leeuw, after an examination of income and rent-rise patterns in various cities over the years, has concluded that only "one quarter to one third" of the increased housing demand stimulated by a comprehensive allowance system would act to drive up costs in relation to services received. "Most of the increase in housing demand—say two thirds or three quarters of it—would in the long run lead to better housing."

But de Leeuw concedes that this is "a highly tentative judgment." Other experts hold that more meaningful precedents can be seen in the previously mentioned welfare program, the shelter-allowance portion of which has had little effect on improving the quality of housing for the poor, and in the nation's experience with medical care. Referring to the adoption of such programs as Medicare and Medicaid in recent years, Anthony Downs, senior vice president of the Real Estate Research Corporation, remarked:

Recently, we did not use money to expand the supply side of the market—which would be equivalent to building more houses —but only to expand the demand side of it. The supply happened to be inelastic, it did not rise with demand, which resulted in a terrific increase in the price of medical care. So a large part of the increase in the public cost of medical subsidies simply represents income for doctors, hospitals, and so forth.

As a result, Downs and others feel, any direct-grant strategy in housing "must be accompanied in many markets with some action to expand supply. . . ."

Allowances and Racial Integration

The ability of an allowance to promote racial integration is also debatable. As long as racial discrimination in the sale and rental of housing remains entrenched—and it persists, despite laws and court decisions to the contrary—it is ludicrous to think that putting a few more dollars into the hands of poor minorities will provide them with *real* "mobility in the marketplace" (a favorite phrase of allowance proponents).

As for avoiding the frequent controversies that erupt over plans to build low-income projects in middle-class areas, how long would it be before a large-scale allowance system produced equally bitter controversies over providing the minority poor with "handouts" so that they could compete *en masse* for housing in middle-class neighborhoods? The truth is that *any* vigorous attempt by the Government to help break down the barriers of residential segregation will be resisted, whether the attempt is made through subsidizing buildings or subsidizing families.

Similarly, though "stigma-bearing" housing projects might be avoided under an allowance system, they could as well be avoided under construction-oriented subsidy programs if the housing built could be widely scattered throughout the nation's metropolitan areas, and if they could contain design features that made them less "institutional." But that would mean removing the pressures arising from restrictive suburban zoning laws and from the continuing inadequacy of housing funds in relation to need.

How to Experiment With an Allowance System

Given the many unknowns cloaking an allowance approach, and the glaring shortcomings of existing programs, what course should Washington follow in its housing poli-

cies? One course it should *not* follow, many vigorously feel,
is to react as the Nixon Administration has done—by cutting
off virtually all new housing subsidies with one slash of the
knife. (Some critics of the Administration are convinced
that the White House latched onto the recent scandals as an
excuse for abolishing programs that some powerful members
of the inner circle have long disliked on ideological grounds.)
It would be equally unwise for the Federal Government to
succumb prematurely to the lure of a cure-all that could
turn out to be as toxic as the present remedies. The rational
course is to experiment fully and carefully with such uncertain alternatives as the allowance, and, meanwhile, to
reform existing programs drastically.

As noted, Washington has begun to test the allowance
approach, but there is a good deal of worry, both inside and
outside the Department of Housing and Urban Development, that the experiment will not be permitted to run its
full course, and that a policy decision will be made in favor
of allowances before all the meaningful returns from the
pilot project are in.

As now conceived, the experiment will involve about
twenty thousand families in a dozen metropolitan areas.
Three basic matters will be examined: the effects of an allowance on participating households, the best ways to administer an allowance program, and the impact of an allowance on the local housing supply. The first two inquiries
will be pursued in pilot projects expected to run for as long
as three years. The third—the all-important market experiment—is scheduled for five years, because of the longer time
needed to assess the effects of allowances on the cost of housing. Furthermore, that test will be conducted on the largest
local scale, with some five thousand households being involved in each of two areas—the Green Bay, Wisconsin, metropolitan area (population 158,000) and a second area,
similar in size, still to be announced.

Those conducting it feel that the scale of the market-
impact experiment—about one tenth of the population in

the areas involved are to receive housing allowances—will be sufficient to provide reliable indications of the potential effects of a general allowance system. However, some aspects of the experiment make one wonder whether it really will uncover all the inherent problems in a national allowance program.

The HUD project is being carried out with the least possible publicity, to avoid the premature ballyhoo that has often accompanied new housing programs in the past. While this discretion is certainly desirable, it introduces a factor that could be crucial. The general public awareness that would accompany a fully adopted allowance program will have a marked influence that cannot be measured in a quietly pursued experiment. How much more active would speculators, blockbusters and other potential abusers be amid a widely discussed system of allowances? How stable would middle-class areas near minority ghettos be amid such a system? Quiet experiments will not necessarily indicate all that could occur under an allowance setup that was a generally recognized staple of Government housing policy.

That is one reason for caution when evaluating such previous allowance experiments as one that has been under way in Kansas City, Missouri, since 1970. Involving some two hundred families as part of the local model-cities program, the project—believed the first of its kind in the country—has been deemed successful by its sponsors, who say it has provided participating families with sound housing at costs lower than under earlier programs, and has avoided exploitation by realty interests and resentment in middle-class neighborhoods. But the Kansas City project has been deliberately muted, with publicity held to a minimum, because officials felt that such an approach would cause less uproar and would escape charges of blockbusting.

The Kansas City experiment must also be taken with a grain of salt because of its scope. The effect on the market in a locality the size of Kansas City of two hundred poor families whose rent-paying or home-buying ability has been substantially improved is far different from the impact of such sharply increased capability when thousands of poor families are involved.

In short, large-scale experimentation is the only real test —pilot projects in which a few entire cities serve, in effect, as laboratories for an allowance approach on a national scale. Granted, such a procedure must seem agonizingly drawn out to those frustrated by present programs, but only patient experimentation can give the nation some reasonable assurance that a housing-allowance approach does indeed offer more promise than peril.

Needed: Reform of Present Programs

Meanwhile, reform of present programs cannot wait, and the following changes are needed as a minimum (and, many hope, will be sought by Congress as the preferable alternative to the Nixon Administration's wholesale freeze):

1. All connection between the FHA and subsidized housing programs must be severed. Although the current abuses stem partly from basic weaknesses in the programs themselves, maladministration by FHA has contributed probably even more than have the structural flaws. And the reason goes beyond simple venality. Ever since its establishment four decades ago, FHA has been "industry-oriented and industry-controlled," as Representative Shirley Chisholm [Democrat, New York] put it. It has proved itself utterly incapable of understanding the housing needs of the poor, and it looks to be incorrigible in this respect. An entirely new apparatus, staffed by consumer-oriented people with an appreciation of the urban crisis, is urgently needed. FHA should be limited to underwriting mortgages for middle-income housing in sound areas.

2. The approach whereby the Government subsidizes interest on market-rate mortgages obtained from traditional lenders—the heart of the Section 235 and 236 programs—should be replaced by direct Government loans to developers and purchasers of lower-income housing. Although the lat-

ter method is more costly in the short run (the amount of the full loan immediately appears as a charge to the Government), it is cheaper over the long run. According to Controller General Elmer Staats, such a change could over the next five years save Washington as much as $2.2 billion (an amount that reflects a subsidy for banks and not people).

3. The tangle of existing federal subsidy programs should be consolidated into a single setup that would apply to all federally aided rental and purchased housing, whether built by local public authorities, nonprofit organizations or limited-profit developers. If that were done, separate developments would no longer be built for poor and lower-middle-class families; rather, *any* family certified as unable to afford decent quarters in the private market would be eligible for residence in the subsidized housing. Apart from bringing rationality to Washington's housing policies, this approach would permit subsidized developments to include a relatively broad range of incomes and would contribute toward racial integration.

4. The "housing problem" must be viewed not simply as a matter of replacing bad structures but as part of a totality —the urban or rural slum—whose elements cannot be remedied separately. This may seem obvious in 1973, especially to those who have seen the futility of putting up new housing in areas that remain as depressed as ever in regard to jobs, schools, drug abuse and municipal services. But it never was obvious to the Nixon Administration and still isn't. While striving to realize the production goals of the 1968 Housing Act, the Administration was also seeking to cut back sharply on the provisions of the Act which relate to such programs as model cities and urban renewal. Flawed though these programs are, they still reflect a basic need for comprehensive approaches to community redevelopment that Washington cannot abandon.

5. The management of subsidized housing must be given equal emphasis with the creation of such housing. It is not

a sufficient federal role to provide funds for housing construction and then leave it to the private sponsors to tend the results. That is especially true when—as is often the case today—sponsors of subsidized housing are attracted more by short-term tax-shelter advantages than by the prospective returns from long-term ownership. Top priority, not just public relations lip service, must be given to operations such as the newly formed National Center for Housing Management which, if you can believe the HUD press releases, "will be instrumental in training sixty thousand housing managers needed to operate the 5 million federally assisted rental housing units to be occupied by 1980."

Other steps are also required (the above list is not meant to be inclusive), but these alone will require a revolution in Congress and the Administration. Yet it would be far safer to spark that revolution than succumb prematurely to the lure of a promised remedy—like the housing allowance—that could turn out to be just one more massive dose of bad medicine.

NIXON'S NEW HOUSING PROPOSAL [4]

President Nixon's new "wide-ranging" housing program will benefit Middle America first and low-income Americans later on.

This tilt, officials insist, derives not from bias, but from the nature of the actions which the President can take without new authority from Congress.

The first to benefit will be Americans who are finding it hard, or impossible, to buy or sell a home because mortgage money is unavailable.

Mr. Nixon is directing the Federal Home Loan Bank Board to launch a "forward commitments" program whereby the board will promise to lend savings and loan associa-

[4] From "A Boost for Home Mortgages," by Harry B. Ellis, business-financial correspondent. *Christian Science Monitor.* p 1+. S. 20, '73. Reprinted by permission from *The Christian Science Monitor* © 1973 The Christian Science Publishing Society. All rights reserved.

tions up to $2.5 billion to cover mortgage commitments made now.

On subsidized housing, the President proposes a radically new approach—"direct cash assistance"—to help low-income families. A poor family would be given an appropriate amount of money and then be allowed to choose its own home on the private market. The Government, in other words, would furnish cash, not a dwelling unit in a subsidized housing project.

Scaled Payments Planned

"The payment," Mr. Nixon told Congress, "would be carefully scaled to make up the difference between what a family could afford on its own for housing and the cost of safe and sanitary housing in that geographic area.

"This plan," he continued, "would give the poor the freedom and responsibility to make their own choices about housing—and it would eventually get the Federal Government out of the housing business." The President told Congress, however, that he would not be ready to present legislation on his new approach until late 1974 or early 1975.

As for mortgage plans, the President said, many savings and loan associations are rejecting mortgage applications because savings deposits are shrinking and it costs the associations too much to borrow more money.

Michael Sumichrast, chief economist of the National Association of Home Builders, says that a current poll of builders shows that "mortgages are not available or only partially available in 88 percent of the country."

Federal Aid Guaranteed

President Nixon now will encourage savings and loan associations to commit themselves to new housing mortgages by guaranteeing them future federal loans if they run short of money.

Separately, the Department of Housing and Urban Development (HUD) will provide up to $3 billion for "FHA-

insured mortgages at interest rates somewhat below the
market level," applicable only to new housing starts.

The Government, in other words, seeks to pump more
than $5 billion worth of new mortgage money into the mar-
ket to stimulate the sagging housing industry. Mr. Sumichrast predicts that, as matters now stand, housing starts
will decline from about 2.1 million this year to 1.6 million
in 1974.

As for the low-income subsidized housing, the President
asserts that existing programs have "produced some of the
worst housing in America" and have made the United States
Government the "biggest slumlord in history."

HUD Secretary James T. Lynn estimates that by June
30, 1974, his department will own "280,000 housing units,"
because of owner defaults on federally insured mortgages.

"Over the years," declared Mr. Nixon, "nearly $90 billion
of the taxpayers money has been spent or committed for
public housing projects and other subsidized housing programs."

This new cash-assistance approach is based partly on
HUD's conclusion that "it costs between 15 and 40 percent
more for the Government to provide housing for people
than for people to acquire that same housing for themselves
on the private market."

After stating the case for a direct cash assistance approach, with first priority being given to the elderly poor,
the President warned of the need for further study of the
whole concept.

The Government, said Mr. Lynn, would not wish to
arouse hopes which might later be dashed. Thus, before an
"operational program" is presented to Congress, HUD will
pursue the matter further.

Information Being Gathered

"I believe," the President told Congress, "we will have
the basic information needed to make a final decision concerning this approach late in 1974 or early 1975."

Meanwhile, HUD will continue to process applications for federally financed housing, which had "moved most of the way through the application process" by January 5, 1973, when the President suspended most subsidies for new housing.

Mr. Nixon also has authorized HUD "to process applications for an additional 200,000 units, 150,000 units of which would be new construction."

To encourage banks to commit more money to mortgages, Mr. Nixon is asking Congress to grant financial institutions "a mortgage-interest tax credit of up to 3.5 percent," somewhat analagous to the existing 7.5 percent tax credit which corporations receive for new investment.

Banks and savings and loan associations, under the plan, would receive tax exemption on 3.5 percent of their mortgage-interest earnings, if at least 70 percent of their total lending portfolios were in mortgages.

HOUSING OR FACADE? [5]

The need for new approaches to public housing is incontestable. The deterioration and abandonment of costly high-rise developments in some big-city slums have brought even well-run projects into disrepute—often unfairly.

President Nixon's long-delayed housing message to Congress is innovative in its emphasis on giving low-income families money with which to find their own apartments and help pay their rents, instead of depending on Government to operate subsidized housing for them.

That approach would have much to commend it if the President were not once again substituting pie-in-the-sky projections for any sizable investment either in rent subsidies to the poor or in programs aimed at encouraging private developers to expand the supply of housing into which poor and middle-income families might move.

[5] From editorial. New York *Times*. p 44. S. 20, '73. © 1973 by The New York Times Company. Reprinted by permission.

Since 1970 the Federal housing authorities have been experimenting with rent subsidies on a small scale in a half-dozen communities. What Mr. Nixon proposes for the next year represents no significant expansion in the over-all scope of these on-going experiments.

The subsidy program presents problems as well as potentialities, and the President indicates little disposition to guard against them in his enchantment with the idea of reinstating free-market concepts in housing. He says that existing programs have made Uncle Sam "the biggest slumlord in history," but even the most superficial study of what happens to welfare families—living with the equivalent of rent subsidies—indicates how quickly such subsidies can turn into massive underwriting of slumlords, far beyond anything yet experienced.

Whole neighborhoods in this city and many others have slid into ruin, even in places where local authorities are socially concerned and rent controls operate as some check on gouging by greedy building owners. The Administration's program, if it ever attains the dimensions Mr. Nixon envisages for later years, will have to be accompanied by safeguards to insure enforcement of housing codes and to restrain rents—either through plentiful availability of decent housing or through limits on rent increases.

For the present Mr. Nixon is obviously more concerned with holding down the budget than with responding to the acute need of millions of Americans for better housing—now.

UNLEARNED LESSONS OF HOUSING [6]

Men make mistakes, but, as has often been observed, a wise man rarely makes the same mistake twice. He learns from his errors.

[6] From "Unlearned Lessons in the History of Federal Housing Aid," by M. Carter McFarland, formerly with the Department of Housing and Urban Development, now director of urban affairs and housing programs for the American Institute of Architects. *City.* 6:31-4. Winter '72. Reprinted by permission from *City*, Magazine of Urban Life and Environment. Copyright 1972. The National Urban Coalition, 2100 M St. N.W., Washington, D.C. 20037. All Rights Reserved.

The same cannot be said of those who have been responsible for federal housing policy during the past four decades. Far too often the same mistakes have been repeated again and again.

This shortness of memory in housing is not easy to explain. It may be related to the fact that housing policy is made by Congress and the Executive Branch in an atmosphere highly charged with politics. It may be related to the frequently changing political leadership in housing and an unwillingness of this leadership to listen to career professionals who should and often do know better. It may be that the housing bureaucracies, like all bureaucracies, generate their own verities and myths which they are reluctant to change. It may be that Government has never developed a capacity for objective self-criticism and a realistic method for examining and evaluating the consequences of its own actions.

Whatever the reasons, those responsible for administering federal housing programs have displayed an uncommon tolerance for repetitive error and a surprisingly short span of recall. These are some of the lessons in the history of federal housing programs that are often forgotten today:

Good Housing No Cure-All

1. *Good Housing Cannot Do It All*: In recent months [former Housing and Urban Development] secretary [George] Romney's speeches and testimony have frequently been devoted to a description of the processes of inner-city decay and the related problems of housing abandonment. Invariably these passages have ended with the statement that improved housing alone cannot solve all the problems of the slums. This is a profoundly true statement. But it is not a new truth. As far back as the 1930s the same observation was being made. . . .

It may be that among the members of the early public housing movement were a smattering of environmental determinists—those who honestly thought that the provision of decent, safe, and sanitary housing could solve all the problems of poverty and erase all the conditions that cause slums. In congressional testimony and elsewhere the public housers made much of the relationship between poor housing and health, between inadequate space and unstable marital relationships, between a child's performance at school and the availability of adequate study and sleeping space.

But even in the 1930s the wiser heads knew that poor housing is not the sole cause of poverty and slums and that the provision of good housing will not get rid of the deeper causes of the slum condition. Indeed, bad housing is as much a symptom of slum conditions as it is a cause. Unemployment, poverty, and a lack of marketable skills cannot be solved by housing. Good housing alone will not solve social maladjustments or broken families. Racial discrimination, drug addiction, vandalism, crime, social alienation are problems of human behavior over which the provision of decent housing has little or no influence. They must be solved by education, training, jobs, motivation, social and psychological counseling and perhaps other remedies as yet undiscovered.

Yet despite all the experience to the contrary, the myth still persists that good housing will eliminate slums. Such a myth is certainly implicit in the national housing goals established by the 1968 legislation and the rhetoric which accompanied them. According to these goals, the country was to gird itself for a ten-year production drive to produce 26 million units (6 million of which were to be subsidized) which would at last fulfill the promise made in the 1949 legislation to provide "every American with a decent home *in a suitable living environment.*" It was more than implied, it was declared that the production of this much housing over a ten-year period would rid America of slums.

The fact is that the housing goals promise more than they can achieve. The desired production levels may be achievable. But this is hardly likely to produce a slumless

America unless many other things are also done which are more accurately aimed at the root problems which cause the slums today. Thus, it should not be surprising that in 1972, four years into the goals period, the inner-city problems seem to be worsening despite the very high levels of housing production which have been achieved.

It is about time we recognized what good housing can accomplish and what it cannot accomplish. It is about time we turned our energies seriously to finding remedies for the deep-seated problems of poverty and slums. It is about time, too, that we recognized that providing everyone with a decent home in a decent environment is an impossible dream —and an expensive one too—until we find solutions to the more fundamental causes of slums of which bad housing is only the most visible symptom. Indeed, it can be argued that building new housing in certain slum neighborhoods—without much more being done to change behavior patterns—is a waste of the taxpayer's money.

Volume Versus Abuses

2. Excessive Emphasis on Volume Alone Leads to Abuses: The well-adjusted bureaucrat is one who has worked out a tolerable balance between two strong and conflicting pressures. The first pressure is to follow the rules and regulations meticulously, carefully, and to the letter, and to reject applications for federal aid which do not meet the most conservative interpretations of these rules. The second contradictory pressure, which comes both from sponsors and often from superiors, is to produce results—"to get the cases out," to be liberal and imaginative, and to produce in volume. This is a cruel and difficult dilemma, and it is made more so by the knowledge that there are always private groups shrewd and rapacious enough to exploit to their own advantage any relaxation of the rules, any sign of processing weakness.

The effective bureaucracy is one in which most of its operating employees have achieved a fine tuning between these conflicting pressures. In the ideal and rare case these two opposite forces can be reconciled to produce both volume and quality.

If the bureaucratic balance point veers too much toward a careful, slow, and literal interpretation of the rules, the organization will be accused of being stodgy, conservative, "bureaucratic," and unresponsive to the public need. If the balance point goes too far in the direction of speedy production, flexible and imaginative decision making, the organization can look for criticism of another kind—that it is being too lax and allowing its clients to get away with too much. It is almost certain to be accused of sloppy administration. It may also be accused of maladministration. Claims of scandal and the reality of scandal can also characterize this phase. It is the nature of bureaucracies that a liberal phase is usually followed by a conservative phase.

FHA is experiencing such a crisis, or turning point, today. Local newspapers, national magazines, the *Congressional Record*, and [former] Secretary Romney's speeches are full of reports of serious abuses and even scandals in the subsidized programs, particularly in 235 and 236. [For explanation of these programs, see "A Critique of Housing Allowances," by Joseph P. Fried, above.] The abuses are particularly grave in the use of Section 235 for the purchase of existing homes. Sharp operators have purchased older homes in the slums, applied a few coats of paint, and, with the help of a favorable FHA appraisal (plus a favorable and sometimes doctored credit report on the borrower), sold them to poor families at prices thousands of dollars above the cost. The poor purchaser soon finds he has bought a house with many defects. Having hardly enough money to keep the payments and none at all to pay for often expensive repairs, the purchaser soon abandons his new house, the mortgage is foreclosed, and the house comes back to FHA.

FHA is being charged with sloppy, irresponsible processing in these cases and sometimes with criminal collusion in the transaction. Section-235-financed purchases of existing housing is not the only part of the subsidized programs receiving criticism. Deficient construction of new 235 homes also is charged. Many 236 rental projects are said to be of inferior construction, poorly located, poorly managed, and more expensive than comparable conventional apartment construction.

There can be no doubt that the FHA processing system has broken down seriously in too many cases. How could this happen? Evidently, FHA's capacity to process cases in an orderly, efficient way has not been enhanced by the several wrenching reorganizations through which HUD and FHA have gone in the past few years. But the principal cause of the problem is the passion for volume production at any cost.

The national housing goals, once again, call for the production of six million subsidized units in ten years. The new Secretary was production minded and determined to meet the goals and even organized a special production department. Thus, during the past four years, the word in HUD has been production and more production. Production goals were set for each FHA office and substantial pressure was put on them to meet the goals and meet them on time. Directors were told in no uncertain terms to get their subsidy funds allocated to acceptable projects or give them back so they could be put in the hands of other offices which could use them within the time limits that had been specified.

It is not surprising that under this fierce pressure for volume (without corresponding increases in personnel) the FHA processing system faltered. Under the pressure to produce, appraisals were done hastily and carelessly, and FHA's normally careful review of market, location, construction and related matters were hastily and superficially performed. The mystery is that no one foresaw that the system would break down under such pressure.

The past history of FHA is full of warnings that just such results could be expected. FHA's "608 scandals" of 1954 provide an almost exact counterpart if anyone had bothered to look. There was the same pressure to produce in volume. In fact, President Harry Truman himself had publicly exhorted FHA to speed up production under the 608 program to house returning veterans. There was the same pressure put on a limited staff. There were the same processing short cuts applied to speed production. All of FHA's normal processing reviews were made more quickly and more superficially than before. And the whole thing ended in a cry of scandal, congressional and executive investigations, and all the other things which are now happening to FHA.

After the 608 storm broke, the pendulum swung back and FHA became stricter and more deliberate in its application of the rules as it returned to conservative, cautious administration. For reasons which are all too human, FHA personnel became excessively cautious. A number of years passed before the effects of this trauma subsided.

The same thing is likely to happen today. In reacting to criticism, investigations, and the cry of scandal, FHA personnel may well stick their heads too far into the sand as an act of simple self-protection. [Former] Secretary Romney has signaled the retreat by saying he would sacrifice 200,000 units of volume this year [1972] if that was what was necessary to achieve quality. In an organization that has achieved the right balance between daring and duty, this kind of over-reaction should not be necessary.

The lesson is that you cannot push an organization too far too fast toward volume production without risking trouble. And the trouble is twofold. First are the scandals and maladministration that are likely to result. Second is the after effect which is likely to be several years of overly-cautious program administration with slower and fewer results than are required.

The Folklore of Homeownership

3. *Homeownership Is Not Necessarily Uplift*: **One of** the oldest verities in the housing field is the belief in the

benefits of homeownership. It is part of our folklore that owning one's home builds character, responsibility, thrift, stability and all the middle-class virtues we cherish so much. This doctrine was often proclaimed by FHA during the 1930s and 1940s when that agency was helping make us a nation of homeowners. There can be little doubt that most Americans aspire to homeownership. In recent decades, also, homeownership certainly proved to be a financial boon to millions of families who have benefited from persistent inflation in house prices.

Yet it would be hard to prove that the behavior of the typical middle-class homeowner is much different from that of the typical middle-class renter. While as a nation most of us prefer homeownership, we probably falsely attribute to it an important role in generating middle-class virtue. It is more likely the middle-classness which causes the behavior we applaud rather than the form of housing tenure.

Still, the homeownership myth persists. Its most recent and dramatic expression came in the housing legislation of 1968 and the passage of the Section 235 program. The purpose of this legislation was to make homeownership available to low- and moderate-income families. During the hearings on this legislation, many a senator and congressman waxed lyrical about the prospect of uplifting poorer families by making them homeowners and sharers in the American dream. So anxious was the Congress to spread ownership among the poor that it passed Section 237 which authorized FHA to accept families with poor credit records, provided they were given personal counseling to teach them to manage their affairs better and to develop the kind of responsible behavior required for ownership.

The drive for ownership for the poor was not limited to the Section 235-237 programs. It became a principal objective of public housing through the Turnkey III and IV programs. Housing authorities throughout the country began to try to make homeowners of public housing tenants no matter how poor they were and no matter how much their family resources and behavior varied from middle-class norms.

The theory was very simple. Homeownership is something good in itself. It has the capacity to change human behavior, generate hope, ambition, and responsibility. If the family does not appear ready for ownership, then provide them with counseling in money management, homemaking, and related virtues and make them homeowners anyhow, in the expectation that the experience will cause them to develop and expand their middle-class habits, thus breaking the poverty cycle.

It is ironic that at the very time when Section 235 was being debated in the Congress, HUD had in its possession a report on a HUD-financed experiment in homeownership for the poor. The results of this experiment scarcely supported the thesis on which Section 235 and public housing ownership efforts rested. In fact, it showed there was very little correlation between family counseling and successful homeownership among the poor. Beyond that, the experiment was not very successful in creating successful homeownership among poor and disorganized families. Such factors as poor family budgeting, unemployment, and marital difficulties among families of marginal incomes made successful homeownership unlikely and these factors were influenced little, or not at all, by whether or not the family had received counseling.

The one lone voice who publicly questioned the wisdom of an indiscriminate drive to give ownership to the poor was that of former HUD Secretary Robert C. Weaver. On numerous occasions he expressed his doubts that homeownership was a universal panacea and questioned whether many poor families would benefit from the responsibility which homeownership would impose.

Experience so far with the Section 235 program seems to reveal, or force us to rediscover, certain basic truths about homeownership and its applicability. First, successful homeownership can be achieved by low- and moderate-income families who possess the qualities to make them upwardly mobile, who know how to manage their finances, and who have enough income to make the mortgage payments and to cover normal maintenance expenses as well as unexpected contingencies such as the breakdown of a water heater or a furnace.

It is such people, for the most part, who are using Section 235 to purchase new homes in the suburbs. These are predominantly young families on the way up, who have steady jobs with good prospects for advancement, and who enjoy stable family relationships. Experience so far suggests that these families are becoming successful homeowners, with no higher foreclosure rates than would be expected. For these families it appears probable that Section 235 will prove to be a successful instrument for helping them to buy a new house which they could not afford without such assistance.

On the other hand, the use of Section 235 to make owners out of poor, ghetto families with uncertain income and other problems, so far has proved notoriously unsuccessful if not catastrophic. These families have proved to be easily victimized by sharp speculators, have demonstrated no strong desire or capacity to continue as owners, and have often been unable or unwilling to keep up the mortgage payments much less pay for expected or unexpected maintenance expenses. To many of these poor families the dream of becoming a homeowner through Section 235 has proved to be a nightmare.

Many of these families have been cheated by speculators with the passive or active consent of the FHA and sold homes in poor repair at greatly inflated prices. It must be assumed that HUD will find a way to put a stop to these abuses. These families should not be blamed for the fact that they have been exploited. Yet the fact that they were so easily exploited says a good deal about their readiness for the responsibilities of ownership. The experience so far with Section 235 ownership for the very poor hardly leads one to be sanguine that ownership can be made a boon for every poor family.

It is unfortunate that HUD's first big attempt to provide homeownership to the very poor should have been muddied up with scandal and abuse. For we still do not have a clear answer on how many of the poor can be made successful owners. It is also unfortunate that HUD, for some unknown reason, has never asked for funds to carry out the home-owner counseling contemplated by Section 237. We cannot be sure to what extent proper counseling might have pre-vented some of the abuses and made successful homeowners of the families involved.

But events under the Section 235 program so far make Secretary Weaver's warnings seem more relevant than ever. This warning is simply that some poor and moderate-in-come families can achieve successful ownership. Many others cannot. Implicit in this warning is another truth worth re-membering: homeownership is not quite the instant panacea that some of the past (and present) rhetoric of its advocates would have us believe.

Excessive Reorganization

4. *Reorganization Is Not the Road to Redemption:* Since the mid-1940s secretaries of HUD and heads of its predecessor agencies have been struggling with the problem of how to organize the elements of an ever-growing bureau-cracy. Many variations have been tried, from a loosely knit confederation of relatively autonomous (as in the National Housing Agency in World War II) to the extensive co-mingling and merger of program elements (which charac-terizes the Romney era).

From this extensive history, several important lessons should have been learned. Among these are: First, that the formal organization rarely, if ever, coincides with the in-formal organization—that is, the way things actually get done and the way decisions actually get made. This is true because the formal organization represents an idealized and theoretical arrangement of people, functions, and lines of authority, while the informal organization reflects the actual practices, habits and capacities of the people occupying the various organizational boxes. For example, during the late 1940s it could accurately be said of HHFA [Housing and Home Finance Agency] that it had an effective deputy administrator, but the person who discharged these functions was never the person who carried the title "deputy administrator." It often occurs that the informal organization is not only different from but better than the formal organization.

Second, no form of organization, however theoretically perfect, can transcend the quality of the people who make up that organization. If the people are poor, or mediocre, the performance will be poor. If the people are skillful and knowledgeable and good bureaucrats, the performance will be good, often despite an illogical organizational structure.

Third, in any organization of any size, there will always be a tension between the administrator or secretary and his staff, who are concerned with broad policy and the smooth coordination of the various organizational elements, and the line operators who focus on their individual functions and whose organizations coalesce around their special mission and tend not to want to be bothered with broad policy and coordination. The ways these natural tensions are resolved and reconciled nearly always measure the success of the organization and the skill of the people who run it. There is no single organizational formula yet discovered which automatically reconciles the centrifugal forces which prompt the coordinators and central administrators and the centripetal forces which work with an individual line-operating organization.

Fourth, any reorganization which realigns what have become familiar ways of doing things will be disruptive of morale and efficiency in the short run. A quick series of basic reorganizations can only lead to short-run chaos.

NEEDED: REGIONAL GOVERNMENT UNITS [7]

As city and suburban problems increase in degree, kind, and intensity, their interests become complementary rather than conflicting.

The suburban community wants to remain suburban, placid, and accessible; the city to remain urban, exciting, and available. The suburbans in a desperate effort to meet rising costs that come with more people and more services, seek to attract industry to suburbia. The result has proven to be counterproductive. Industry robs the suburban area of its semirural charm, increases the need for services to accommodate the new industry (often resulting in greater costs than the taxes it can produce) and promotes urban sprawl, suburban slums (slurbs), and uncoordinated development.

The city on the other hand, loses industries which it is better equipped to accommodate, loses its tax base, and loses jobs for its marginal workers. The suburban communities are not equipped emotionally, financially, physically, or strategically to take on these low- or moderate-income workers fast enough to serve their imported industry. Nor do the suburbans appear willing to zone land or plan its use to meet the problems which confront them.

The city has demonstrated greater understanding and sensitivity to these problems and needs of low-paid workers. However, a lack of funds and resources slow the city's efforts to meet their needs, or to effectively deal with accommodating industry within the city.

In New York City and its suburbs, the impact of these land and tax problems is not limited to New York State. It fans out over the three-state metropolitan area composed of thirty-one counties in New York, New Jersey, and Connecticut. This region constitutes the Greater Metropolitan

[7] From "Urbs, Slurbs, Suburbs—and Regional Government," by Martin Gallent, a member of the New York City Planning Commission. *Christian Science Monitor.* p 16. O. 25, '72. Reprinted by permission from *The Christian Science Monitor* © 1972 The Christian Science Publishing Society. All rights reserved.

Area, as defined by the Regional Plan Association [RPA], a private group created to seek solutions to problems of the New York Urban Region. The association attempts to formulate regional goals, to forecast problems and solutions, considering open space, airport policy, metropolitan centers, housing opportunities, and public transportation.

The regional approach of the RPA is the only way to resolve the basic problems caused by suburbia enticing industry from the city, eroding the city's tax and employment base, and by the same means creating for itself an urban problem not resolvable on a suburban scale.

By looking to a regional area of interest, we can direct our zoning, employment, and tax-base interests. This could best be accomplished by a regional government built upon the RPA regional concept. To make such a government practical and realistic, the federal revenue sharing program should not be split among the states, cities, and suburban counties, but rather directed to a new form of regional government. In all probability, this new governmental structure would have to be created by a congressional act in the same manner as the Port Authority of New York, which is a bistate compact authorized by the Congress.

One solution to the industrial-tax-base problem, based on a regional approach, is for the region to create industrial-park areas. These industries would pay taxes to the regional government, which would deal with the related regional problems. The parks would be located in areas best suited for transportation, sanitation disposal, housing density for workers and management, proximity to horizontal and vertical suppliers and industries. The areas best suited to a suburban environment could be supported by the regional government without setting up a rival series of complex bureaucracies.

A proportionate amount of the taxes could be used to help meet the city's problems increasing the city's attractiveness to suburbia and thereby helping to resolve some of the problems faced by the city, both financial and social.

The suburban character, so prized by its residents, can be assured and supported by a tax contribution by the regional government with realistic population-density controls.

The current situation can give neither the city nor suburbia much comfort. One-acre zoning is under relentless and persistent attack. The New York Urban Development Corporation has proposed a very modest scatter-site plan, but even this has set suburban teeth on edge. Top management wants industry in its nearby neighbor's backyard. Local residents want the industrial tax base, but not the low- and moderate-income workers required by the industry. The sprawl continues and farms become factories, parking lots, and subdivisions, resulting in a net loss to both city and suburbia.

The time is at hand not to demand answers, but to innovate the answers based on our own experience and creative ability.

RESHAPING METROPOLITAN AMERICA [8]

If I had to sum up the source of much of our domestic dissatisfaction today, it would be in the conflict between where we have chosen to live and the arrangements we have inherited for determining how we shall live. Our problems are immediate and acute, and they have a way of ignoring all lines on our maps, of spilling over from one jurisdiction to another, of refusing to adapt themselves to the pigeon-holes of political subdivisions.

Let me be blunt: Our major cities are at once too big and too small to serve their people. They are too big to respond to the needs of neighborhoods, and too small to marshal the political and economic resources of a metropolitan area to improve the life of their residents. Our states, with few exceptions, have become unresponsive to the problems of an urban nation. And the Federal Government, in its

[8] From article by Sol M. Linowitz, chairman of the National Urban Coalition. *City*. 6:64-5. Ja.-F. '72. Reprinted by permission from *City*, Magazine of Urban Life and Environment. Copyright 1972. The National Urban Coalition, 2100 M St. N.W., Washington, D.C. 20037. All Rights Reserved.

role of financier, is pumping money into a tangle of programs and projects that too often permit the most parochial jurisdiction to undercut the progress of an entire metropolitan economy, or allow private interests to benefit at the expense of the public good.

If the competition of the states animated the founding of our nation, the survival of our urban environment and, indeed, our coherence as a nation demand an equally imaginative act of statesmanship today. And it must start with the Federal Government, the instrument created almost two hundred years ago to overcome the jealousies and fears among other levels of government. *The reshaping of metropolitan America is the great unfinished job of American federalism.*

Our first census in 1790 counted four million people in the United States; 95 percent of those people lived in rural areas. So the founders of the Republic wrote our Constitution and established the nature of our federalism in an agrarian setting. The principles that sparked their debates were not the problems of cities. The federal union was primarily a response to the fears of foreign invasion and debilitating commercial rivalries among the states.

For the next one hundred years our national policy and our literary and cultural traditions were based on our self-image as a rugged and rural society. With the crowded cities of Europe as a reminder, our great thinkers regarded cities as inherently immoral, as breeding places for social and physical pestilence. Jefferson distrusted city dwellers. Tocqueville, looking at riots in New York and Philadelphia, predicted that ultimately the residents of American cities would have to be controlled by armed forces responsible to the wishes of a majority who would presumably live elsewhere.

So it is not surprising that during the first century of the Republic the Federal Government undertook various programs to encourage the dispersal of the eastern urban population to the West. It gave away the public lands to help the railroads extend their lines to the West, or to promote education in these far-flung settlements. The Congress enacted the Homestead Act to open up new lands in the West by offering 160 acres to those willing to work them. In those days people were sought to tame the wilderness and to build the frontier towns. Today, as we so well know, most communities look on additional people as a mixed blessing at best.

Fifteen years ago this inherited distrust for cities as places to live was renewed when urban centers became hostage to the atomic bomb. We passed the national defense highway legislation ostensibly to enable our population, our industry, and our military defense forces to disperse from cities before they were destroyed by atomic attack.

Over the past few years there has been a resurgence of interest in depopulating metropolitan areas under the guise of something called "national urban growth policy." We hear it said that they are too big, that they are being inundated by undesirables, that we ought to devise a way to keep people from moving to them or to lure them away. In short, we are being urged to adopt a new national urban growth policy that is really a national urban *non*growth policy.

Present Population Trends

It is worth recalling that the 1970 census confirmed the overwhelmingly metropolitan nature of our population growth. The population living in metropolitan areas grew by 20 million, accounting for nearly 85 percent of the entire increase in US population over the last ten years. As a result, over two thirds of our population now lives in such areas. Indeed, over half of the population of the United States now lives in metropolitan areas of 500,000 or more. By far the largest part of this growth occurred outside the central cities.

The moderate growth of the nation's central cities was due almost entirely to increases in the black population. For cities of 500,000 or more, the white population declined by 1.9 million during the decade, while the black population increased by 2.2 million. If present trends continue, by 1985 over 80 percent of our black population will live in metropolitan areas, mostly in the central city and in the older, close-in suburban jurisdictions.

Most of the current further increase in our urban population is coming from natural increase rather than rural-to-urban migration. More people reached our metropolitan areas from foreign shores in the last ten years than from our own hinterland. Consequently, we have become not only a metropolitan nation but, alarmingly, a nation of residential apartheid.

So the first hard fact to recognize and accept is that the pattern of migration within our metropolitan areas presents us with a far greater problem than the pattern of migration from rural to urban areas or from one region of the country to another.

The second major fact to recognize is that our large urban areas will fuel our economic growth in a postindustrial society. With greater size comes the ability to invent, promote, and finance new products and services. With greater size comes the diversity that contributes to stability, that generates new employment and a greater overall choice of economic opportunity for our people. Therefore, when we permit the environment for our future economic strength to decay we weaken our ability to meet competition in the world's marketplaces.

Our society cannot indefinitely endure the tensions created by a nation half ghetto and half split-level. The ghettoization of the poor and minorities may be welcomed by some who believe this will concentrate "power." But, in fact, concentrating the helpless will more likely make them easier targets for neglect and hostility than turn them into potent political forces.

A New Urban Inventory

Sensing that this may be true, last year the National Urban Coalition took inventory of our center cities to determine what progress, if any, had been made in dealing with the problems that led to the 1967 and 1968 riots. We established the Commission on the Cities in the '70s, co-chaired by two men who had served on the original National Advisory Commission on Civil Disorders: Senator Fred Harris of Oklahoma and Mayor John Lindsay of New York City.

Recently we issued the commission's findings. We issued them with a deep sense of regret and shame. For the commission's basic conclusion was that despite earlier findings that the deplorable conditions of life in our cities were a major cause of the civil disorders of the 1960s, most of these conditions have worsened since 1968—in housing, in education, in health, in the spread of crime, in unemployment, in drug addiction, in the number of people on welfare, in the hostility between citizens and police. And these conditions worsened during a time of intensified residential racial segregation.

In the face of such findings, how can we organize ourselves to promote the kind of economic and human relationships we will need in our metropolitan areas over the next century?

As I think about this, I find myself wondering if we don't have too much land in this country to permit the growth of civilized cities. I wonder if we are destined to keep on hacking away at nature to make for ourselves even more escapes from having to live together as a people. I wonder if we don't have too much land and too little sense of history. Other nations, with a better sense of history, have managed to preserve their cities as places of national pride, while we have permitted ours to become simply places where only strangers pass in the day and hope even to avoid passing in the night.

Many of our problems are beyond the capacity of the cities to solve alone, demand too much from the suburbs, and cannot wait for a response from the states. For example, the land and housing market in many of our central cities has broken down. Investment is being virtually sucked out of the central-city housing market. Had this occurred by the force of a tornado we would regard it as the true disaster it is, and would be rushing resources in to deal with it. But how we deal with it will work against a past policy to clear the slums and bring a middle class back into the city that has proved unsuccessful, in part because we have no corollary policy for upgrading the opportunities of the poor on a metropolitanwide basis.

We have built highways between our cities that are the envy of the world, but in our great metropolitan areas we too often seem unable to develop a coherent transportation program that serves everybody. Meanwhile, jobs are being generated in outlying areas that are literally beyond the reach of those who need them because of the resistance of suburban jurisdictions to lower-income housing.

A New Urban-Growth Policy

We have, in short, been building a new metropolitan nation in a way that excludes the less advantaged and the minorities from participation in the benefits of urban growth. In doing so we have been wasteful of our human and natural resources. We need a national urban-growth policy that is not caught up in piecemeal central-city and suburban approaches.

The genius of our form of government has been its ability to adapt to change. Maybe it is given to the United States to live on the leading edge of history, to keep alive the hope that where strangers congregate today, communities and neighborhoods will grow tomorrow. I believe we have the ability to forge new ways of governing ourselves to overcome the difficulties of metropolitan life if the Federal Government will provide the leadership.

I think it is time for the Federal Government itself to bring into being new metropolitan-development agencies to stimulate and carry out new patterns of community development with federal resources.

In every aspect of community development sooner or later we are going to have to recognize that neither rational nor truly democratic approaches to our problems can be fashioned in the balkanized and competitive compartments and political fossils that pass for local jurisdictions. We have known this for a long time and yet seem unwilling to recognize where the pressure for change must be directed: the Federal Government.

Within a few years federal outlays for a variety of urban-development programs may reach a level of $20 billion a year. Federal funds will supply the capital for much of our future urban growth. But supplying the capital is not enough.

New Urban Agencies Needed

The Federal Government must also forge new instruments for metropolitan planning and development. These new instruments should be elective metropolitan-development agencies, politically accountable on an areawide basis and capable of reconciling regional and community needs.

These agencies must be able to acquire land for three forms of development: (1) improvement of inner-city neighborhoods, including rehabilitation or replacement of abandoned dwellings; (2) development of needed housing outside of the city, near centers of job opportunities; and (3) creation of new satellite or minicommunities within their metropolitan areas.

These are tasks that can only be undertaken successfully if planned and carried out by the same agency on a coordinated basis, so that they strengthen one another in the process.

The metropolitan-development agencies also should plan and install transportation systems within their areas, and install the water and sewer lines that determine directions of development.

They should have the power to preempt local zoning and building regulations under appropriate circumstances, and the power of eminent domain.

They should be able to tap private capital by issuing special-purpose indebtedness bonds backed by federal guarantees. And they should have the resources to provide the social services that are often the key to the successful operation of physical developments.

A Government that created TVA, that chartered Comsat, and that organized the effort to reach the moon has the undoubted authority to develop such new organizations to reduce racial and economic polarization in our metropolitan areas. The only question is whether it has the will.

What I am proposing would not supplant general-purpose local government, nor would it be some superagency of unresponsive professionals. As a democratically elected agency, it would, however, give both central-city and suburban residents an additional stake in new ventures using primarily national resources to improve their environments.

For a Birthday Present

This task I have described is as demanding, as fraught with uncertainties, as controversial, and as crucial as that which faced the draftsmen of our Constitution almost two hundred years ago. The greatest birthday present we could present to ourselves to mark the start of the third century of this nation would be a totally new way of governing ourselves in an urban and metropolitan environment.

The Federal Government was designed to represent all of us, and we must look to it for the initiative the designers intended, to give the people once again the chance to live together under a system in which cooperation pays off for all.

This should be the essence of a new national urban growth **policy.**

Charles Abrams, a wise and experienced observer of America, once wrote: "The history of civilization from Memphis, Egypt, to Memphis, Tennessee, is recorded in the rise or demise of cities."

Unlike the citizens of early Egypt, however, we are conscious of this truism.

The question facing us is whether, in the light of this knowledge of history, we will stand paralyzed and watch our civilization rot away, or whether we will build anew by thinking anew and acting anew—while we still have the chance to save our cities and our society.

III. NEW HOUSING PROGRAMS

EDITOR'S INTRODUCTION

That many innovative housing projects have been undertaken in the past two decades attests both to the need for them and the great concern that has been generated by America's housing problems. Some developments, like the proliferation of mobile homes and the erection of high-rise crime-inducing housing, have brought new problems. Other plans, only in part futuristic, point to the growth of "suburbs" on coastal sea areas and the erection of new ocean-cities.

One response to meeting housing needs has been the emergence in many cities of citizen action groups concerned with housing and community development. The work of one such organization, Cincinnati's Better Housing League, is explained by its executive director, Charles G. Stocker. In the next selection, a fresh approach to racially integrated housing is proposed by Charles Hammer, a reporter for the Kansas City *Star*.

The bulk of this section includes articles on specific projects underway or trends only newly emerging. Gail Bronson, staff reporter of the *Wall Street Journal*, reports on a new version of homesteading. The growing preference for condominium housing is noted by Martin Skala, business and financial correspondent of *The Christian Science Monitor*. Cooperative housing is explained by Richard J. Margolis, a columnist for the *New Leader*. And an article by Marie C. Maguire from the official magazine of the Department of Housing and Urban Development (*HUD Challenge*) presents a summary of design requirements for the elderly. The

final selection, an article by Elaine Kendall, deals with the
growing numbers of boat dwellers in floating suburbs.

A CITIZEN ACTION GROUP FOR HOUSING [1]

Since its beginnings in 1916 Cincinnati's Better Housing
League—the nonprofit citizens' organization serving a five-
county area, has been involved with people, their neighborhoods, and their structures. Its 2,000 members are dedicated
to helping people obtain adequate shelter, maintain that
shelter properly, and receive the most for their housing dollar. In a sense, we serve as the conscience of the community
in matters of housing, alerting public officials and the citi-
zenry to problem conditions and encouraging them to find
solutions.

Information and Counseling

For more than half a century the Better Housing League
[BHL] has provided information and counseling to residents
in the Cincinnati area. Its members have worked toward
improving housing without reference to political affiliation
or involvement. It has brought together neighborhood rep-
resentatives and city staff members. It has supported new
legislation on tenant-landlord relations; it has won the Cincinnati City Council's approval for a law making it illegal
for property owners to shut off essential utilities in occupied
buildings. Through its efforts, others have come to know
the Better Housing League and have sought its guidance in
developing similar programs in their area.

The League has received inquiries from such major cities
as Spokane, St. Louis, Boston, Washington (D.C.), Gary,
Omaha, and Tacoma, including many communities in its
home state of Ohio. The brochures explaining its programs
and operations are simply written and illustrated to make
its message easily understood. During the past year more

[1] From "Cincinnati's Better Housing League," by Charles G. Stocker, executive director of the Better Housing League of Greater Cincinnati. *HUD
Challenge.* 4:24-5. Je. '73.

than 14,000 of its various publications were distributed "with the conviction that the greatest force for better housing is an informed consumer."

Of particular interest is the League's *Tenant Handbook,* developed in cooperation with tenant-managers as part of the tenant-education program. This provides key telephone numbers, facts about the tenant's lease agreement, how to pay rent, who makes repairs, and tenant-landlord responsibilities. A three-page check list assists the tenant in understanding responsibility with respect to utilities, fire safety, housekeeping, and garbage disposal.

Innovative Programs

Four years ago there was little work being done in the field of tenant education. Although the City of Cincinnati had provided funds for the program with the intent to co-ordinate efforts in this activity, the main thrust was in the area of encouraging and training persons to become involved professionally in this endeavor. The League's effort in promoting the program of tenant education with other agencies during this initial period has paid dividends.

Today BHL is coordinating the work of L. M. Primack, Inc., a Cincinnati management firm, and the Cincinnati Board of Education in developing a management-training program utilizing a mobile unit, developing a training course for Cincinnati's Model Cities Neighborhood Development Corporation offered through the University of Cincinnati's College of Community Services, and providing leadership training to officers of tenant councils around the metropolitan area.

The staff designed and instructed the first management course offered at the University of Cincinnati—a ten-week course conducted by the College of Community Services in the spring of 1972.

"Over the years the Better Housing League staff has been a catalyst in proposing innovative programs and in conducting major activities to help improve housing con-

ditions for the people of Cincinnati," says Arnold J. Rosemeyer, housing development officer for Cincinnati's Department of Urban Development.

Rosemeyer tells of BHL's assistance in developing specific plans for experimental rehabilitation in East Washington Park and Dayton-Linn Triangle areas. "This concept
initiated by BHL," says Rosemeyer, "was the first local inducement for inner-city rehabilitation. The League can also
be credited with developing a relocation plan for the
Queensgate II renewal area."

In recent years the League has centered much of its activities around homeownership counseling. Because of its
work in this field, we were invited in 1971 to meet in Washington with HUD staff members to discuss redesign of the
Section 237 program. [See "Unlearned Lessons of Housing,"
by M. Carter McFarland in Section II, above.] The League
was among the agencies to receive an award from former
HUD Secretary George Romney for its work in voluntary
counseling.

In the City of Lincoln Heights, a predominantly black
community of some 7,800 persons, BHL staff member Tom
Cade is working with William Korte, the City's urban renewal director, who is on a one-year leave of absence from
HUD's Columbus Area Office under the Intergovernmental
Personnel Act. Korte believes that the homeownership
counseling provided by BHL is a protective key for those
being displaced by the Lincoln Heights renewal program.

"We view the Better Housing League as representing
the buyer rather than the seller in seeking proper housing
for our relocatees," Korte says.

Annually, BHL counsels some three hundred families in
homeownership and others seeking help when confronted
with problems that arise after purchasing a house.

In spite of its fifty-seven years of existence and acknowledgement of its worth in the greater Cincinnati area and
elsewhere, the Better Housing League has seen some lean
years, and funding of its counseling program is still not per-

manent. Requests for assistance from other agencies have
not been accompanied by offers of financial assistance. Only
through its contracts with clients such as Lincoln Heights
and Cincinnati has its counseling program continued to
function . . . [in 1973]. Our budget of $130,000 consists of
some $50,000 from the Greater Cincinnati Community
Chest, of which the League is a participating member, and
the balance is derived from contracts or grants. The current
programs of neighborhood coordination, tenant and homeownership counseling, education, research, and public information are manned by a nine-member staff of full-time
employees.

Looking to the future, the League has on the drawing
board a regional management-training center which it hopes
to establish in cooperation with the University of Cincinnati's College of Community Service.

A NEW APPROACH TO INTEGRATED HOUSING [2]

Once upon a time it was the big thing for white idealists
to demonstrate brotherhood by moving their families into
a racially changing neighborhood. And almost invariably
they soon found themselves the last whites in an otherwise
all-black neighborhood, a situation no more "natural" than
its all-white opposite. So the rest of us caught on (me included) and joined the flight to the stable suburbs. I am
here to argue that despite all the sweat and seeming futility,
those sweet idealists were dead right.

Try imaginatively to put yourself in one such racially
changing neighborhood of Kansas City, Missouri, where I
have written as a newspaperman for more than a decade.
Like hundreds of similar city-neighborhoods in the forties
it was modest, attractive, separated physically from the
jammed black ghetto only by one street. For years racial
covenants in deeds had prevented the crossing of that street.

[2] From "Racially Changing Neighborhoods," by Charles Hammer, a reporter for the Kansas City *Star*. *New Republic*. 169:19-21. S. 15, '73. Reprinted
by Permission of The New Republic, © 1973 Harrison-Blaine of New Jersey, Inc.

Then, as 1950 approached, the United States Supreme Court declared those covenants unenforceable and the ghetto began expanding southward. Real estate brokers and mortgage bankers cooperated to prevent any scattering that might have resulted in permanently integrated neighborhoods. Block after block was emptied of whites to be filled with blacks.

So swift and chaotic was the change at times that the ratio of black children in one elementary school soared from 25 to 65 percent in a single year. Physical deterioration started when whites saw the wave coming, for they suspended all maintenance of property. The early black arrivals—middle class and nearly always better educated than existing white residents—struggled to keep up their homes. It is no reflection on them to say property values plummeted, since the market was glutted with homes put up for sale by desperate whites. The wave continued, bringing poor blacks from the inner city.

Here we created—are still creating—the worst possible situation for the neighborhood meeting of the races. Even poor black families would have responded better in a stable community where old residents could have monitored them with a critical eye. They came instead to neighborhoods in disorder, and they were treated to a destructive vision of themselves as the pariahs who had caused it. "The thing I dread," said a black judge, "is when I have to explain to my little girl about that kind of thing. That's a cutting thing for a parent to have to tell a child."

Whites who might have been willing to accept integration were never offered a choice. They could flee or prepare to live in a virtually all-black neighborhood. Courageous resistance in the name of understanding invariably proved useless, since there was no metropolitan plan which might have made such gestures successful.

In the wake of neighborhood turnover has come most of Kansas City's other urban problems—loan foreclosures, widespread housing abandonment, new slums, sharp de facto school segregation and a black pupil ratio that has now soared beyond 50 percent.

In 1950 no Kansas City census tract in which the population was more than 24 percent black extended south of 31st Street. In 1970 one tract with a population 39 percent black reached south to 77th. Between lay five miles of neighborhoods, some virtually all black now, the rest still changing. In twenty years some 67,000 whites—equal to almost one fifth of the city's entire 1950 white population—left Southeast Kansas City.

Much has been said about the white flight to the suburbs. Little has been said or done about its origins, which lie here, in the changing neighborhood. Kansas City may be considered among a lucky few: its ratio of black citizens grew only from 12 percent in 1950 to 22 percent in 1970. Consider the consequences in Chicago, where the comparable figures are 14 and 33 percent; Philadelphia, 18 and 34 percent; Detroit, 16 and 44 percent; or Washington, D.C., 35 and 71 percent.

It is a mathematical axiom that as a circle expands the area of isolation inside grows faster than the line of contact around its circumference. No surprise, then, that the American metropolis is more segregated than ever. In 1950 only one fourth of Kansas City's blacks lived in neighborhoods more than 90 percent black. In 1970 nearly half lived in such areas. Chicago's principal segregating years came between 1920, when none of the city's blacks lived in tracts more than 90 percent black, and 1950, when 67 percent did.

The segregation of cities is becoming segregation of suburbs as the Washington, D.C., ghetto pushes eastward into Prince Georges County, the Cleveland ghetto expands tentatively into DeKalb County, the Baltimore ghetto begins its break westward into Baltimore County. The pattern of ghetto formation and expansion holds even in suburbs such as Media, Chester and Darby outside Philadelphia, Maywood west of Chicago, Grandview outside Indianapolis.

All this would be fine if blacks wanted compact, fortress neighborhoods that could be defended in race war—and if whites wanted handy concentration camps that could be ringed with wire in emergencies. But even die-hard racists on each side don't want that. Yet that is what we have and are getting more of.

Citizens Must Organize

Racial turnover begins anew tomorrow and continues forever. But not if citizens organize to stop it. It will take more than the old liberal appeals to human decency, however. Needed now are appeals to interest, appeals to black and Chicano families weary of neighborhood turbulence, to middle-class and working-class whites whose neighborhoods are threatened by turnover, to suburban whites willing to accept integration if it comes with a guarantee against their greatest fear, racial turnover. We need to shift black buying out of the changing neighborhood into stable, outlying areas where scattered purchases by blacks will cause no panic. Here is the rallying cry: "Stop resegregation. Keep East Cleveland integrated. (Make it Prince Georges County or Media or Maywood.) Open cities everywhere."

In nearly every area undergoing turnover there are organizations, usually interracial, which can be useful—Serena Hills Neighbors in a Chicago suburb; the former Dayton View Stabilization Project in Dayton, Ohio; South DeKalb Neighbors near Atlanta. Such groups need alliances in outlying white neighborhoods. Many have found them in the fair-housing councils that have sprung up across the country. Blacks can make common cause with whites in the changing neighborhood only when the purpose clearly is not simply the exclusion of blacks. The charge that whites in the changing area only want to move blacks elsewhere can be blunted best by suburban whites eager for new black neighbors.

Such alliances should demand for the changing neighborhood its share and more of city services. If economies are to be made in garbage collection, housing, law enforcement, city beautification, they should be made by neighborhoods without the worst problems. The changing area must be first on the list for tree-planting, city-financed street improvements, park recreation-programs and high-quality moderate-income housing. It should be last on the list as a site for low-income housing. It must be protected by city ordinances against blockbusting and the real estate "for sale" signs that tend to increase anxiety.

When racial change in housing begins, citizens should demand of their school board that the schools change more slowly or not at all. Switching individual school boundaries a few blocks often can prevent the swift change in school population that frightens white families. Busing can accomplish more, and busing to stop turnover is far more likely to be tolerated by whites than busing for integration.

The city-suburban alliance could also awaken local government to new options. One idea being discussed by certain city planners would help the changing neighborhood by guaranteeing every resident the return of his home investment there. By easing fears that homes will lose value, the plan would take countless houses off the market, bolstering prices sufficiently that the cash outlay might be relatively small.

Another plan calls for administrators to define neighborhoods likely to undergo racial turnover—white to black, black to white. Government would then pay substantial bonuses—call them "open city" payments—for home purchases there by qualified families whose presence tends to reverse the trend. This would almost always mean paying whites to fill vacancies in changing neighborhoods near the black ghetto. The more controversial obverse side of that notion would have government reward families whose purchases integrated a neighborhood where their race was in a specified, tiny minority and where there was no future danger of racial turnover. This would be positive encouragement for black purchases in the suburbs and—for that matter—white purchases in the heart of the ghetto. Some such scheme would create new white buyers for the changing neighborhood, stop the drop in values, stiffen resistance by the old residents and push black families into outlying areas.

This pattern of dispersal—the pattern of an integrated society—already is emerging. It may be clearest outside Washington, D.C., where more than half of the 460 elementary schools in suburban districts showed percentage increases in black enrollment even before 1969. Chicago suburbs such as Skokie, Highland Park and Park Forest exhibit the same pattern, as do a few areas in nearly all of the nation's metropolitan areas.

The ghetto and changing neighborhood are one market, divided up among black real estate brokers and certain white brokers. Outlying neighborhoods are another, served largely by a separate group of brokers, almost all white. Black families usually find their way voluntarily or are steered to brokers of the first group—a fact that predetermines the housing they will be shown. But interesting things happen when the dual housing market is cracked—when a broker with access to black buyers gets listings in all-white neighborhoods. A pair of black brokers in Kansas City, Kansas, put together such an effort in the mid-1960s and lightly integrated the formerly all-white west side of that city. In 1966 one of the two, Donald Sewing, bought a home for himself in the nearly all-white bedroom suburban area of Johnson County, Kansas. Since then he has negotiated sale of more than forty homes there to black families, making a conscious effort to scatter them.

The force of such adroit personal effort can hardly be overestimated. In 1965 Dorothy Davis, a white housewife from an outlying Kansas City neighborhood, began to wonder why . . . homes [foreclosed by the Federal Housing Administration] in all-white neighborhoods were never sold to blacks. She learned that on market day, when black brokers called in to bid, they were always told the house was already sold. So Mrs. Davis bought one herself, proving in the process that the FHA managing broker had been "preselling" these homes to whites before they officially went on the market. She carried the story to a newspaper. Suddenly the foreclosed homes began to sell to black families.

Her work underlines the necessity for citizen scrutiny of federal housing agencies such as FHA and the Veterans Administration. Former HUD Secretary George Romney startled these fusty organizations with new guidelines that helped put some federally subsidized housing for low- and moderate-income families in the suburbs. Inept administration cost the nation much of the good Romney sought. But there is still opportunity for citizens to make something out of the remnants of the Romney era.

The Case of Dayton, Ohio

In few places around the nation has the trend toward integration taken shape as well as in Dayton, Ohio. The first question to be settled by the Miami Valley Regional Planning Commission there was whether dispersal of low-income housing was necessary and right. The staff of the five-county commission studied the problem for more than a year and in 1970 answered, "Yes." The staff proposed a plan for building 14,000 federally subsidized housing units for low- and moderate-income families. The units were to be dispersed on a formula almost the reverse of past practice: the richer the community, the richer and less crowded the schools, the fewer families of low income, the more low- and moderate-income housing that suburb was assigned. The member cities and counties on the commission approved the plan 30-0. Virtually no subsidized housing had been built before in the metropolitan area outside Dayton. Today 800 units are completed or under construction outside Dayton, and another 2,700 are in process. In Dayton itself another 1,800 units have been completed or are under construction, with 665 others on the way. All are scattered and well away from the ghetto.

Dale Bertsch, Miami Valley executive director, says the major reason for the acceptance the plan has won is that people know each area gets its share of subsidized housing—no more. Miami Valley halted plans for a 465-unit project in Madison township, which is substantially integrated and lies directly in the path of northeastward black movement from Dayton. By opening themselves to racial integration, the Dayton suburbs have gone far toward protecting themselves from racial turnover.

Not directly connected with the Dayton plan but one reason for its success is the former Dayton View Stabilization Project, a city agency set up to battle racial turnover. Its first director, Joe Wine, is another example of how personal weight can help tip the scale. He left a job as department store executive and later became a community organizer of modest national reputation. While leading Dayton View, he helped convince Dayton citizens that only by opening the suburbs could they prevent resegregation of the city.

The Dayton plan is the flying prototype of a machine that could be mass produced across the nation, just as the locally developed Philadelphia plan or variants of it were multiplied to increase minority employment in construction. The first Dayton copy came off the line in 1972, when the Washington Area Council of Governments adopted a fair-share dispersal plan. Your town could follow.

The Dayton plan leads inevitably into economic integration, which is precisely where it should. But citizens must demand that when the poor meet the better-off in outlying neighborhoods, they do so under the best of circumstances. That rules out the sort of high-rise, completely low-income project that caused a revolt among middle-class residents of Forest Hills in New York. Far better would be a garden-apartment development on a suburban corner, with perhaps forty moderate-income families and ten low-income families. Every possible help should be extended to the families, but a landlord should hang in the background, ready to evict any family that fouls the nest. The few that cannot succeed even with major help simply must find a place in inner-city public housing.

The development described here will work—already is working in many outlying neighborhoods across the nation. In it both the poor and the moderate-income families gain housing far better than they could otherwise afford. And the old residents of the neighborhood console themselves that at least it is new construction, that the situation is under control—far better than the sweep of poor and black through crumbling neighborhoods half a century old.

The Dayton Public Opinion Center in one poll asked a cross-section of Montgomery County residents (the county is 14 percent black) whether they agreed or disagreed that their own neighborhood should have a mixture of races and economic groups. Five percent replied they agreed strongly, while 56 percent merely agreed—a total of 61 percent on the integration side. Asked whether subsidized apartments should be built only in Dayton or scattered into suburbs as well, 81 percent of Dayton residents—not surprisingly—said they should be scattered. But 69 percent of the suburban people also voted for scattering.

"It's a natural thing for people to be provincial and protective and frightened," says Joe Wine, "particularly when there is no public ethic. Conversely, if people can be brought to understand the rightness, the essential rightness—witness what Miami Valley has done—people can be matured to understand moral purpose. That's why the work we've been involved in is so exciting."

URBAN HOMESTEADING [3]

Maybe you can't get something for nothing, but Bill Trainer and his wife got a house the other day for only a dollar.

[3] Article entitled "The Old Homestead—Abandoned Houses Are Given Free to People Willing to Restore Them," by Gail Bronson, staff reporter. *Wall Street Journal.* p 1. S. 21, '73. Reprinted with permission of *The Wall Street Journal* © 1973 Dow Jones & Company, Inc. All Rights Reserved.

It isn't much to write home about. At least not yet. The house is located in a rundown section of the inner city . . . [in Wilmington, Delaware]. The brick facade is cracked, the steps are rotting, most of the window frames are broken, and there isn't any heat or electricity.

Even so, "We are ready to drop out of the world for eighteen months to fix the place up," asserts Regina Bonney, Mr. Trainer's wife.

It may take that long. Mr. Trainer and Miss Bonney are one of ten families who were awarded similar houses under an "urban homesteading" plan that Wilmington and a number of other cities are experimenting with. Under most of the plans—Wilmington's is the first to be put into effect—individuals will be given title to abandoned center-city homes in return for fixing them up and living in them for a certain number of years. In Wilmington, the residency requirement is three years; also the houses must be rehabilitated according to local building code standards.

A Lawyer and a Longshoreman

Urban homesteading harks back to the Homestead Act of 1862, which awarded 160 acres of land free to anyone who remained on it five years. The result of the 1862 act was to stimulate one of the great mass migrations in history. City officials have much more modest hopes for urban homesteading, but clearly they view it as a potential antidote to urban blight, lack of low-income housing, and middle-class flight to the suburbs.

Some of the winners in the Wilmington drawing were a Du Pont Company lawyer now from Main Line, Pennsylvania; a nursing home aide who will renovate with her grandson, and a longshoreman who has six children and a wife to help him. Bill Trainer is studying art at the University of Delaware. His wife, Regina (who retains her maiden name), is an office worker who supports the two on her $7,900-a-year salary. The couple currently live in a small suburban apartment. They figure it will cost about $6,000 to fix up their homestead even if they do a lot of the work themselves. But they are confident that it will be worth it. "We want to make the third floor into an art studio, so we won't have to move Bill's projects off the kitchen table every time we have dinner," says Miss Bonney.

Homesteading is being studied or adopted in cities from Rockford, Illinois, to Boston. In Baltimore, a historic downtown section was saved from the urban-renewal bulldozer at the last minute, and houses are being turned over to homesteaders for rehabilitation. In Washington, city officials are negotiating with the United States Department of Housing and Urban Development for an inventory of abandoned homes that could be homesteaded; nationwide, HUD holds title to or mortgages on some 250,000 houses and apartments, many of them abandoned.

Swamped With Requests

And in Philadelphia, city officials were swamped with more than two thousand requests for homesteading application forms even before the program had gotten underway officially. Only a few hundred homes will be doled out initially.

Not everybody is enthusiastic about the idea. For one thing, city-planning experts doubt that sufficient numbers of homesteaders can be enticed into rehabilitating houses to make a dent in urban blight. Wilmington alone has over fifteen hundred privately owned abandoned houses, while Philadelphia has nearly thirty thousand. Moreover, getting clear title to the houses for transfer to a homesteader can be a problem. Philadelphia owns outright only about three hundred houses, while a federal-city agency—the redevelopment authority—has several thousand available lots and dwellings. To complicate matters further, in some states a delinquent taxpayer can reclaim his house up to two years after it has been foreclosed upon.

Also, rehabilitation can be an expensive proposition. "In areas where homes sell for $8,000, an abandoned house might require $15,000 minimum to restore," estimates William Grigsby, a University of Pennsylvania urban-planning professor. He terms homesteading a "terrible" idea. "Unless there is public subsidy (for rehabilitation), the homesteader is being led into a bad deal."

Subsidies in Boston

City officials in Philadelphia and elsewhere retort that homesteading is at least worth a try. "I haven't seen any urban experts solve city problems," says Wilmington's thirty-one-year-old mayor, Thomas Mahoney. City officials from across the country are understood to be taking a look at the Philadelphia and Wilmington experiments.

To ease the burden of rehabilitation, subsidies are indeed being considered for homesteaders. The Massachusetts legislature will consider a bill this session to be introduced by Boston delegates to include guarantees on rehabilitation mortgages given to homesteaders. In Wilmington, four churches and a bank are making available loans of up to $4,000, repayable in five to ten years at relatively low interest rates. Philadelphia lending institutions have expressed interest in the homesteading project.

Wilmington officials say they are proceeding slowly with urban homesteading—another ten houses will be assigned to homesteaders later this month—in order to see what problems crop up and to avoid any big errors that could cripple the program. A homestead board of city officials reviewed some 70 applications for the first lot of houses. The field was narrowed to 40 heads of households over eighteen years old, with sufficient monetary resources or do-it-yourself ability to rehabilitate the houses, and the names of 10 winners were drawn from a fishbowl. The Philadelphia homestead board must now go through similar proceedings and will attempt to make housing assignments in a few months.

THE GROWING POPULARITY OF
CONDOMINIUMS [4]

A surging demand for condominiums is adding extra zip to the homebuilding outlook this fall.

Ranging from luxury oceanfront high-rises in southern California to colonial-style town houses in the western Connecticut hills, "condos" are currently the housing industry's hottest product. "The most successful housing innovation in years," enthuses Irving Rose, president of Advance Mortgage Corporation, a Detroit-based organization that keeps close tabs on homebuilding trends.

Much of the unexpected strength in multifamily housing starts this year stems from the growing popularity of the "condo" concept. Statistically, condominium activity is hard to measure precisely.

For reporting purposes government bodies usually count them as apartments along with rental units. But in its latest survey of housing trends, Advance Mortgage predicts that builders will lay foundations for more than 235,000 condominiums of all types this year, including town houses, garden apartments, and high-rises.

Triple 1971 Level

This level of activity would be triple . . . [the 1971] figure and would account for about 10 percent of total US housing starts. Outside of Florida, more condominiums are under construction than have been built in all the years to date.

In cities where condominium ownership is relatively new, such as Philadelphia, and Washington "demand is fantastic," Advance Mortgage reports. "Any well-planned development has strong presale and some are sold out before the first model apartments are even finished," the survey says.

[4] From "Condominiums Booming All Over," by Martin Skala, business and financial correspondent. *Christian Science Monitor.* p 14. O. 5, '72. Reprinted by permission from *The Christian Science Monitor* © 1972 The Christian Science Publishing Society. All rights reserved.

Condominiums are said to be capturing a "striking variety of market segments around the nation." In Chicago, Atlanta, and Detroit more than a quarter of all new multi-family apartments now have "for sale" signs hanging on them.

Many younger families who might otherwise be looking for $25-30,000 single-family homes are opting for a town house or garden apartment that cost 10-20 percent less, builders say. In Washington, D.C., low-rise and garden-type "condos" have preempted the $25-35,000 market from the one-family home, Advance Mortgage says.

Luxury Sales Booming

Despite some scattered problems with overbuilding, luxury condominiums selling for $60,000-$100,000 are going over big in resort areas such as San Diego and Boca Raton, Florida. Many of the developments are aimed at affluent retirees and offer easy access to golfing, swimming pools, and waterfront marinas. As an extra inducement for second-home owners, developers offer rental arrangements which may produce extra income and tax deductions.

In an effort to hold homebuilding costs down and reach families that can't afford the detached house costing $25,000 or more, many developers are building garden apartments and town houses on large-scale tracts.

Dallas-based Centex Corporation, which claims to be the largest US builder of condominiums, says that only one third of the close to 2,500 living units it will build . . . [in 1973] will be of the single-family detached variety. Centex's condominiums range from one-bedroom garden apartments selling from $60,000 up in St. Petersburg, Florida, to elegant $90,000 three-bedroom units on the Hudson River overlooking Manhattan.

Thomas Cooper, marketing vice president for Centex's homebuilding arm, attributes the swing toward condominiums to "changing life styles, particularly among the young.

Many younger families no longer dream of a split-level house surrounded by an acre of land," he says.

Mortgages Widely Available

"Condominiums satisfy the homeowning instincts of people who don't want the burdens of property maintenance," Mr. Cooper says. Getting mortgage financing in most areas is no more difficult now than for single-family homes.

For builders, three- to four-family town houses and garden apartments help overcome a problem of land scarcity in urban areas. Many of Centex's developments include outdoor recreational facilities—usually in an attractive parklike setting. Owners pay a monthly charge that takes care of maintenance of common properties as well as the typical homeowning chores such as lawn care and exterior painting.

From the buyer's viewpoint the income tax shelter available from the deductibility of interest and real estate taxes is a major attraction, according to Mr. Cooper.

Tax savings are also one reason why many apartment buildings are being converted to condominiums in some large cities. The tax shelter aspects of apartment ownership diminish over the ten-to-fifteen-year period.

Thus landlords are encouraged to convert rental units to condominiums, especially since they find that individual apartment sales in the aggregate can bring as much as 25 percent more income than the sale of the whole building to another landlord.

COOPERATIVE HOUSING [5]

The unofficial capital of cooperative housing in America is New York City; its "White House" is on the Lower East Side at 465 Grand Street, headquarters for the United Housing Foundation (UHF); its Founding Father is the late Abraham Eli Kazan, an immigrant from Kiev who began

[5] From "Housing," by Richard J. Margolis, staff columnist. *New Leader*. 50:27-32. Ap. 17, '72. Reprinted with permission.

his career as errand boy for the International Ladies Garment Workers Union (ILGWU); and its most astonishing achievement thus far is Co-op City, a new, gigantic complex of apartment buildings, town houses and stores rising improbably from the marshes of the East Bronx.

Kazan, who died last year at the age of eighty-two, organized the nation's first housing cooperative in 1926, when as manager of the Amalgamated (Clothing) Workers Credit Union he persuaded that organization and the Jewish Daily Forward Association to finance and sponsor the unlikely experiment. Few observers at the time were betting on his success. . . .

By 1927 the Amalgamated Co-op was fully owned and occupied by 250 workers and their families; they paid carrying charges of $11 per month. (The building, a five-story walkup, was torn down four years ago to make way for two twenty-story cooperative towers built by Kazan's original organization, Amalgamated Housing. It is the oldest cooperative housing sponsor in the United States, and it is the only one to have survived the Depression.)

Toward a Better Life

Kazan pushed ahead with construction of more co-ops during the next two decades, teaming up with such New York labor and political luminaries as Sidney Hillman, Jacob Potofsky and Herbert Lehman. Like the organizers of Seattle's health co-op, Kazan was able to draw strength from the labor movement, but his principles were pure Rochdale. In 1951 he helped found the United Housing Foundation [UHF], a consortium of co-ops and trade unions aimed at sponsoring new housing. "All that we do," announced the founders in their statement of purpose, "is directed toward utilizing the methods of cooperation to enable people to enjoy a better life and to achieve a better society."

In twenty-one years the Foundation has brought "a better life" to more than 100,000 New Yorkers, sponsoring an unrivaled procession of middle-income cooperatives. These have ranged in size from the **Park Reservoir Housing Cor-poration** (273 apartments) to Co-op City (15,382 units).

Co-op City is home to some 60,000 persons. Each adult has a legally equal voice in directing the community's affairs; each is a shareholder in the co-op stores he patronizes; each is an owner, a voter and a full participant in the nation's most interesting housing experiment since the invention of the log cabin.

At present the community, a combination of skyscrapers and town houses, looks as raw and primitive as any frontier settlement. But the cooperators, assisted by UHF, are doing all they can to speed the mellowing process. They have filled in the swamps, planted 22,000 trees and left intact the hills and rocky outcroppings that surround their homes. The street names—Brook Farm Place, Bellamy Loop—are not the sort one is likely to find in a suburban subdivision.

The cooperators also have started to heat up that peculiar social brew which invariably marks the successful co-op. "The place vibrates," says Sidney Weinberger, who with his wife and two daughters has been living in Co-op City since last August. "I can only say this: If suddenly there were no television, most of New York City's population would go nuts. But not us. We don't need the boob tube. We got too many other things going for us."

Niagara of Activities

One thing they have going for them is Co-op politics, a process which residents take at least as seriously as presidential politics. After a recent election of board members, supporters of a losing candidate charged one winner with "electioneering near the polls" and bade the board not to seat him. The insurgents lost, but by stirring up a fuss they reminded everyone that democracy was the name of the game at Co-op City. . . .

Between elections co-op members spawn new organizations at a remarkable rate. These range from the Camera Club to the Black Caucus. In a single issue of the cooperative's weekly newspaper, the following organizations announced they had scheduled meetings for the coming week: an Art Club, Co-op City Senior Citizens, the Mr. & Mrs. Club of Section #2, a day camp, an ambulance corps, a modern dance group, the American Legion, a glee club, a Jewish folk-chorus, a Spanish-American club, a horticulture hobby group, the Singles Club, the Married Couples Club, the Black Caucus, B'nai B'rith, the Knights of Pythias, and a miscellany of temple and church groups.

The niagara of activities can be a mixed blessing. Residents accustomed to the anonymity of apartment-house living are sometimes overwhelmed by Co-op City's small-town social pressures.

> Before I came here . . . [says one tenant] I used to complain that "nobody knows my name." Now my main complaint is that *everybody* knows my name. The phone is constantly ringing, and there's always someone on the other end asking me to raise money to fight cancer, or to campaign for someone running for some kind of office, or take up *ballet*, for heaven's sake. It's friendly and sweet, but sometimes I just like to be left alone.

The Rest of America

Critics of Co-op City have deplored its "monolithic design," its "excessive sterility" and its "appalling isolation." But no one who lives there believes it. On the whole they like the village atmosphere; they also like the convenient shopping, the central air-conditioning, the private terraces and the relatively low tariff. Weinberger, for instance, pays $232 a month for a seven-room town house on [Heywood] Broun Place. His initial down payment was $3,150 or $450 per room. That is not inexpensive, but it is considerably cheaper than rates most New Yorkers must pay for comparable living space and amenities. "All I can tell you," says Weinberger, "is this: It should only happen to the rest of America."

The rest of America, alas, remains mostly a marshland bereft of decent, reasonably priced housing, with only a scattering of cooperatives to grace the grim landscape. The Cooperative League estimates that fewer than a million Americans live in co-ops (probably one quarter of them in New York). The United States Department of Housing and Urban Development (HUD) has hazarded a guess that of the nation's 65 million dwelling-units, less than one half of 1 percent are cooperatively owned—and these include dozens of unsubsidized luxury co-ops crowding the shores of the Potomac, the Hudson and other urban watering places. Strictly speaking the residents of these posh places are part of the "cooperative movement," but in truth their interests run less to Rochdale than to real estate. . . .

Of interest here are low- and moderate-cost cooperatives, and the signs that they are catching on. . . . [In 1971] HUD's Special Assistant for Cooperative Housing, Philip R. Thompson, gave out the news that for the first time, "we at HUD are really taking housing cooperatives seriously."

Last Hope

Thompson's boss FHA Assistant Commissioner Eugene A. Gulledge, had gone still further in a speech delivered . . . [in 1970] to the National Association of Housing Cooperatives. "For a great many people in this country," he said, "some type of cooperative concept is perhaps their last and only hope of being able to have a decent place to live." But then, while pledging to promote and finance more cooperatives, he unintentionally discouraged a lot of people. "We will achieve . . . the same type of satisfactory results," he predicted, that "we've been able to produce in such things as the Indian housing program, the elderly housing program, and [other] subsidized programs."

Gulledge was as good as his word. . . . [In 1971] builders completed 1,500 new, HUD-supported cooperative units, using up *one fifth of 1 percent* of all HUD's available insurance and loan funds. No one now can doubt that the Government's cooperative housing program equals its Indian housing program, which, at present rates of construction, will rehouse the entire Indian population in 281 years.

The truth is, we have drifted into a dreadful housing crisis brought on by decades of Federal indifference and papered over by a pastiche of Federal nonprograms. In 1968, the Congress committed the nation—in principle anyway—to the "construction or rehabilitation of 26 million housing units" during the next ten years. Six million of those units were to be subsidized—that is, slated for low- and moderate-income families who couldn't afford decent housing at going market rates.

But no sooner was the goal enunciated than it began to recede. Construction lagged; housing costs soared. Suddenly not 6 million households but 25 million—40 percent of all the households in the nation—became technically eligible for Federal housing assistance. As the Administration conceded last summer in its *Annual Report on National Housing Goals,* "It appears unlikely that the housing needs of the nation's poorest families would be fully met, even if the numerical goal of producing 6 million new units during the 1969-78 decade is achieved." (The congressional goal of 26 million new or rebuilt units, obsolete as it is, also exceeds our grasp. Since 1968, construction has fallen behind by 20 percent; for *subsidized* housing, the lag is 35 percent.)

Needless to say, co-ops cannot singlehandedly cure the nation's nagging housing headache. The cure will come when Federal agencies, at present armed only with empty congressional promises, have money to spend and a firm mandate to get the job done. Much of the evidence, however, suggests that cooperatives could do that job best.

Item: Cooperatives cost less to maintain. Recently the Urban Institute, a Washington-based research organization, compared maintenance and operating expenses of HUD-sponsored co-ops with those of HUD-sponsored rental projects. The co-ops' expenses ran from 15-35 percent lower per unit.

Item: Cooperatives cost less to build and sell. Nearly everyone in the housing profession concedes that cooperative sponsors tend to create more housing for less money than do their profit-oriented competitors. HUD officials estimate the difference to be 5 percent; Paul Golz, president of the National Association of Housing Cooperatives and founder of the Mutual Ownership Development Foundation (MODF), says 15-20 percent is more like it.

Item: Cooperative sponsors provide greater space. Urban Institute investigators found that one third of the co-op units studied, but only one fourth of the non-co-op units, contained three or more bedrooms. Moreover, the density for co-ops was 15 units per acre, compared to at least 21 units per acre for other types of subsidized housing.

Item: Cooperators meet their payments. The same study compared payment default rates among families participating in a variety of HUD programs. The co-op families had the best record.

Item: Cooperators tend to stay put. The turnover, or move-out, rate among cooperative families studied was 16 percent; among other families, about 30 percent.

Item: Cooperators often behave better than their neighbors. In Watsonville, California, Golz's MODF sponsored a one-hundred-unit cooperative for Chicano farmworkers next door to a straight rental project. In one typical month local police had 2 calls from the co-op and 58 calls from the rental project.

Section 213

In the light of all this, one wonders why more cooperative housing does not get built. The answer appears to lie in the biases of our Federal Government and in the wasteful ways it subsidizes low- and middle-income housing. In New York, co-operative sponsors like United Housing can rely largely on state subsidies; but in most other places the fate of cooperative housing is directly linked to the success or failure of Federal housing programs.

This has been true since 1950, when Congress amended the National Housing Act to make cooperatives eligible for Federal loan insurance. The amendment, known as Section

213, was as important to cooperative builders as the Capper-Volstead Act had been to cooperative farmers three decades earlier. For the first time, it gave co-ops a reasonable shot at Federal subsidies. But the subsidies are shrouded in a bureaucratic maze that has grown increasingly complex.

Since the passage of Section 213, as Congress has periodically tinkered with the housing crisis, new subsidy programs and new section numbers have proliferated. For example, Section 221 (d) (3) sets the interest rate on mortgages at 3 percent, far below the conventional market rate, with the Government paying commercial lenders the difference. Similarly, Section 236 reduces interest rates on a sliding scale, to as low as 1 percent for the poorest families. These and other programs are not specifically designed for co-op housing; but each makes room for cooperatives in parceling out its largesse, giving rise to a system of cooperative sponsors ready and eager to tap into any program that promises to provide capital.

Co-op Entrepreneurs

Sponsors began to appear as soon as Section 213 became law, for it was instantly clear that if proposals for new cooperatives were to make progress through the Federal maze, they would require professional packagers: experienced, well-connected organizations capable of speaking plainly to bankers, land developers and Government officials. Indeed, most of the cooperative housing being built today is sponsored by one or another of these entrepreneur-type groups, such as the Foundation for Cooperative Housing (FCH) in Washington, D.C., Cooperative Services in Detroit and Paul Golz's MODF on the West Coast.

It is they who coax in the subsidies, manage the money, buy the land, hire the builder (or do the building themselves), screen the applicants, negotiate the insurance rates and lawyers' fees, and finally—O blessed day!—hand over the keys to the new cooperators. In return, sponsors receive a guaranteed service fee, usually about 3.5 percent of total costs; sometimes they are hired by residents to manage the new co-ops.

At their best, cooperative sponsors are both educators and advocates, teaching families the cooperative way and protecting them from the ordinary plunderings of profit-oriented contractors, bankers and attorneys. All this works well on paper, but in practice it sometimes breaks down. The Government seldom allows a sponsor sufficient funds to educate new cooperators, to school them in both the Rochdale principles and the art of apartment management. The result is that many people who are, in theory, cooperative owners behave as if they are tenants: They take no interest in the proceedings, and they tend to think of the landlord as "them" rather than "us."

I have visited co-ops where residents were not aware they were owners. In a co-op in Atlanta, sponsored and managed by FCH, some of the occupants were considering staging a "tenants' strike" to protest shoddy conditions in the project. It would have been a strike against themselves, but no one had bothered to tell them.

The sponsor's advocate role is equally difficult. Federal subsidy programs are so deviously designed as to immediately invite a parade of middlemen, each with his hand outstretched, each claiming he is indispensable to the housing process. . . .

Housing the Elderly

Despite the bureaucratic hurdles, a handful of hard-pressed sponsors and hopeful college students persevere in their labors for a cooperative commonwealth. One of the sponsors is Cooperative Services, Inc., in Detroit, which began in 1960 as an optical co-op—dispensing glasses and eye care to members—and soon branched into cooperative housing for the elderly. "It took us five years to get our first loan applications through HUD," says Fred Thornthwaite, founder of the cooperative and its executive director, "but we stayed with it."

One reason they stayed with it was their determination not to abandon all those applicants who were counting on them. "We found an appalling need for housing among the elderly," says Virginia Thornthwaite, Fred's wife and co-worker. "They had no money and no place to go." The Thornthwaites came upon rooming-house tenants who were so poor that when a neighbor up the street died, they went there to take food from the icebox. One woman told Mrs. Thornthwaite, "I got $3,000 in the bank and Social Security of $67 a month. I hope I die before it runs out."

Eventually, Thornthwaite and his organization succeeded in completing two cooperative apartment buildings in Wyandotte, a blue-collar suburb south of Detroit. Three more co-ops are in construction. I visited the Bishop co-op in Wyandotte, a nine-story building of 204 apartments, most of them with a view of the Detroit River from their living rooms. I was greeted at the door by several members of the co-op Building Council, including Viola Doty, a short, energetic woman who did most of the talking. . . .

We looked into a few apartments which Mrs. Doty knew were unoccupied just then. The apartments were either one-and-a-half rooms or two-and-a-half rooms, all "light, airy and attractive."

Everyone likes his privacy [Mrs. Doty said]. But sometimes when a person comes back from the hospital, privacy is not a good thing. The person might be too weak to take care of himself. That's a problem. We want a halfway house for people to go to from the hospital, before they come back here. A halfway-house cooperative. People really need that kind of a home.

By now we were back in the front vestibule. I asked Mrs. Doty where she would be living if Bishop had not been built.

Oh, probably with one of my kids [she said]. It wouldn't be good. Not for them and not for me. Years ago I took it for granted that if my husband died, I'd live with one of my children. I didn't know about cooperatives. If I'd known about co-ops when I was young, I'd have devoted my life to them.

Born in Controversy

Paul Merrill is young (twenty-seven), knows about co-ops and may be devoting his life to them. He quit graduate school at the University of Minnesota last year to become general manager of Commonwealth Terrace, a student housing co-op of four hundred units. "We thrive on controversy in our organization," says Merrill. "After all, we were born in controversy." The housing had been under University control, but two years ago officials casually announced a $10 rent hike, and the students were quick to respond. With their wives and small children they converged on the steps of the State Capitol in St. Paul and asked the governor to support their efforts to turn Commonwealth Terrace into a student-managed cooperative.

The governor approved, and so, eventually, did University officials. "The University still owns the housing," says Merrill, "but we manage it. In our first year as a co-op we were able to reduce rents an average of $5 per month; we closed the year with a $4,000 surplus. This year we had to raise rents $7—but when you add it up, that comes to only a $2 net increase over two years." Residents pay between $88 and $100 per month. According to University officials, that is 50 percent less than what most other married students must pay.

Members help keep rents low by taking on such minor maintenance chores as mowing the lawn, changing light bulbs, cleaning laundry rooms, and sweeping stairwells. In addition, co-op leaders engage in hard bargaining for goods and services. The coin-operated laundry, for example, now yields considerably more revenue than it did under University auspices.

"When we took over," says Merrill, "a vending service had the contract and was paying 10 percent of its take to the University. It amounted to $2,500 a year. We didn't ask for the 10 percent. We asked whether we could get 50, 60 or 70 percent." The cooperative negotiated with other companies and ultimately settled for an even split. Last year residents made $10,000 from the coin-operated laundry; this year, after more negotiations, they are guaranteed $15,000.

Commonwealth Terrace has its problems. Members engage in much bickering, and Merrill complains of their reluctance to get involved—"apathy," we would have called it twenty years ago. Sometimes even the Board of Directors fails to muster a quorum.

Yet the co-op seems likely to endure. It was born in protest, reflecting a conviction among students that they are their own best advocates. Cooperative supporters can find encouragement, not in the protest *per se*, but in the direction it took. If the University had tried to raise rents twenty years ago, student response would have been diffuse and ineffective—at most, the Dean of Students might have been hanged in effigy. In the mid-sixties a rent hike might have sparked a demonstration; students might even have drawn up a list of nonnegotiable demands; but they would not have organized a cooperative.

After College?

To students nowadays the idea of organizing a cooperative may be more natural than that of joining a sorority or fraternity. In fact, the cooperative resurgence on many campuses has paralleled a "Greek" collapse, with many new co-ops taking over the abandoned houses of once-flourishing Betas and Kappas. In Madison, Wisconsin, university officials estimate that at least one third of the students live in co-ops and communes, most of these being informal arrangements in which students pool their rent and food money. At the University of Michigan in Ann Arbor, the Inter-Cooperative Council has built eight new houses in three years, and still has a long waiting list of co-op aspirants. (Michigan is the cradle of student cooperative housing. The Inter-Cooperative Council was founded in 1932, an offshoot of the campus Socialist Club.)

It now remains to be seen whether students, on leaving the campus, will take their cooperative experiences with them. Or will they, like many of their parents, seek the solitary joys of suburbia—a private patch of lawn, individually owned and individually mowed? While chatting with Merrill in his office, I asked him this question. He smiled mysteriously and pointed to a sign on the wall, a small bit of inspiration from President John F. Kennedy: "United, there is little we cannot do in a host of new cooperative ventures."

HOUSING FOR THE ELDERLY [6]

In the design of housing for the elderly and handicapped, factors of comfort, safety, and well-being must be considered. Such factors go beyond HUD-FHA minimum property standards that have proven their worth over the years and continue to constitute a yardstick and a spur to structural quality in the entire homebuilding field.

Housing for the elderly is more than a shelter program. Both design and management should reflect understanding of the characteristics of the older person. The housing which HUD assists should respond in types, amenities, and services to older Americans' varying needs and life styles. To accomplish this, we must apply the techniques of psychology, sociology, architecture, and planning to the development and management of their housing.

Just as any other segment of our population, older people have varying tastes in housing. Some prefer to stay in the old family home. Some seek mild climates. Some want to continue homeownership but want smaller quarters. Some want to rent in midtown areas, others in the suburbs. Some need in-house medical facilities and food service; others do not want reminders of frailty nor will they be deprived of the opportunity to decide independently when or where

[6] From "Housing Design for Elderly Needs," by Marie C. McGuire, an adviser for housing programs for the elderly and handicapped in the United States Department of Housing and Urban Development. *HUD Challenge.* 4:5-9. My. '73.

they will dine. But whatever the differences of taste and style, we need to recognize that age groups of 65 to 75, 75 to 90, and over 90 are marked by substantially different characteristics.

To be sure, many older Americans satisfy their needs and make their choices in the commercial market. But for those for whom HUD programs alone can provide, we have the obligation to see that design meets their needs fully. HUD's experience should perhaps be translated into a set of standards that take into account the special needs, psychological and physical, of the older population, much as the FHA property standards guide housing generally.

How do we proceed to write design guides that reflect our understanding of the needs of the older population and assist developers, builders, architects, and engineers?

I think we can begin by using our experience to guide us to the positive, but experience can enable us to avoid repeating mistakes that have been made over and over again and which, in the absence of a record, are likely to be repeated in the future.

Here I will give an abbreviated overview of what I've observed around this country and abroad in housing for the older population and the handicapped, some of it good, some bad, but all of it to be considered when planning housing for the elderly.

The desirability of housing—regardless of cost or design —is influenced by its location—a fact that cannot be overlooked in examining critical features of environments for the elderly.

This is especially true at a time when we are dispelling such myths as that elderly people want isolation and removal from areas of activity.

Today it is generally accepted that housing for the elderly should be in lively, stimulating locations convenient to a variety of services and facilities, or, at least, close to public transportation when land costs require an outlying site.

Another lesson for the future has been learned from the programs that failed to make effective use of areas surrounding projects for the elderly.

Historically, designers have overlooked the value to residents of the out-of-doors areas surrounding multifamily residential housing. The effects have been an unnecessary limitation of healthful, outdoor opportunity in most projects for the elderly.

Unfortunately, consideration has been limited to areas for sitting, which, too frequently, amount to uncomfortable, flat concrete benches without backs, regularly spaced, fixed so that they cannot be moved and making impossible any degree of social interaction.

Location of sitting areas makes a bad situation worse. Some are placed at the quiet rear of the building, thus isolating the user from neighborhood or project activity and revealing on the part of the designer an unfortunate lack of understanding of the isolation concept. It should be kept in mind that when residents want quiet they go to their apartments. Observation of activity is essential as participation in activity decreases.

Other examples of the prevalence of the isolation myth can be seen in the popularity of not only rear, quiet sitting places, but in the number of enclosed gardens, inner patios, rooftop community centers, floor to floor sitting areas—all with minimum potential for watching human activity.

The built-in failure of such isolation techniques of design is apparent in projects across the country, where expensive and beautifully appointed recreation and leisure-time areas are ignored—to the bafflement of management, who themselves become victims of planning that failed to recognize that older persons do not want to be cut off from a world which already finds them with serious life-space limitations. Thus driveways, lawns, and sidewalks are used by older persons to observe life, relate to it, and have something to talk about.

The practice of ignoring outdoor space also ignores the benefits of outdoor health pursuits so vital to physical and emotional well-being. The aesthetic value of well-planned outdoor areas is of paramount importance in projects for the elderly since much time is spent indoors peering from one's window.

If one is frail, carrying a bag of groceries, or using a cane or walker, the chances of opening the heavy wooden or glass doors that are so popular are slim indeed. Automatic doors are, of course, the answer. Security must be given equal weight but it is still unnecessary to have heavy doors reminiscent of western stockades.

And once inside the front door one sees what Dr. Powell Lawton of the Geriatric Research Center in Philadelphia considers the most important of all spaces—the lobby.

At their best, lobbies serve as a social, traffic, and visual stimulation center. They should, in fact, provide places to sit, walk, play, watch, buy conveniences, and permit management to monitor access to upper floors. (The manager's office should look out upon but not dominate the lobby; it belongs to the residents.)

A hostess desk manned by tenants provides a sense of welcome and security. Yet some lobbies have no furniture on the theory that old people sitting around are a discouraging sight when, perhaps the only pursuit possible is sitting and watching.

An extension and, indeed a central part of the lobby could be the mail box area where, unfortunately, one rarely finds facilities for comfortable sitting or coffee while waiting for the mail. One project that has recognized the potential of this area separated the mailboxes from the lobby by a half wall, put up a big sign which reads "gossip corner," provided coffee, newspapers, and fashion magazines. That section is always full.

Pool, card playing, checkers, TV, and seeing who comes and goes make the lobby an inviting place rather than sitting alone in one's small room. Make it gay, happy and popping with activity. And what harm if someone naps in his chair or uses scented pipe tobacco?

Services for the Elderly

Keep in mind that the laundry room may be a primary social area. It does not belong in the basement. The same is true of storage areas, which ideally should be located in the tenants' apartments.

The hazards of improperly designed elevators and corridors are innumerable. Safety factors, such as rubber-edged doors, slower operation, electric eyes, ventilation, and a direct voice-contact in cases of emergencies should not be overlooked in elevators intended for elderly residents. If a bench for resting packages or for sitting is impossible there should, at least, be a railing for support. Floor numbers on elevator panels should be very large and panels placed low and horizontal so it is possible to reach the top button from a wheel chair.

A word about corridors. Vary colors from floor to floor. Include plants, art work, such as sculpture or whatever is pleasing to the eye and will serve as landmarks and guides for tenants. Cheer up corridors with windows to admit daylight.

No room holds greater potential for accidents and injury than the kitchen, and it is here that principles of safe design and equipment cannot be exaggerated. The stove is a good example. Broilers at the bottom of the stove are difficult to clean and are often impossible for use by the handicapped.

Proper lighting and large calibrated numbers on front controls will help eliminate needless accidents and allow easier cooking. All cooking facilities should be operated at or above the work level to minimize bending. Levers instead of round knobs should be used on all plumbing fixtures and doors. A rule of thumb would be to have all work levels lower than usual. Shelves should be kept at minimum heights with reaches of sixty-three inches and not lower than

eighteen inches, which is all that can be expected of older
people and far safer for persons of any age.

Double-hung windows, cleanable from the inside, have
proven better than casements that require a twisting action
to open. Think of the arthritic hand. Windows that extend
to the ceiling are too hard to dress. Those extending to the
floor cause fright. Draperies should be of durable materials,
shrink proof, and so hung that they do not impede the use
of other inner curtains.

Other Elderly Needs

A word about other important areas. To eat alone is bad
enough, but to eat alone in interior space with no window
will cause loss of interest in eating and possible erosion of
health.

The bathroom is one of the most critical areas in terms
of safety needs. Over and over we see bathroom doors opening in, wedging a body in the small space when accidents
occur. Always open the doors outward or have sliding or
curtain doors and no locks. The shower over tub is universally used although it can be a very dangerous arrangement. Plan instead to install a well-designed shower—not a
cubicle—but a shower that is long, has a comfortable seat
with arms that let down, has the controls outside the shower
stall and delivers the mixed water to a testing spout. The
shower should have tempered glass doors, a metal foot rest
flush with the inside wall which may be pulled out for ease
of foot washing. Given this kind of shower, the frail older
person or handicapped person can take care of himself over
the years.

In one study where showers were substituted for baths
against the wishes of four hundred older women, they reported that sitting comfortably with the flow of water on
the body was more relaxing than immersion and considerably safer.

Toilets should be wall-hung and higher than normal for
the handicapped with space enough to manipulate a wheel

chair on at least one side. A grab bar at the commode is essential. Grab bars and their installation are costly. As a rule only two or three at most are called for—in the shower stall, at the tub and at the toilet. They should not be too large or resemble a "jungle gym."

Generally, an emergency alarm bell is included in plans for elderly housing. Studies would indicate that it should be at arm height next to the commode. Yet they are frequently seen high on the living room wall, in a hallway, or other places not related to emergency experience. If two bells are possible the second one should be at the bedside. These alarm bells should also open the front door when rung.

These guidelines for sound and thoughtful design of housing for the elderly are by no means exclusive or absolute. They do, however, offer some considerations beyond minimum property standards for comfort and safety and a measure of hope for more years of independent living in an environment that makes this not only possible, but enjoyable.

FLOATING SUBURBS [7]

The idea of living aboard a boat is just at that intriguing stage between phenomenon and trend: too well established for headlines, but not yet widespread enough to be called a new American life style. America's boat dwellers seem to be enjoying their ambiguous status: they think of themselves as a club, not a minority.

Of some 8 million pleasure craft in this country, about one fifth, or 1.6 million, could conceivably serve as homes. Probably no more than 20,000 actually do, and even this figure is no more than a rough estimate based on information supplied by marina managers in California and Florida, who put the full-time live-aboard population at 5 to 10 percent per harbor.

[7] From "Our Floating Suburbs," by Elaine Kendall, a free-lance writer. *Horizon.* 15:14-15. Autumn '73. © 1973, American Heritage Publishing Company, Inc. Reprinted by permission from *Horizon*, Autumn 1973.

Not that American boat dwellers are confined to warm waters. New York City has the 79th Street Boat Basin. . . . Seattle's Puget Sound has several colonies of live-aboards, and there is a small and attractive development of houses on pontoons in Portage Bay. A fair number of boat dwellers live in Chesapeake Bay, and the Gulf of Mexico is filling up with houseboats. Rivers, ponds, and creeks all over America are being reconsidered as home sites.

The definition of a live-aboard can vary from strict and narrow to loose and broad. Purists restrict the term to people whose sole residence is a self-powered vessel: they insist that people who live on towable houseboats or in condominiums on pontoons belong in other categories. The retired couple moored in a Florida port for the winter don't count; nor do the pair who take a motorized houseboat on a long meander down the inland waterways; nor do yachtsmen. They can all go home if they like. To the truly committed live-aboard, these are frivolous types. Genuine "sailors," furthermore, tend to look down on houseboat dwellers.

Partly as a result of this attitude, and partly because older marinas cannot accommodate them, houseboaters have found their own havens. Clusters of them bloom along Florida's gulf coast, and many have seeded into Texas, Louisiana, and even Mississippi and Alabama. Still, the greatest concentrations of authentic, no-other-address boat dwellers are along the California and Florida coasts. There, where marinas are to be found at intervals over hundreds of miles, it's easy to believe that another kind of Woodstock nation—a formidable naval power—already exists. The western enclave of that nation is very active: on water as on land, California sets the trends.

Until recently, boat dwellers were found only at the opposite ends of the economic scale. The rich had yachts, and, invariably, houses on land. The boat-dwelling poor must once have been numerous, or the word *shantyboat* would not have entered the language, but they kept well out of the way—on backwaters and creeks, tucked into the hidden bends of rivers, or perhaps on bayous. Middle-class people simply didn't consider living on boats until the last decade or so, with the introduction of the fiberglass hull. Fiberglass and the newer acrylics make the boat-buying dollar go 15 to 20 feet farther, reduce maintenance time and cost, and permit a once impossible dream to come true. Owning enough boat to live on—at one time just a caprice of the super-rich or the shift of the independent poor—has rather quickly become a practical alternative for the vast numbers in between. Pleasure craft account for the greatest single sporting-goods expenditure in the country—about $2.5 billion a year including fuel and accessories. The figures come from the boating industry, but these men see no need to exaggerate: "In fact," one California yacht broker said, "we'd play down the numbers if we could and keep that old aura of exclusivity. People will resist buying a boat if they think the Pacific is going to look like the Santa Ana Freeway at rush hour."

Why Live on Boats?

What draws people to boats? In 1955 Dr. Ernest Dichter of the Institute for Motivational Research investigated American attitudes toward various sports for manufacturers seeking to expand their markets, and he supplied the boat makers with a number of helpful hints. Men seek outboard power "in an almost sexual way," Dr. Dichter reported. As a recently retired live-aboard said, "There are two great pleasures in life, and fooling around with boats is the one that lasts longest." Work and play overlap for the boat dweller. "I used to spend all week waiting for Saturday," another veteran live-aboard said. "Now that I've moved in, I can take her out any time and work on her every night." (Did Dr. Dichter say *almost* sexual?)

Pent-up sexuality is hardly the major reason for living on a boat. Though individual reasons may differ, most members of the marina community invariably profess a sincere love for the sea.

There are all kinds of motives [says Charles Thomas, president of the Jensen Marine Corporation in Costa Mesa, California, and a permanent live-aboard]. I just love the freedom and the water, but people who come here to buy boats have different rationalizations. They may want to trade a smaller boat for a larger one, and figure that they can afford it only by moving aboard and giving up their house. A boat suitable for full-time living and serious cruising can run to about $75,000, fully equipped. There's something else, too. A great many people get to be forty or so and see the free life that kids have today. They envy them. It looks like more fun and less work. At this point, they start to feel they've missed out. The sensible ones buy a boat and move onto it. That way, they have a feeling of changing their whole lifestyle.

Marina life is village life, and—like the small towns that many Americans long to return to—marinas can accommodate a surprising range of humanity. Those for whom a boat is home constitute a group within a group, and in the larger marinas they usually have a kind of civic association that convenes periodically, like a town meeting. The topics discussed are many of the same ones that concern townspeople: trash collection, police and fire protection, parking space for cars, recreational facilities, representation in the larger community. Yet, even when the talk runs to assessments and surcharges, there's noticeably less rancor and dissension than one finds at town meetings in the suburbs. Boat people are bound together, not only by common practical concerns, but by that emotional attitude toward the sea.

To the outsider and inlander, life on a boat may seem paradoxical: the illusion of adventure, of space and liberty, is there, all right, but often the actuality is not, for a boat tied up in a marina most of the year surely can't feel too different from a house in the suburbs, particularly if the occupant commutes to work or school. In town, people worry about heating or air conditioning; on board, it's the engine or the pumps. Then, too, a marina may be a congenial enclave with a strong sense of community, but what if it isn't? The long waiting lists for desirable moorings make moving away less easy than it might seem.

Nor do the shortcomings end here. The rules of marina life eventually irk those who have come in search of autonomy. The word *prohibited* turns up on almost every walkway, dock, wall, and public room. The Long Beach Marina's rules, for instance, cover everything from swimming (forbidden), to fishing (no bait on the docks), to children (none under ten allowed on the docks unless accompanied by an adult), to bikes and motorcycles (none), and so on in the manner of the bylaws of a small sectarian college in the hinterlands; one almost expects compulsory chapel. Those who move onto a boat with the idea that a marina is the perfect place for a nonconformist existence are soon disabused of the notion.

Life Aboard Boats

People who own a sliver of the San Andreas fault overlooking the Pacific regard the live-aboard movement in purely economic terms. To them, 20,000 live-aboards in all of America seems a very conservative estimate; they are sure they can see at least that many from their patios, enjoying a whole deckful of costly sea, sun, sky, and air for what seem to be bargain rates. The view can be profoundly unsettling to someone who has just overextended himself to acquire a quarter-acre of dusty brown hilltop. To a growing number of Californians, therefore, a $75,000 boat has abruptly come to seem a splendid economy. For no matter how huge and houselike the boats may be, they continue to be taxed as personal property rather than as real estate.

This apparent economic discrepancy has created a distinct division between those who live on the land and those who live on the water, but if the tax question is the real irritant, ecology has become the respectable rallying cry for the landlubbers. "I wouldn't mind providing them with free municipal services if they didn't pollute the water," is the way the more tolerant phrase it. The intolerant *do* mind the idea of free provisions, and rarely hesitate to say so. The thought of boat dwellers taking full advantage of public schools, fire and police protection, hospitals, libraries, and other tax-supported services as virtual guests of the community at large is a source of constant friction, and a topic that local politicians have been quick to exploit. In fact, live-aboards *do* pay their own way; most marinas, for instance, provide a private security force, their own fire-fighting equipment, and reliable daily refuse collection. Fees covering these services are included in dockage rates or added as a surcharge. Nor have the schools been overloaded with the children of live-aboards. Large families simply don't live on boats: the logistics are too complicated, and the space too limited.

To those now in residence on boats and to many more who might like to be, living aboard is the answer to a basic problem of life: finding a home one likes and can afford. To the rest of us, the movement can be a threat, a fad, an option, or even a scenario of the future. The floating suburb is obviously a congenial idea, already tested and found workable. It is unrealistic to expect one-acre zoning and two-car garages out beyond the Verrazano and the Golden Gate, but one *could* have dwelling units rather like boats, with adequate headroom, cleverly designed built-ins, and generous deck space. Architects have already drawn the plans for such developments, and the Japanese government expects its offshore housing project to be under way within the next year. America is not as land-poor as Japan, but a great many Americans would prefer the open sea to the Dakota Badlands. And this generation of live-aboards can teach us how to manage.

IV. HOUSING IN THE URBAN FUTURE

EDITOR'S INTRODUCTION

As noted in the Preface to this compilation, the housing crisis is but part of what is increasingly recognized as America's wider urban crisis. Accordingly, this last section includes articles dealing with the more general problems of urban life.

At the outset a note and map indicate the growth of population expected for the nation by the year 2000. Essentially, two huge urban regions are developing: one extending from Illinois and Wisconsin to the East Coast from Maine to Virginia; the second, that of the urban California area from San Francisco to San Diego. The other articles in this section should be read against the background of that knowledge, especially those concerned with the pros and cons of population density, governmental agencies and programs for dealing with housing and urban problems.

Three articles constitute a debate regarding urban America's future: Are we becoming an urban civilization without cities? Does the traditional city have a future? And can a case be made for high city-density? The first question is dealt with by Irving Kristol, Henry Luce Professor of Urban Values at New York University and co-editor of the *Public Interest*; the second, by Bennett Harrison, associate professor of economics and urban studies at the Massachusetts Institute of Technology. William H. Whyte, author of *The Last Landscape* and *The Organization Man* argues the case for high-density cities.

Constantinos Doxiadis, the noted city planner, next sets forth his ideas on the crisis of urban civilization and his prescriptions for dealing with it. The following article, by Senator Edmund S. Muskie, outlines a rather detailed list

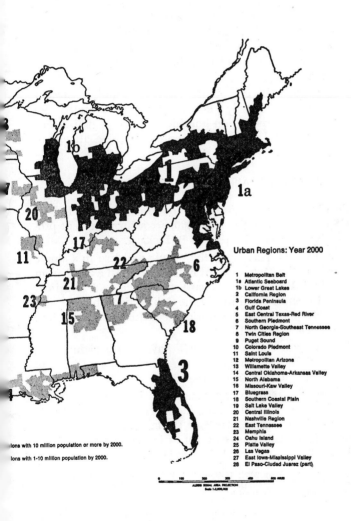

Urban Regions: Year 2000

1   Metropolitan Belt
1a Atlantic Seaboard
1b Lower Great Lakes
2   California Region
3   Florida Peninsula
4   Gulf Coast
5   East Central Texas-Red River
6   Southern Piedmont
7   North Georgia-Southeast Tennessee
8   Twin Cities Region
9   Puget Sound
10 Colorado Piedmont
11 Saint Louis
12 Metropolitan Arizona
13 Willamette Valley
14 Central Oklahoma-Arkansas Valley
15 North Alabama
16 Missouri-Kaw Valley
17 Bluegrass
18 Southern Coastal Plain
19 Salt Lake Valley
20 Central Illinois
21 Nashville Region
22 East Tennessee
23 Memphis
24 Oahu Island
25 Platte Valley
26 Las Vegas
27 East Iowa-Mississippi Valley
28 El Paso-Ciudad Juarez (part)

ions with 10 million population or more by 2000.

ions with 1-10 million population by 2000.

0   100   200   300   400   500 MILES
ALBERS SONAL AREA PROJECTION
Scale 1-5,000,000

of proposals for an all-encompassing urban growth policy. This scheme is included here rather than in Section II, which deals more narrowly with governmental housing policies, for Senator Muskie is concerned with tax policies, welfare and employment, new towns, environmental concerns, housing, racial integration and other problems—all part of the impacted-area crisis.

Last, to close this compilation, a realistic and, in present circumstances, necessarily pessimistic, note is sounded: Joseph P. Fried, a reporter on housing and urban affairs, tells why he is doubtful that America will meet the challenge of its housing crisis.

AMERICA'S URBAN FUTURE [1]

Two huge urban regions will contain more than half of the US population in the year 2000, according to recent projections by urbanologist Jerome P. Pickard.

More than 40 percent of the people will live in a single superregion—the Metropolitan Belt—which will extend from Illinois and Wisconsin eastward to Maine and Virginia. Another 13 percent will live in the California Urban Region and nearly 5 percent in the Florida Peninsula Urban Region. [See map, pages 180-181.]

All told, the United States will have twenty-eight urban regions with more than one million people apiece. Eight out of ten Americans will live in them.

During the past forty years, Pickard notes, the urban regions of the United States have grown explosively. If trends continue, by the year 2000 the land area of the urban regions will be 2.5 times as great as it was in 1960 and the total population will be 2.4 times as large.

[1] From "By the Year 2000: Half of U.S. People May Live in Two Urban Regions." *Futurist.* 6:238-9. D. '72. Copyright © 1972 World Future Society. P.O. Box 30369, Bethesda Branch, Washington, D.C. 20014. All rights reserved. Reprinted with permission. For further information on the issue of national growth, see the special report on population distribution in the October 1970 issue of *The Futurist.*

Pickard's projections, prepared for the President's Commission on Population Growth and the American Future, are based on population growth in the period between 1940 and 1970.

Population growth, says Pickard, is based on three factors: the birth rate, the death rate, and net migration. The death rate is fairly well stabilized and migration has been reasonably stable so that Census Bureau projections assumed net immigration of about 400,000 a year. By contrast, the birth rate varies widely and recently reached a new low. Because of the decline in the birth rate, Pickard adopted the second most conservative series of Census Bureau projections (Series D), and on that basis foresees a total population of 287 million people in the United States by the year 2000. The projections for that year range from a low of 270 million to a high of 320 million; the 1972 population is 208 million.

AN URBAN CIVILIZATION WITHOUT CITIES? [2]

The very idea sounds preposterous. How can there be such a thing as an urban civilization without cities? Is it not a contradiction in terms? These questions are inevitable—but not quite so unanswerable as they seem at first glance. A very good case can be made to the effect that much of what we call "the urban crisis" in the United States is really a misnomer for a historical, popular effort to create an urban civilization without cities. Indeed, it can be argued that the basic impulse throughout our history has been in this direction, and that what the textbooks call "the urbanization of America" is not at all the same thing as "the citification of America."

Before we can see this matter in clear perspective, we must rid ourselves of a couple of mischievous misconcep-

[2] Article by Irving Kristol, Henry Luce Professor of Urban Values at New York University, co-editor of *Public Interest. Horizon.* 14:36-41. Autumn '72. © 1972, American Heritage Publishing Company, Inc. Reprinted by permission from *Horizon,* Autumn 1972.

tions. The first is that, as President Lyndon B. Johnson majestically proclaimed, we are today what we have never been before: "a nation of cities," with some 70 percent of our population residing in what the Census Bureau calls an "urban place." What President Johnson did not mention—perhaps because he did not know it—is that the Census Bureau's definition of an "urban place" is any settlement with more than 2,500 residents. That definition may once have made some sense. Today it can only confuse us, as it apparently confused the President, by obscuring the distinction between the categories of "urban" and "city."

In fact, less than 30 percent of the American population lives in places with a population of more than 100,000, which is what we ordinarily regard as a city. This is approximately equal to our "rural" population, living in settlements of fewer than 2,500 inhabitants. Moreover, the proportion of our population that lives in big cities, those of over one million, is the same as it was in 1920.

True, there has been an *absolute* increase in the big-city population, reflecting the overall growth of our total population. But even so, a good part of this absolute increase has *not* taken place in the big cities of yesteryear—the most troubled cities of today. New York, Chicago, Philadelphia, and Boston have not experienced any remarkable population growth in recent decades. (New York, in fact, has experienced no growth: its population today is almost what it was in 1950.) The increase in our big-city population is largely the consequence of the furious expansion of such new cities as Los Angeles and Houston. These are, as we shall see, very special kinds of cities in that they are by traditional standards not proper cities at all. Some critics have even called them "anticities," which is not far from the truth.

What the urbanization of America over the past half-century really amounts to, then, is the movement from the farm *toward smaller cities,* most of them clustered in metropolitan areas, i.e., areas in the center of which there is a city of at least 100,000 people. The urbanization of America is thus more accurately described as the *suburbanization* of America.

Suburbs As Self-Sustaining

What hinders us from grasping the full import of this process is the conventional antisuburban bias of most writers on urban affairs. It is assumed that a suburban town is some kind of "satellite" of the central city—embittered critics would call it a "parasite"—and that it is not a serious urban phenomenon in its own right. This assumption might hold for the relation between most European cities and their suburbs, which is, in truth, where the idea comes from, but it has no application to the American experience.

Though many American suburbs begin as "bedroom suburbs," they very quickly move in the direction of self-sustaining communities. Only about 30 percent of the working population of Westchester County, for instance, now commutes to a job in New York City, and this percentage is sliding steadily downward every year. Moreover, the suburbs of our newer cities never even pass through this kind of transformation. In Los Angeles or Houston the suburbs *are* the city, with the "inner city" being, in effect, one suburban area among others.

The second mischievous misconception obscuring America's actual urban condition is the notion that Americans would really prefer to live in the cities if only they were more attractive and agreeable. Behind most of the literature on city planning there lurks the conviction that Americans have been forced out of the city by circumstances beyond their control, that suburban living is for them *faute de mieux,* and that such things as picturesque shopping malls, efficient rapid transportation, and a civic cultural center will draw them back.

Most city planners certainly and sincerely love city living; they are authentic city types, which is, perhaps, as it should be and must be. But most Americans do not feel this way at all. In a 1968 Gallup Poll, only 18 percent said they preferred to live in central cities; 25 percent chose the suburbs; 29 percent wanted to live in small towns; and 27 percent actually said they wished they could live on a farm. In terms of the popular ideal, one could more accurately speak of an agrarian crisis than of an urban crisis.

It would be tempting to dismiss these expressed opinions as an ideological hangover, a case of "cultural lag," a futile nostalgia for an unavailable past. But that would be an error. These are no idle fantasies; they are genuine preferences—and Americans act upon them. Moreover, the evidence is overwhelming that Americans have always had a similar attitude toward cities. How else can we explain the extraordinary American decision, almost without precedent or parallel, that the capitals of our states should only rarely be the largest or most important cities? Such "peculiarities" are not mere oddities. They tell us much about the American way of life and about how it differs from the traditional European ways of organizing societies.

Cities in the American Tradition

A city may exist for three types of reasons: (1) economic-commercial; (2) political-administrative; or (3) cultural-intellectual. In Europe, it has always been assumed that, ideally, a city should combine all three *raisons d'être;* and the outstanding European cities—a London, a Paris, a Madrid, a Budapest, a Vienna—do, in fact, combine them. Surely, too, one of the reasons Italy has so many memorable cities is that until national unification only a century ago, they were all capitals, combining the three urban purposes.

Such a combination gives a city a power of attraction that is close to irresistible. Europeans feel a possessiveness toward, and identification with, their major cities that is unknown in America. These cities are an integral part of their national identity; frequently, they antedate the national identity, and have played a crucial role in creating the nation itself. No Frenchman can imagine France without Paris, but it is not so hard to imagine the United States without New York—millions of Americans indulge in this fantasy every day, with no great pain.

Clearly, what we have here is an important difference in urban values. This difference reaches far back into American history and has deep roots in the American character. Unless we take this history and this character seriously, we are not likely to get very far in understanding why American cities are the way they are. Nor are we likely to understand why it is that Americans live most happily and contentedly in precisely those cities—Los Angeles, Houston, San Diego, Tucson, Las Vegas—that are the despair of any properly educated city planner.

For such an understanding, one must begin with a plain fact: Americans have always regarded their cities—with the unique exception of nineteenth century Boston, an exception that proves the rule—from an utterly utilitarian perspective. The American city, unlike the European city, has never been thought of as a nucleus of civilization. As Professor Daniel Elazar of Temple University has emphasized, the American city has been regarded as, and has been treated as, a focus of economic activity—to put it bluntly, as a kind of service station. Americans have always *used* their cities, and more often than not, in a casual and even brutal way.

Cities as Service Stations

One service, in particular, has been of the utmost importance: the absorption and integration of rural immigrants—mainly, but not only, foreign—into American life. American cities have been very successful in performing this service and are still performing it quite well. But to evaluate this service, we must first understand what "success" means in American terms. It does *not* mean making urban citizens of these new immigrants. It does mean making them sufficiently urbanized—sufficiently acculturated, trained, and educated—that they can *leave* the city.

The American city is an entrepôt, importing people and exporting citizens, usually to the suburban towns and smaller suburban cities. That is why it is so misleading to try to measure the state of the blacks, the newest immigrants to the city, by looking exclusively at the conditions of life in the inner city. Such conditions always look bad, always are bad, because the inner city is mostly populated by people who have not yet succeeded. If we wish to know if the city is working, then we must, paradoxically, look at the rate of emigration to the suburbs. This rate is moving up sharply for the blacks today, and it will certainly continue doing so throughout the 1970s. We can then say that our cities have been functioning as they were intended to.

That *this* intention is radically different from the intention that city planners or most writers on urban affairs would ascribe to the city is another matter. The latter long desperately for a traditional kind of urbanity, for cities with grace, with style, with charm, with elegance—cities, in short, where cultivated persons like themselves can live in comfort. These people may even be right in believing that without such cities any civilization will be deficient and limited. But all this is not really relevant. It is quite impossible for the city to be a processing depot for immigrants and at the same time strive for a traditional European kind of urbanity. The wear and tear is enormous; urban life is inevitably too messy and turbulent and more than a little sordid. One cannot say that Americans *like* this process; but it is obvious enough that they are willing to use up their cities in order to achieve this purpose.

The common explanation of this callous, utilitarian attitude toward cities is in terms of frontier individualism; it is seen as an anachronistic survival of a time when each American dreamed of having land, lots of land, underneath the Western skies, and when he scorned those effete conformists who could live their routine lives cooped up behind city walls. There is something in this, of course—but less than meets the eye that has seen too many Western films. Americans are individualistic, to be sure, but one of the ways they express their individualism is by setting up voluntary communities and associations.

Put a bunch of Americans on a desert island and the first thing they will do is enter into a new Mayflower Compact, draw up a constitution, and form a PTA. The American West was explored by rugged individuals, but it was settled by communities that were more or less identical in their legal and social structures. All of this is but another way of saying that the instinct of American individualism is *also* an instinct for voluntary community. Americans are unquestionably a nomadic people—one in five moves every year. But these nomads move from one interchangeable and nearly identical community to another, and the speed with which they sink roots in their new communities is astonishing. These roots may be—more often than not, must be—shallow; yet they are nonetheless real, and it is important to the individual that they exist.

It is this instinct for voluntary community that, more than anything else, explains the American suspicion of cities, big cities especially, as good places to live in. Cities are by their very nature involuntary and haphazard *aggregations* of people. These people are anonymous—it is an important aspect of the city's "free" life style that they be so. The city is, and always has been, the place where people go when they wish to escape from community and its confining conventions, its precise definition of one's identity in terms of family, friends, and neighborhood. The city is the place where one mixes with strangers; where one experiences excitement and risk; where one is liberated from the bonds of conventional thinking and conventional morality. The city is very much like the frontier in that it permits, even encourages, a kind of uninhibited individualism. But while the frontier is a disordered preliminary to community, the city is a standing challenge and alternative to it.

The City Versus Community

True, the city has its own kind of "society," but society is not community. It is no accident that Robert Park, the founder of urban sociology at the University of Chicago, could write: "Urbanity is a charming quality, but it is not a virtue. We don't ever really get to know the urbane person, and hence never know when to trust him." This is a typically American sentiment, expressing a traditional anti-urban bias. At least, we are inclined today to think of it as a bias, but it is really something much more than that—both more authentic and more important. For behind this anti-urban impulse, this preference for community over society, there lies a theory, a political philosophy. It is a *republican* political philosophy, as distinct from a merely *democratic* one, and that distinction is anything but academic.

The democratic political ethos celebrates the sovereignty of the popular will, and there is nothing inherently anti-urban in it. The republican ethos, in contrast, *defines* this sovereignty in terms of individual participation in popular government. For such participation, a relatively small, self-governing community is needed, not a large, bureaucratically governed society. A big city may be democratically governed, but from Aristotle to the black militants of Harlem it has been generally agreed that no big city can be governed in a republican way. The anonymous multitude that inhabits a city cannot give birth to a republic, in which the individual citizen is personally involved in the tasks of self-government. Indeed, the people who live in large cities rarely think of themselves as "citizens" of those cities; the term seems inappropriate and is rarely used—because, one suspects, it *is* inappropriate.

This republican tradition has shaped all of American social thought, whether it be conservative, liberal, or radical. Washington and Jefferson were at one in their distrust of big cities, as were Lincoln and Jefferson Davis, Henry George and Henry Adams, William Jennings Bryan and Calvin

Coolidge, John Dewey and Herbert Hoover. Our greatest architect, Frank Lloyd Wright, despised them, as have many of our novelists, poets, and playwrights. It is the power of this tradition that makes American cities so American—which is to say, so lacking in urbanity as compared with the cities of Europe.

Some fifteen years ago there was a movement—much favored by regional and city planners—to enlarge the dominion of the city, to incorporate the suburbs within its political boundaries to bring their financial resources within reach of the city's budget makers. This idea had strong support among members of the new upper-middle class created by post-World War II prosperity, who felt entitled to the kinds of urban amenities that European cities offered. These people—more numerous than ever before, wealthier than ever before, and frustrated as never before—also wanted chic downtown shops, a glittering cultural center, fine restaurants and convivial cafés.

Since they dominated the mass media, in which so many of them make their professional careers, they were for a time able to impose their perspective upon public opinion. "Urban renewal" was their battle cry; the "revival of downtown" their declared purpose; the "good urban life" in the European style their ultimate dream. For a while it looked as if they would have their way—but only for a while. Their dream was punctured by the bristling realities of American life; and no reality was more destructive than the republican ethos itself, which experienced a powerful and quite unexpected revival, both in the nation at large and *within* the city.

The Demand for Participation

Today, the demand is not for greater urbanity but for participation by the individual citizen in the decisions that affect his life. Such participation is almost impossible to achieve in a big city—simply because it is so big and because there are so many decisions, the consequences of which are remote and yet intertwined. Moreover, such participation is death to the idea of an urbane city—we do not get opera houses or concert halls or subsidized theatres by a popular referendum of the neighborhood they are to be built in. These institutions have to be imposed by nonlocal governments, as is the case in Europe. There, the imposition has been of such long standing that popular opinion accepts it as natural, can even take a kind of civic pride in it. Here, it is seen simply as an imposition from above, is resented, and in the end is defeated.

The problem of American cities today is not how to consolidate their civic powers for urbane purposes but how to prevent them from falling apart under the impact of a revived republican ethos. It is the centrifugal forces that predominate, not the centripetal ones. And even among the upper-middle classes the impulse to urbanity has faltered and become uncertain of itself. Back in 1952 a committee of the American Political Science Association reported that the merger of cities and suburbs into new political units ("metropolitan governments") was desirable and probably inevitable. Fifteen years later, the newly elected president of the association, in his inaugural address, vigorously challenged the idea that humane and responsible government was possible in a political community of more than 200,000 people.

Simultaneously, the idea of "community control," both of neighborhoods and of governmental programs as they affect neighborhoods, has become enormously popular and is finding embodiment in more and more legislation. Community control certainly increases the number of people who are involved in the decision-making process, and makes for far greater participation in self-government; but it also creates perpetual conflict within the city and the near impossibility of any large-scale planning.

The Declining City Economy

These political developments are taking place at a time when the economic significance of the central city is steadily declining. Manufacturing has been moving out of the central city for the past thirty years, and the trend is as strong today as it was in 1950. The garment industry in New York City, once the city's single largest source of employment, is only a shadow of its former self, and the shadow daily grows paler. As a transportation hub, the central cities are declining along with the railroads, which were their vital arteries. And the advent of containerization in sea transport is also bad news for the old central cities, many of which came into existence as ports. (Containerization requires vast areas of "backup" space, which is difficult to provide in New York.)

It is true that during the 1950s and 1960s there was an extraordinary movement of corporation headquarters, with all of the jobs necessary to their functioning, into the central cities. But this movement has by now reversed itself, and more corporate headquarters are leaving than are coming in. Our nation's greatest metropolis, New York City, today stands on three precarious economic pillars: financial services (above all, the stock market), the media (television, book publishing, national magazines, advertising), and the older, declining industries. It is not hard to imagine circumstances in which financial services and media-associated activities will find it sensible to emigrate from Manhattan to more pleasant and less troublesome locations.

Should this occur, the inner city would become something akin to an Indian reservation, with part of the population being paid by the Government to provide necessary services (medical, social, educational) for the rest, who are dependent on welfare and Social Security. Indeed, in New York City at the present time about one third of the population is either employed by the government or is dependent on welfare and/or Social Security.

Politically weakened and economically enfeebled, the central city is also in the process of declining as a center for cultural activity. In this case, the movement is not toward the suburbs or smaller cities but toward the thousands of university campuses throughout the country. The writer-in-residence, the artist-in-residence, the composer-in-residence—all are familiar figures on the college campus of the 1970s. These people used to be regarded as intrinsically urban types; they still are urban types—only they no longer live and work in an urban setting. Bohemia itself, the urban artistic milieu par excellence, now tends to be a campus and off-campus phenomenon rather than a unique inner-city phenomenon. If we could envisage such a census, we would surely discover a larger population of bohemians in Berkeley than in Greenwich Village. And the off-Broadway theatre flourishes nearly as successfully at Yale and on other university campuses as it does in New York.

The New "Doughnut" Cities

The "natural" configuration of the American city today is revealed by such new cities as Houston and Los Angeles. Though these cities provoke apoplexy among city planners and are not without their problems, they are nevertheless successful in the most elementary and primitive sense of that term: the people who live in them are disinclined to leave, and more people are moving in than are moving out.

The shape of these cities is that of a doughnut. Each has a hollow center in which are located official buildings (city hall, the courts, state and federal agencies), some corporate headquarters, and perhaps a cultural center (with a museum, concert hall, and theater). Around this hollow center are concentric rings of inner suburbs, quasi-suburbs, suburbs, and exurbs. It is in these rings that everyone lives and most people work, do their shopping, and find entertainment. "Downtown" is where you sometimes have to go; it is really just another suburb, centrally located and with high-rise buildings. Even the urban poor no longer live there in large numbers. They have their own suburbs in which to be miserable.

What is happening is that our urban areas are taking up more and more space, but are becoming steadily less densely settled. According to Professor Lee Rainwater of Harvard

University, the population per square mile in urbanized areas will have decreased from 6,580 in 1920 to around 3,800 in 1985. We are not, as some commentators on the city seem to be saying, all being squeezed into a constricted urban space. On the contrary, each of us is getting more space than he ever had before. (Even in the New York metropolitan area the average resident today has more square footage of living space than he did ten years ago!) But the space we are getting is a new and special kind of space. It is an *urbanized* space, with an urbanized life style and an urbanized mode of thought. (Needless to say, the word *urbanized* here means something rather different from what we usually mean by *urbane*.)

Though Americans were certainly first attracted to the suburbs because they felt they were getting closer to the "grass roots," and though many Americans doubtless are still of this mind, the crucial fact is that our suburbs and exurbs are inexorably being transformed into what Melvin M. Webber [a writer on city planning] calls "undifferentiated urban space." The evidence of this transformation is nowhere more evident than in the family-style television serial. Patty Duke and Dennis the Menace were popular folk heroes of only yesterday; but they and their families are already of another world—distant, quaint, archaic. One can say, in retrospect, that they represented the last, desperate, and ultimately futile efforts of an older "provincial" culture to withstand a newer, "metropolitan" culture.

The New "Metropolitan" Culture

The den mother of yesteryear now trots off to see *Hair* when a traveling troupe or the students of a nearby college make it available to her. The den father of yesteryear now ponders, not whether he should build a new porch, but whether there might be something worth looking into in this new idea of "swinging couples" who indulge in occasional mate-swapping. Their neighbors used to be families; now a colony of "swinging singles" is likely to be nearby. Ameri-

cans have been fleeing their cities to find refuge in a more
traditional style of American living—only, ironically, to find
themselves captives of what has been called "the tradition
of the new."

This liquidation of the older, provincial American culture is probably the decisive event of twentieth century history. If anything can be described as America's coming-of-
age, this is it. The two cultures whose conflict and tensions
had been the fundamental experience of the American arts
—the traditional "square," provincial, more or less philistine
culture and the urban, sophisticated, avant-garde, elite culture—have coalesced in the past ten years.

The catalyst for this event has been the enormous expansion of higher education—or, to be more precise, of college
attendance—which brought masses of young people together,
exposed them to "the tradition of the new," and encouraged
them to create a "youth culture" that was both urban-so-
phisticated and popular. The prosperity of the postwar years
also permitted these young people to support this new cultural mode (movies and the record industry are now "con-
sumed" mainly by younger audiences) and eventually to
impose it on the nation as a whole. It is not, in some respects,
a particularly attractive popular culture, but then, neither
was the popular culture it replaced. On purely esthetic
grounds, it is not easy to choose between *Candy* and Patty
Duke. That choice, however, is no longer offered us; it has
been made for us by the developments of the postwar years.

How to Combine Urbanity With Small-City Life

The question that confronts us, therefore, is: how do you
combine an urban life style and an urban culture with a
small-city and suburbanized population? No civilization in
history has ever had to address itself to this question, and
we ought not to be overdepressed if we find it a hard question to answer. One's instinctive response—that such a combination is impossible—is almost certainly wrong. After all,
fifteen years ago one's instincts would have been to assert
that it was impossible for such a question to arise.

There are already a few signs of the direction in which things *might* drift. It seems to be the case, for instance, that the republican ethos has been suffusing the arts themselves, which until now have been dominated by a talented elite who subscribed to "high" standards. One of the most striking tendencies of the present age is the desire of large numbers of people, especially young people, to participate in the arts instead of merely enjoying or experiencing them. There is an urge to make one's own movies rather than simply attend movies; there is, similarly, an urge to make one's own music, write and read aloud one's own poetry, write one's own plays and put on one's own production of them, and so on.

That such amateur efforts are almost invariably inferior to the best professional efforts is not regarded as all that important. People, it is said, get more out of participating in artistic activities, no matter how amateurish, than out of being spectators of the most polished and expert performances. Whether this is true is open to argument. (The fact that it *sounds* plausible to American ears, and utterly absurd to Europeans, is not decisive one way or the other.) What is not open to argument is that this kind of thinking corresponds closely to the new urban condition of so many Americans. In a smaller city or on a college campus you will either make a virtue of amateurism or be deprived of culture altogether—and this deprivation is no longer tolerable, as it once was.

There are other possible developments we can contemplate—though we cannot attach a specific degree of probability to them. For example, it is not unthinkable that *new* nuclei of cultural activity will emerge in our undifferentiated urban space. Yesterday's suburban shopping center—serving several towns at once—is being transformed into today's suburban mall: a place for shopping, to be sure, but also a place where young people informally congregate, where there is likely to be a cinema and a paperback bookstore, and where there could easily be a small concert hall, library, and theatre. This is one prospect that cannot be dismissed out of hand.

Another, and at the other extreme, is that our culture will be completely democratized as well as republicanized; that informal, amateur activity will come to be regarded as the only proper kind of cultural life; and that the very idea of polished professionalism in the arts will become repugnant.

The Decline of the Central City

But whatever turn events take, there is one eventuality that is too utopian to expect in the twenty years or so ahead of us. This is the revival of the central city as the nucleus of American urban civilization. No doubt more civic centers and museums and attractive shopping malls will be built downtown, in a heroic effort to reverse the existing trend. But we have already had enough experience on this score to say with some certainty that though these schemes may work in a few cities, they are not likely to be universally successful, and even where they do work, they may have only a temporary success.

Lincoln Center in New York may be a nice addition to the city, and those of us who live in the city, and who also like operas and concerts and repertory theatre, are grateful for its presence. But we are becoming fewer and fewer with each passing year. If the circulation of the New York *Times* in the central city drifts downward every year—as it is doing —the attendance at Lincoln Center cannot be far behind. The *Times* is trying to counter this trend with an appeal to suburban readers, just as Lincoln Center is now appealing for suburban subscribers to its various programs. But fewer and fewer suburbanites find the idea of a trip to New York —of an expensive (and perhaps dangerous!) evening "in the city"—so overwhelming in its appeal. By contrast, Shea Stadium, located, like practically all new stadiums, on the border of the suburbs, is a resounding success. The trend seems to be unmistakable.

A candid recognition of this trend will not come easily. Not only are there powerful business and political interests that still have a stake in the central city, but our mass media are populated by upper-middle-class people—incipient patricians, as it were—who have an authentic longing for the more traditional kind of city and the more traditional kinds of urban amenities. They all adore London; as well they might, since it is in truth an adorable city. But the United States has never had a London, and though it was widely assumed that at some point we would be "mature" enough to have one, history has prescribed otherwise.

This makes for disappointments and frustration and for a shrill insistence that we do something big and expensive about our "urban crisis." But it is close to impossible to do anything big and expensive when each neighborhood and each activist group participates in its version of community control. The sad history of urban renewal—a term in such disfavor that it is already passing into disuse—is sufficient testimony to this point. And even if it were possible to do something big and expensive, there are good reasons for thinking it would not be very effectual. The trauma of our central cities has such deep, organic causes that the proposed therapies seem trifling.

It is just possible that in the distant future our central cities will assume a more significant role in American life—even if we cannot now imagine what kinds of cities these would be or who would live there. But in the foreseeable future, we can say with fair certainty that we are moving toward an urban civilization without great cities—and that this movement is so without precedent that prophecies of doom or hopes of utopia are both premature.

IN DEFENSE OF CITIES [3]

The American central city is sick and possibly dying. That much is generally conceded. Where we go in policy

[3] From "The Once and Future City," by Bennett Harrison, associate professor of economics and urban studies at the Massachusetts Institute of Technology. *Challenge.* 16:8-15. S.-O. '73. Reprinted with permission.

terms with that information depends, however, on how we diagnose the illness and how we value the patient.

If the illness is incurable, then all that remains is to provide the city with a decent funeral. If, on the other hand, we decide that the city can be saved, we must determine whether the task is worth doing as well as possible. If we then decide against treating the patient, we shall be burying not only the existing city but the idea of urban life as we have known it.

It is my thesis that the central city is not dying a natural death, but rather is being killed by misguided public policies. The city can be saved by reversing those policies—if we choose to do it. But should we do it, or is the city in any case obsolete?

I believe we should save the central city—by which I mean a place of high-density population and mixed land-use —because the city is the home of the future. For reasons of conservation of resources and quality of life, the central city is better adapted to our needs than the suburb. It is the suburb—by which I mean single-family dwellings and single-use zoning—that is becoming obsolete.

The Case Against the City Rebutted

The contrary view is prevalent today. We are repeatedly told that the central city is defunct as a social organization: impractical, inefficient, an environment that is suffocating and even dangerous to life and lung. The white middle class and, more recently, some blacks have voted with their feet for suburban living. Employers are moving to the suburbs in search of open space for their modern one-story plants. The only workers and employers left in the city are those who cannot find a way out. All this, we are told, is the inevitable result of the workings of the private economy. In the view of Professor John Kain of Harvard, it may not be possible to reverse these processes, nor is it obvious that we should want to do so.

A prominent exponent of the conventional view is Irving Kristol, of New York University and *The Public Interest,* who set forth his views in the Outlook section of The Washington *Post* for December 3, 1972. [See preceding *Horizon* article by Mr. Kristol, in this section, expressing the same views.—Ed.] Kristol observes that the great majority of Americans do not live in the large central cities, and he implies that our concern for urban well-being is therefore disproportionate. (This seems a strange position for one who always identifies himself as a pluralist.)

Kristol writes that a "mischievous misconception obscuring America's actual urban condition is the notion that Americans would really prefer to live in the cities if only they were more attractive and agreeable." Not so, says Kristol, and he cites the familiar fact of the postwar flight to the suburbs and Gallup polls showing that most people want or prefer suburban living. He also cites the antiurban bias of state legislatures, though that seems to tell us more about the political process than it does about the viability of cities. People leave the city because it has served its function for them. That function, Kristol argues, is to provide a staging area for unskilled rural or foreign migrants who, once the city has "processed" them, want to move up and out into the suburban middle class.

In Kristol's view, the " 'natural' configuration of the American city is revealed by such new cities as Houston and Los Angeles." This is "doughnut city": the core contains mainly government and corporate headquarters and cultural activities, while the poor live, like everyone else, in the ring of suburbs. The revival of the central city as anything other than a place where "you sometimes have to go" is simply "utopian." The only reason we discuss it at all is because the media and the planning profession are dominated by "incipient patricians" who exhibit a weird hang-up about city living. Here we get a hint that there is more at issue than urban economics. Kristol's shafts seem aimed at a number of people who disagree with him on a variety of political and cultural issues other than the quality of urban life. Many of them doubtless live on the West Side of Manhattan.

Kristol's notion that hardly anyone wants to live in the central city will come as news to anyone trying to find a townhouse in Georgetown or an apartment in Manhattan. It will also come as news to those working-class people—like the Italians of Newark, the Poles of Jersey City, and the blacks of Oakland—who cling by preference to their city homes. Of course, these are also the part of our population least likely to own an automobile. And therein lies a clue to the truth about the decline of the city.

Kristol's "city of the future" is built around the automobile. Places like Los Angeles depend crucially on the private car. But that dependence is not "natural"; it is the result of decades of public policy. It hardly needs demonstrating here that government policy discriminates in favor of the auto and against any other form of transportation. Each year, the United States spends ten times as much on highway construction as on mass transportation. That this need not be is clear to anyone who has seen the quality of mass transit in other industrial societies. Thus it makes little sense to say that Americans "prefer" to do all their traveling by auto. In the suburbs, at least, they have no choice in the matter: the car is the only means of transport available to them, and hardly any place is within walking distance.

Similarly, the apparent preference of Americans for suburban living is in large measure the consequence of public policy. Suburban residents are subsidized at the expense of city residents. Federal tax deductions for mortgage interest and property taxes provide a massive subsidy for homeowners, who are mostly suburban; tenants, who are mostly urban, are denied that subsidy. Because local government depends mainly on the local property tax and because the poor are concentrated in the core, city taxpayers bear the burden of services for the poor. The suburbs, which zone out the poor, escape that burden. Thus Americans who choose the suburbs need not be expressing a preference for suburban over city living as such. They may simply be recognizing that public policy rewards them for living in one place and penalizes them for living in the other. In fact, research shows that most white migrants to the suburbs are responding to these tax pressures rather than to racial mixture or fear of crime in the cities. In these circumstances, it is remarkable that so many people are willing to pay the price to live in cities.

The Kristol case is based not only on consumer preference but on the question of jobs. Research in urban economics conducted during the early 1960s seemed to show that jobs were leaving the city, perhaps at an accelerating rate, and that those which remained behind required skills not held by the large numbers of blacks and members of other minority groups who were not able to follow "their" jobs out to the suburbs because of residential discrimination. The suburbanization of jobs and the skill mismatch in the urban core were thought to contribute to the deterioration of the tax base of the central city, while the city's growing low-income population required more, and more expensive, public services.

In reality, the decentralization of urban people and jobs is a complex business indeed, not well represented in the picture painted by Kristol and others. Rather than dealing with a bottle (the city) whose bottom has fallen out, which explains why there is water on the floor, we seem to be dealing with a bottle which, having been filled up, is now simply spilling over. Clearly, the planning problems and possibilities differ dramatically between the two models.

People and Jobs

Certainly there is a trend toward decentralization of both people and jobs going back at least a century. But decentralization of employment does not necessarily imply the physical relocation of plants to the suburbs. The share of metropolitan employment located in the suburbs is indeed rising over time, but this is due to a combination of circumstances. For example, the ratio of urban jobs located in the core may fall because plants in the core reduce their employment or move out altogether. But core plants might not be moving at all; on the contrary, new plants might even be moving *in,* and plants already located in the core might even be expanding, and *still* the central city's share of total metropolitan employment could be falling, because of the even more rapid growth of suburban jobs. A more accurate picture would show plants moving into and within as well as out of the core; similar starts, short-distance relocations, and closings in the suburbs; and—most important of all—cyclical expansions and contractions of employment in *plants which aren't moving at all.* Over time, the net growth of jobs is greater in the suburbs than in the central city, but this is a sign of economic health. It means that the urban area is producing more income and more jobs and is therefore searching for more space.

This more complex, less naïve picture has important policy implications. It suggests that we can affect the decentralization of jobs by economic policies which expand consumer demand (and, consequently, the demand for labor), as well as by policies explicitly addressed to location, such as the provision of a public infrastructure in areas having difficulty attracting or retaining plants.

Some sectors are decentralizing more slowly than others. Office, service, and, especially, public sector employment are growing quite rapidly in central cities, as was predicted almost fifteen years ago by Raymond Vernon [an urban affairs specialist]. These are activities in which most jobs require very modest skills—although this fact is not easily perceived because employers in these sectors often require inflated educational credentials. This suggests that reducing "credentialism" can reduce the purported skill mismatch and lower black unemployment in central cities. Another finding on the mismatch hypothesis—this by Charlotte Fremon [another urban affairs specialist]—is that, far from there being insufficient numbers of unskilled jobs in the core, there are apparently more than enough such jobs to provide work for unemployed residents of the inner city, but most of them are held by white workers who move to the suburbs but keep their old jobs in the city.

Beneath the trend toward decentralization lies a very pronounced cycle. During recessions, cities lose ground to their suburbs in terms of net job growth. During periods of recovery, they may actually *gain* ground on their suburbs. Between 1958 and 1963, for example, all but the outermost areas of Chicago lost jobs, the losses being greatest in the inner-city ghettos. Between 1963 and 1968, all of Chicago's neighborhoods, including even the innermost areas, experienced significant net growth in employment.

One explanation of the cycle phenomenon is that firms with plants in both core and suburban areas decide during recessions to reduce capacity and lay off workers in their older (and therefore presumably less efficient) plants first; normally these are the plants located in the city. During recovery, these firms generally prefer to restore capacity in their existing plants before building new capacity (probably in the suburbs). Thus, policies which reduce the severity of the business cycle may also improve the economic status of central cities by smoothing these variations in employment in plants located in the core.

Significant tax or space differentials between central-city and suburban sites may induce prospering plants to relocate. The modern plant employing people with high skills at high wages and providing on-the-job training for its workers can afford to outmigrate. It belongs to a company which has access to the capital with which to make the move and can probably find its kind of labor force in the suburbs. But the technologically stagnant, low-skill, low-wage plant providing little training and generally producing in a competitive industry cannot move out: it lacks the capital, or the power with which to acquire capital; many suburban middle-class residents would be unwilling to take the jobs it offers; and, in any case, suburban communities generally zone out such plants. These plants are forced to remain in the core; they have no choice. As their relative profitability declines, the real wages they are able to pay probably decline as well, with a predictable impact on central-city economic conditions. Thus differential tax and space development policies induce the firms offering the better jobs to leave the city.

Nor is suburban residence likely to be a sufficient condition for improving black economic well-being, an assumption apparently widely held by the advocates of open housing. While no one to my knowledge has studied actual city-to-suburb migration of blacks, I have been able to compare the economic circumstances of blacks living in three different areas within the nation's twelve largest standard metropolitan statistical areas in 1966: central-city ghetto, nonghetto central city, and suburban ring. Unlike the whites in my sample of over 11,000 persons, the earnings, unemployment, occupational status, and returns to education for blacks showed virtually no correlation with residential location. If there was any best area for blacks, according to these characteristics, it was the nonghetto central city, *not* the suburban ring, although even here any differences were very small. This evidence suggests that job discrimination follows blacks out to the suburbs.

If there is any single message that emerges from this review of recent research on the location of people and jobs, it is that central cities are far from dead.

First Aid for Cities

How long central cities will continue to be viable depends very much on the directions public policy takes in the near future—advocates of "benign neglect" notwithstanding. There are forces—including the auto and tax policies touched on earlier—acting to undermine the viability of central cities. If we do not deal constructively with these forces, then Kristol's forecast of a future built on the Los Angeles model is likely to be all too accurate. . . .

Public transportation is an obvious area in which collective action is needed. Whatever the mix of auto, rail, bus, taxi, or more exotic modes of transport that each city chooses for itself, we must provide adequate resources to cities to enable them to make that choice; for the private market will inevitably continue to place virtually all of its emphasis on the automobile, since that seems to be the only highly profitable form of transportation.

Another area for public action is employment. I perceive (especially at the federal level, with the possible exception of the Pentagon) an almost total disregard for the local consequences of the employment (or lack of it) generated by national fiscal and monetary policies. It takes the 12 per-cent unemployment of Seattle to make us see that federal spending decisions affect things closer to home than does the GNP or the balance of trade.

I submit that both the kinds of jobs created—the skill mix—and the *location* of those jobs ought to be explicit ob-jectives of public policy along with the usual national goals involving employment and inflation. Until we adopt such a policy, we place the fate of our central cities (and, for that matter, of all lagging regions, rural as well as urban) entirely in the hands of the private market, hoping that decisions based entirely on private profitability will create good jobs in the places that need them most. It is precisely because the market has been consistently unable to do this that we need social indicators to guide public planning.

Future manpower policy need not repeat the errors of the recent past. All of the efforts of the 1960s seem to have been based on what . . . [the late Representative William Ryan, Democrat, New York, called] "blaming the victim": those who are poor, unskilled, and "present-time oriented" are encouraged to change their behavior in order to become unpoor. The best way to become unpoor, in this view, is to participate in education and training programs which, by augmenting the so-called "human capital" of the poor, will presumably increase their attractiveness to employers. By following this path, the poor can work their way out of poverty.

It is my conviction that the critics of such an antipoverty strategy have successfully demonstrated that developing the skills of the poor in an economy suffering a chronic shortage of jobs paying better than poverty wages leads only to increased frustration and discontent among the underclass that is the target for these programs. Evaluations of the manpower programs of the last ten years present a picture of a revolving door: people are pulled out of the class of low-skilled, low-paid workers, whirled through some form of training, and then returned to a job (or hiring queue) not substantially different from that to which they had access before they underwent the processing. What we must do, by contrast, is design a strategy based on the creation of more jobs and on-the-job training at nonpoverty wages. Nothing less will do.

Except for zoning laws, which are often drawn up by or for the interests that own and control land, we still indulge the almost totally unrestrained private manipulation of land. This means that land uses are determined mainly by private profitability, without regard to their true social costs and benefits. Some land uses impose what economists call external diseconomies on neighboring areas; an outstanding example is the large-lot, low-density suburban development, which reduces the availability of open space to others; makes sewage and waste collection, treatment, and disposal more difficult and expensive than would be the case in a higher-density environment; and makes residents dependent on the private automobile, with all *its* attendant costs, from pollution to destruction of neighborhoods by highways. It is a theorem in economics that goods generating external diseconomies will be oversupplied by a profit-oriented market economy, since the full social costs of producing such goods are not brought to bear on the producer.

Conversely, other land uses confer external economies—unanticipated benefits—on neighboring areas. Jane Jacobs [author *(The Death and Life of Great American Cities)* and city-planning critic] tells us that high-density urban streets which mix housing, commerce and light industry provide a valuable free protection service to residents through informal surveillance ("eyes that watch the street"), as well as the more obvious benefit of reduced dependence on transportation. Schools make communities more attractive to young families. Industrial parks accessible to low-income areas provide jobs and activity centers which may reduce local crime, teenage boredom, and (perhaps) narcotics addiction. However, goods and services that provide such external economies are systematically undersupplied by the private market.

Orthodox welfare economists argue that policymakers should interfere with the private market as little as possible, in order to preserve the allocative efficiency which decentralized private markets presumably display. The losers—those who are the victims of the external diseconomies generated by a system pursuing private profit—should be compensated in the form of "transfer payments" from the winners.

In the real world—as every legislator knows—such bribes to the losers are almost always politically unfeasible—if only because the winners in the marketplace typically also win enough political power to protect themselves against being taxed for the benefit of the losers. The usual result is that the diseconomies do get generated, and the victims do not get compensated—and in any case, how do you compensate someone for the loss of an intangible good like community?

The future viability of the central city depends intimately on our fashioning a land-use control policy which maximizes the external economies and minimizes the external diseconomies associated with the uses of urban land. This may well require much more public ownership of that land (again, not necessarily by federal bureaucracies) than the United States has been willing to accept in the past.

Restructuring Taxes

Drastically different tax policies will be needed. Historically, American cities have been able to deal with employment decentralization through two policies: increased property taxes, and annexation of the adjacent areas experiencing
the greatest growth of new jobs. Neither is available any
longer. The taxable capacity of the private property base in
cities seems just about exhausted (except perhaps for church,
foundation, and university property), and the peripheries of
most large cities are now themselves incorporated into towns
that are capable, with the help of their state legislatures, of
resisting annexation. These developments, coupled with
rising social costs, have created a fiscal crisis of enormous
proportions for municipal governments. . . .

At 1972 levels, the total resources available to local governments fall far short of what those governments themselves define as adequate to meet their needs. This means
that cities will probably continue to raise local taxes or
introduce income taxes—assuming that their state governments authorize the latter. But if they do this, then the most
mobile elements of the population—middle-class residents
and private companies producing for regional and national
markets—may move out. Cities will be at one another's
throats in the tax/subsidy competition for industry.

The best way to prevent this is to nationalize all taxes,
thus eliminating tax rates as a factor in the location of industry. I would favor the replacement of all property taxes
—and indeed all wage taxes as well—by a single progressive
income tax and by full taxation of wealth, although a uni-
form national property tax might serve the immediate purpose. The revenues generated could then be returned by the
Federal Government to state and local governments according to formulae based partly on population and partly on
whatever redistributive goals, such as relative unemployment or poverty, Congress chose to establish.

If this kind of plan were put into effect, cities would
compete for new industry not by mortgaging their future

sources of income through competitive tax cuts, but by public investments in the infrastructure and environmental quality they could offer to new plants.

The Power to Govern

Change in the structure of government is also needed. The future viability of the central city is threatened by the unwillingness of existing political bodies (from Congress down to local city halls, but especially the state governments) to create a system of "community control"—a city of neighborhoods with significant powers of self-government—without destroying the ability to plan sensibly for the urban region with respect to such naturally regional matters as pollution, transportation, and (possibly) housing. This sort of change, which Kristol dismisses as impossible, is in fact the subject of much current research. More important, actual experiments are now under way across the country—indeed, across the world—in the politics of local self-government, urban decentralization, community economic development through local development corporations, and similar activities (perhaps the most prominent—and apparently successful —example is taking place in Toronto). . . .

The choice that Kristol presents us with—between the intolerably congested and deteriorating New York or the Los Angeles-style "doughnut city"—is incomplete. We have it in our power to design cities which combine the most useful social functions of high-density regions—environmental conservation, collective consumption, a wide range of choice in personal lifestyles and activities, and opportunity for contact with other human beings engaged in a variety of pursuits—with the amenity and privacy of low-density living. The basic economic system that is the large city appears to be viable. How long it can remain so in the absence of public policies to deal with the forces threatening that viability is a good question.

A CASE FOR HIGHER DENSITY CITIES [4]

[My] thesis is that . . . [our metropolitan areas] are going to look much better, that they are going to be much better places to live in, and that one of the reasons they are is that a lot more people are going to be living in them.

Many thoughtful observers believe the opposite is true. They hold that not only is the landscape of our cities and suburbs a hideous mess, as indeed much of it is, but that it is bound to become much worse. The saturation point has been reached, they say, and unless growth and population trends are redirected, our metropolitan areas will become fouler yet. Some think they are beyond redemption already and that the only real hope is to start afresh, somewhere else, with new towns and cities.

But there is a good side to the mess. We needed it. It is disciplining us to do out of necessity what we refused to do by choice. We have been the most prodigal of people with land, and for years we wasted it with impunity. There was so much of it, and no matter how much we fouled it, there was always more over the next hill, or so it seemed. . . .

In filling out the metropolis . . . we treated land as though we were in fact on the frontier. With the great postwar expansion of suburbia in the forties and fifties, we carried this to the point of caricature. We were using five acres to do the work of one, and the result was not only bad economics but bad esthetics. People began to feel that if things looked this awful, something had gone wrong. At last we were having our noses rubbed in it. . . .

Others have a more apocalyptic vision. Some say that we are on the threshold of a postindustrial society—i.e. it's a whole new ball game now—and that entirely new forms of living must be devised. They see a breakthrough in environmental planning with teams of specialists applying systems

[4] From *The Last Landscape*, by William H. Whyte, author of *The Organization Man*, member of President Johnson's Task Force on Natural Beauty. Doubleday. '68. p 1-12, 375-93 passim. Copyright © 1968 by William H. Whyte. Reprinted by permission of Doubleday & Company, Inc.

analysis and computer technology to create the city of the future. A number of people have already begun jumping the gun, and in the recent upsurge of futurology have been devoting great energy and imagination to anticipating what forms these cities will take. Even the popular magazines are now full of pictures of megacities, stilt cities, linear cities, and such.

Some are to be located far, far away from any place. A Government-aided research project has just been launched for . . . an "Experimental City" to be located somewhere in Minnesota or the Great Plains. Dr. Athelstan Spilhaus, the prime mover of the project, visualizes a self-contained city with a population limit of 250,000 people. The city would test a host of technological advances. Many of its functions would be put underground and possibly a transparent dome two miles in diameter might be constructed. Dr. Spilhaus, who thinks present cities are something of a lost cause, believes that Experimental City can be the progenitor of many such settlements. [Planning is now underway for Experimental City.—Ed.]

What is being fed into the machines is a set of rather questionable assumptions. What comes out is an extrapolation of the trends of the last twenty years—surging population, increasing affluence, and more leisure. Maybe these will continue. Maybe they will not. The very unanimity and assurance with which these projections are made should be enough to make one quite nervous. . . . But faith in the grand design is stronger than ever. . . .

Living With Higher Density

Designs can indeed help shape growth, but only when the designs and growth are going in the same direction. Most of the year-2000 plans are essentially centrifugal—that is, they would push everything outward away from the city, decentralize its functions, and reduce densities by spreading the population over a much greater land area. I think the evidence is staring us in the face that the basic growth trends are in the other direction; that they are toward higher rather than lower density.

There will be no brief here for letting the free market decide how we are going to grow, but where people and institutions are putting their money is a phenomenon worthy of respect, and planning which goes against the grain usually comes a cropper. The English, who have far more stringent land controls than we do, have been doing their best to constrain London, but the beast keeps growing. Most thinking Frenchmen agree that Paris is much too big in relation to the rest of the country, and Paris keeps growing. The Russians have been doing everything they can to curb Moscow, and it keeps on growing. . . .

I think that the bulk of the significant growth is going to take place within our present metropolitan areas. I think we are going to see a build-up, not a fragmentation, of the core cities. There will be a filling in of the bypassed land in the gray area between the cities and suburbia and a more intensive development—a redevelopment, if you will—of suburbia itself. New towns, yes, but I will wager that the ones which work out will not be self-contained and that they will not be somewhere off in the hinterland. We are, in sum, going to operate our metropolitan areas much closer to capacity and with more people living on a given amount of land. . . .

Our densities are not high at all. They are low. In some of the slum sections of the city, to be sure, there are too many people crowded together. But overcrowding—which is too many people per room—is not the same thing as high density. The residential density in most of our cities is quite reasonable.

So is the density of the metropolitan areas around them. By European standards they are enviably underpopulated. The densest in this country are the metropolitan areas along the Boston—New York—Washington axis; the 150 counties that make up this Atlantic urban region contain 67,690 square miles and 43 million people. If this region was de-

veloped to the same average density as the western Nether-
lands, the number of people would be tripled. The comparison is an extreme one perhaps, but so is the difference in
appearance. Our areas *look* more filled up than the ones
that really are. . . .

Our eyes are not a bad guide. The kind of land we find
ugliest is not that which is overused but the land that is
largely vacant or hardly used at all: worked out gravel pits,
derelict waterfronts, obsolete freight yards, the scores of vacant lots, the rubbish-strewn areas underneath the high tension lines. (Probably the dreariest of all urban views is that
of the Jersey flats, with its billboards all the more obscene
for the emptiness around.) Almost as bad are the lands that
are devoted to only one use, and only a fraction of the time
at that. The great seas of asphalt around our shopping centers, for example, chew up enormous amounts of high-priced
land, yet they are used to capacity only four days of each
December.

But the very existence of this waste land means that our
metropolitan areas have a great capacity for regeneration.
The increased competition for land use is not a force for
blight; it is a discipline for enforcing a much more economic
use of land, and a more amenable one. Developers, for example, are now taking to a subdivision pattern that treats
land much more sensitively and is far more attractive than
the conventional pattern; they have been doing this not because planners and architects convinced them it was better
—planners and architects have been trying to do that for
years—but because land prices had finally gotten so high
they had to adopt the new pattern to make money.

The same discipline is going to apply to open space as
well as developed space. We should try to save all the big
spaces we can get our hands on, but there are only so many
left. From here on out we are going to have to work much
more inventively with the smaller spaces, the overlooked
odds and ends; we are going to have to rediscover the obso-
lescent rights-of-way that thread the metropolitan area. We

must use all sorts of devices for conserving key features of the landscape that are in private hands. We must explore much more diligently the use of air rights, and of creating open spaces where none existed before. We must make the spaces more accessible to people—to their eyes most of all. To overstate the case, we will have to jam more people in and make them feel they are not jammed. . . .

The net of what I have been saying . . . is that we are going to have to work with a much tighter pattern of spaces and development, and that our environment may be the better for it. This somewhat optimistic view rests on the premise that densities are going to increase and that it is not altogether a bad thing that they do. It is a premise many would dispute. Our official land policy is dead set against higher densities. It is decentralist, like official policies in most other countries. The primary thrust of it is to move people outward; reduce densities, loosen up the metropolis, and reconstitute its parts in new enclaves on the fringe.

I do not think it is going to work out this way. Certainly, outward movement will continue, but if our population continues to grow, the best way to accommodate the growth will be by a more concentrated and efficient use of the land within the area. The big "if" is whether or not intensity of use will be coupled with efficiency of use. It may not be. But it can be. . . .

The Case for Crowding

The case for higher densities cannot rest on a shortage of land. There is none. It is true that top-grade agricultural lands are being overrun by urban expansion, that open space in the right places is increasingly difficult to save. The fact remains, however, that if we wish to go the expansion route, there is room for it. Expand the diameter of a metropolitan area by only a few miles and enough land will be encompassed to take care of a very large population increase. This may be a poor way to do it, but the option exists.

Nor are our cities running into each other. Metropolitan areas are being linked more tightly, but this is not the same thing as collision. Consider, for example, the great belt of urban areas along the Eastern Seaboard from Boston to Norfolk. It is well that we are paying more attention to the continuities of this megalopolis, as Jean Gottmann [geologist and author of the noted study *Megalopolis: The Urbanized Northeastern Seaboard of The United States*] has done so well, but to call it a strip city, as many are doing, is misleading.

There is no such city, and the proposition can be easily tested. Fly from Boston to Washington and look out the window. Here and there one suburbia flows into another—between Baltimore and Washington, for example—but the cities retain their identities. This is especially apparent at night when the lights beneath simplify the structure so vividly: the brilliantly lit downtowns, the shopping centers, the cloverleafs, the spine of freeways that connect it all. But just as striking is what is dark—the forests of Massachusetts and Connecticut, the pine barrens of New Jersey, the farmlands of the Eastern Shore, the tidewater of Virginia. For many miles along the great urban route you can look down and see only the scattered lights of farms and small towns.

Urbanized sectors in other parts of the country—excepting, always, Los Angeles—show much the same characteristics. They are systems of cities, tied by high-speed rail and road networks, but they have not yet congealed into an undifferentiated mass. There is room outside them for expansion. There is room inside them. Whichever way is best, a measure of choice is still open to us. . . .

The Future of Suburbia

Further out, densities will continue to be relatively low, and on the outer edge of suburbia fairly large lots will probably continue to be the rule for many years to come. Overall, however, there is bound to be an increase in the number of people housed in a given area, and much of this increase will be concentrated in pockets of high-density housing.

So far, cluster has not been used to increase density, but the efficiency with which it can house more people per acre is so great that inevitably it is going to be used for that purpose. Developers already have this in mind, as local governments are only too aware; their density zoning ordinances, roughly translated, mean no more density. For the moment developers are not pushing too hard to up the allowable quota of houses; they are getting enough in return in construction savings to be content. But this happy coincidence of self-interests is too good to last much longer. The next big drive of the developers will be cluster *and* more houses, and if the population increase continues they are going to win.

Another rich source of suburban controversy will be apartments. Most suburbs do not want them, and at rezoning hearings the opposition, often the best people in town, will offer statistical proof that apartment people breed too many children, get more out of community taxes than they pay, have little allegiance to the place, and are in general not the element one would want. But the apartments have been going up just the same. Too many people need apartments, and the pressures have been translated into land prices of compelling force. If a plot can be rezoned from one-family residential to garden apartments, the market price per acre vaults immediately, and if the change is to high-rise, it can leap as much as $250,000 an acre. The possibility of this profit overspill will prompt other local citizens to argue that apartment people have to live somewhere; breed few children, move to houses when the children are school age, are above average in education and income, and are highly desirable in every respect.

But a zoning variance is almost always necessary. Despite the clear warning of the market place, most suburbs are not anticipating apartments; they have their zoning so set that no new apartments will ever get built without a zoning change. They are playing Canute. There will be changes, just as in the density zoning. All in all, suburban zoning boards are in for a rough time.

Using Unused Land

There are other ways to raise the carrying capacity of our urban land than having more people per acre. We can also increase the number of effective acres, and this can be done without pushing farther out into the country to find them. Within the metropolitan area there is a considerable amount of land that is not used at all, and an appalling amount that is used wastefully.

Parking space is the greatest wastage. Even with our present parking technology, backward as it is, we are allocating much more space for cars than is necessary. . . .

Industry is profligate too. The trend to the one-story, horizontal plant has good reasons behind it. Esthetically, the new plants are built to a considerably higher standard than most new subdivisions. But they, too, consume a great amount of space, and as with shopping centers more of it is given over to parking than to the primary activity. Industrial parks pool space more efficiently, and they require no more land for buffering or landscaping than one isolated plant. If industrial expansion continues, it would seem inevitable that land costs would induce more of this kind of concentration. But might there not also be something of a reversal in the trend to the horizontal? Within a decade we may be hearing of the revolutionary new concept of a vertical stacking of manufacturing space, with improved materials-handling making it possible to have factories four and five stories high.

Another possibility is a high-rise shopping center. This would concentrate on one acre what now is spread over many. The goods and services would be grouped by category, stacked in floors one above the other, with vertical transportation systems tying in with mass transit lines underground. No cars or parking space would be necessary. The entire complex would be enclosed and kept at constant temperature and humidity. It could be termed a department store.

Utility rights-of-way should be tightened up too. High tension lines are so unsightly our eye tends to blank them out, and few people realize what a considerable swath they cut through our urban land. This single-purpose use of land is unnecessarily wasteful, and . . . the rights-of-way can be put to good use as connective and recreational space.

Nor does so much land have to be taken. The most striking thing about a utility map of an area is the duplication of effort by different kinds of utilities. Oil pipelines, water conduits, and electric lines angle this way and that along separate rights-of-way, except, as in the central city, where they have been forced into joint routes. Why could they not be pooled? Several new high voltage transmission lines have been laid down over railroad tracks. The kind of right-of-way that has been greediest of space, the superhighway, offers similar potentials. . . .

Bridges can be made to do more duty. Instead of putting up massive towers for a new river crossing, utilities can put electric lines, even oil pipelines, on the underside of existing bridges. Most bridges are forbidden to such uses, but where they have been permitted the lines or pipelines have proved compatible. The bridge authority gets revenue it otherwise would not, the utility saves a great deal by not having to build the towers, and the public does not have to look at them. . . .

Some kinds of underuse will not be so easily resolved. For planners, the most frustrating open spaces to contemplate are the cemeteries of the city. Together, they take up a large amount of space—in some areas, like Queens in New York, they form the bulk of the urban open space. Many a planner has toyed with the thought of all the good things that could be done with the land were there a relocation effort. Those who are wise have kept the idea to themselves.

Title problems are immense, and the whole subject politically explosive.

Reservoir and watershed lands of private and municipal water companies are in many states restricted to any use except the gathering of rain. Pressure for recreational use has been mounting—particularly from sportsmen—and in time it would seem inevitable that these lands will be opened up to multiple use. The delaying action is strong, however, and in one respect it has been quite beneficial. The fact these lands have been unavailable as usable open space has made it easier to get public support for acquisition of other open space.

City-owned land has great capabilities too. In New York City, for example, subway freight yards, together with railroad yards, total some 9,641 acres. These are probably the dreariest acres to look at in the city, and development over top of them could greatly improve the looks of the city as well as its finances. A few starts have been made. Two new public schools are being built over subway storage yards. Since school buildings are customarily low and flat roofed, in some cases it would make sense to go a step further and lease the air rights over the schools for yet another structure. In a project for one new high school in New York, part of the air rights are to be used for the construction of an apartment tower. The lease payments will pay a substantial portion of the interest on the school construction bonds.

City-owned reservoirs can be decked over too. Philadelphia is now considering the proposal of a developer to build a commercial and shopping complex over a city reservoir. The city's planners and engineers like the idea; in addition to the income, the structure would keep the sun off the water in summer and there would be much less loss through evaporation.

Expressways and streets are going to be exploited more vigorously. . . .

There are problems, of course, in this kind of construction. An apartment project built several years ago atop the

Manhattan approaches to the George Washington Bridge, for example, has run into difficulties because of the great amount of noise and air pollution the high concentration of cars beneath sends up. But the technical challenge is not too difficult. The real problem, as the New York *Times*' Ada Louise Huxtable has pointed out, is governmental. "In the city," she notes, "the municipal pipeline is jammed with simple projects unable to clear the hurdles of requests, reviews and multidepartmental jurisdiction." . . .

Coping With Population Growth

Let me turn from the techniques of compression to the matter of whether or not it is justified. In bespeaking a more intensive use of the land I have been accepting the fact of growth. But is it inevitable? And is it good? A number of ecologists and conservationists think not. They are horrified by the specter of a growing population devouring the resources we have left. . . .

Malthusians argue that planners can no longer make sensible plans unless they face up to the issue of population control, and as a minimum, demonstrate to the public the choices involved. They point out that in almost all of the alternative regional-design plans growth is assumed; in the worst alternative presented, unplanned growth, the bad word is *unplanned*. Why not, critics ask, a planned no-growth alternative? The planners could say to people, look, we've shown you different ways we can handle a growing population; now we'd like to show you what a job we could do if the population doesn't grow. . . .

I wonder. On the face of it, it would seem easier for land planners to cope with growth if there were not any, or, at least, much less. But there is a challenge and response equation involved. When growth pressures were less we wasted land and abused it. And were there respite we might be as bad as ever. We are, of course, still enormously wasteful, but we are beginning to feel guilty enough about it to try and mend our ways a bit. . . . It is quite doubtful if we would be now adopting better land use measures except for the pressures of growth.

It is a shame so much land had to be sacrified to force the recognition, but the blight seems a necessary stimulant (it is not by accident that so many of the new approaches have been tried first in California). We have to have our noses rubbed in it. Whether or not, as the Malthusians hope, the discipline leads us to the further step of population control, we are being goaded to a more effective use of space, now, and the process is hardly a palliative.

BUILDING FOR TEN BILLION CITY-DWELLERS [5]

The crisis of urban civilization is a crisis of courage and imagination. If our cities are dying, we should not blame technology, the population explosion, the consumer society or any of the other usual scapegoats; we should blame ourselves.

The urban crisis is not simply a contemporary phenomenon. A hundred years ago, men lost their grip and let their cities develop in a sprawling, anarchic way. Haussmann was one of the last town planners worthy of the name, not because he philosophized about the future of urban civilization or drew up attractive plans—as people are so fond of doing today in order to mask the timidity of what they are actually doing—but because he *built*. In Greek there is no word for town planner; one has to use the expression *town builder*, an apt description of Haussmann, whose main claim to fame is the bold way in which he drove new avenues through built-up sections of Paris. It is often forgotten that he also built in open countryside, extending the city. Haussmann belonged to an energetic and self-confident age which produced figures like Ildefonso Cerda, the inventive engineer who remodelled Barcelona.

[5] From "What to Do With the Cities," by Constantinos Doxiadis, Greek architect and city planner. *Réalités*. No 263. p 20-1. O. '72. Reprinted by permission.

Since then, city-builders as a race have become extinct. In their place we have an army of the timid who cry that the growth of the cities must be halted. Paris was among the first cities to be affected by this anxiety, which is, however, universal. Each autumn the Chinese authorities drive thousands of new inhabitants from the big cities, where they have settled without authorization. In 1970 there was a fierce campaign to drive the young people who had flocked into Shanghai during the preceding months back to their villages. They were officially described as bands of thieves, and since they had been reduced to thieving because they had not been given work permits, this propaganda was easy to sustain.

Ideological differences apart, China today is in the same boat as other countries which, for the last century, have refused to accept the simple fact that people are attracted to big cities and want to live in them. The city offers freedom. Nowhere else can people find the same degree of choice—of work, friends, entertainment. The mass movement into the cities is as irresistible as it is understandable, and those who take part in it are not responsible for the present urban crisis. The blame lies with those whose business it was to foresee the growth of the conurbations.

The urban crisis is one of size, and it is clear that problems will get worse as cities continue to grow. If we assume that the world population will double between now and the end of the century, and if we take into account migration from the countryside, then out of a total population of 7 billion people, 5 billion will live in cities. This means that the present world urban population will be quadrupled. By the next generation, in the year 2030, there will be at least 10 billion city-dwellers out of a world population of 12 billion people.

Building Dynamic Cities

But these figures reveal only one aspect of the urban problem. We must also bear in mind that increased mobility, mainly through the possession of one or more cars per family, will cause an increase in the amount of space required per person. Furthermore, per capita energy consumption is also increasing: while primitive man used up 3,000 calories per day—more than the average for some parts of India today—in the developed countries the figure now stands at 100,000 calories and even 200,000 in the biggest American cities. Demographic increase, mobility and energy are the essential factors in the problem we must solve. And so we must construct an urban system which is truly dynamic.

This is where the planners and armchair administrators come in. They take the line of least resistance and let gigantic agglomerations spread like cancerous growths. This lack of imagination does give free rein to a kind of dynamism, but at the cost of the destruction of the countryside and a lowering of the quality of life, because these urban monsters pose immense working difficulties. Experience has taught us that city-dwellers can only identify with units of limited size, which provide a pleasant environment because they are on a human scale. All the pseudofuturistic talk about the creation of spatial cities, the plasticity of buildings, and transformable spaces is simply hollow theorizing. I see no reason to modify the conception of streets and houses which has brought happiness to generations of people. It corresponds to the needs of the individual, and above all to those of the child—always forgotten—of the famiv, and of human relations in general. One of the favorite aberrations of our time is to build high-rise blocks next to expressways. I believe that urban units should have populations of between 50,000 and 100,000 people—the latter figure should be considered the absolute maximum. And these groupings should be composed of houses, flats, streets and gardens, all on a human scale.

It would be absurd, however, to suggest that we should only build small towns. The small units I have in mind must be interlinked to form vast urban systems which will give ample scope to the dynamism necessary to cope with the growth problems mentioned above. In these *dynapoleis,* or dynamic towns, the constituent parts will remain static while the city as a whole will be dynamic, as more and more units are added to the existing network. The units themselves will be connected by central avenues.

Conceived in this way, the *dynapolis* will one day become the universal city or *oecumenopolis,* because it will allow very different types of people to live in close proximity.

Integration Through Open Space

Large areas of open space must be provided. In the cities of Ancient Greece, the *agora* or meeting place played an important part in bringing together the most diverse elements of a city's inhabitants. This pluralism must be restored and made to work in today's urban systems. Otherwise the city-dweller will be caught between two extremes: the conformism, boredom and social sterility which exist in some American suburbs, inhabited by families whose incomes, activities and life styles are identical; or the intolerance and conflict which break out when very different people are forced to live too close together.

Over a long period of time our cities have become increasingly segregated, and we are suffering from the consequences today. As cities grow, distinct neighborhoods evolve. For example, many cities have a bohemian quarter: the Latin Quarter in Paris, Greenwich Village in New York, Chelsea in London. Other ethnic and social groups have their own areas, while large areas of our cities, especially the fringes, tend to be nondescript in character. Thus cities are compartmentalized like a chess board, emphasizing differences in income, standards of living, and fields of activity between the various groups. Even in America, segregation is not essentially racial in origin. I made a study of Detroit which revealed that the physical decline of the heart of the city was not due to the arrival of the blacks; it began as long ago as 1895, when the first traffic problem caused the richest inhabitants to move out to the suburbs, while different groups of European immigrants—Poles and Italians, for example—formed their ghettos in the city center.

Our cities have become fascist. They impose segregation, and freedom of choice depends on how much or how little money one has to spend. Only the rich escape this restraint, although even they have their own part of town, like all the other social groups. Economic and social pressures decide which section people live in. In this process one can see the resurgence of a new kind of feudal order, with each group shutting itself in with its own lifestyle, ostracizing other groups and throwing up leaders to defend its own interests and prejudices.

This segregation must be broken down, first of all by reintroducing trees and greenery into built-up areas. It is absurd to create green belts around urban agglomerations, as has been the fashion; this is like putting a growing adolescent into a steel corset. Nature must be near at hand for everyone so as to irrigate the entire urban system. One consequence of the green belt principle is that anyone who wants to enjoy some open space must get into a car and drive out of town. Nature then becomes a spectacle accessible only to those with sufficient time to make the journey and enough money to buy a car. If, on the other hand, the open spaces are concentrated into parks, there are other disadvantages, one of them being a tendency towards the aristocratic conception in which segregation is encouraged. The apartment buildings which line Central Park and the Bois de Boulogne are the private reserve of the richest New Yorkers and Parisians. In the city as I conceive it, no dwelling would be more than two minutes' walk from an area of open space.

The essential concern of town planners should be to develop the widest possible range of choices and make them accessible to the least favored sections of the population. If some groups want to live apart from the rest, their wishes should be respected. At the same time, we must not impose large tower blocks on people who would prefer to live in

small apartment blocks or individual houses. It seems to me
that tower blocks are only suitable for old people and for
offices. It is inhuman to force young couples with children
to live in them—even if they are provided with gardens and
play areas—because the mothers cannot keep an eye on their
children from such apartments.

Housing and the Role of Transport

It will be argued that lack of space makes it essential to
build high-rise blocks if towns are to grow. I do not accept
this. We must move out from the city centers to find suitable
areas of land for the small urban units that I have in mind.
Then, when they have reached their maximum size, we
should build new units further afield rather than let the
original ones spread like cancerous cells. We possess the
technical means to connect these units with rapid transport
systems which will leave the countryside unspoiled.

In the long run, urban transport must be underground,
just as the veins and arteries function within the human
body. At one time drainage and sewage flowed through the
streets. Then people realized that this was dangerous and
unhealthy, and underground sanitary systems were devised.
In the same way, the day will come when many of the industrial installations that now disfigure and pollute nature
—from electric cables to roads and railways—will be buried.
For the moment, one of the best solutions is to build highways in trenches that are subsequently covered over. Later
—five or ten years from now—tunnels will be bored directly.
Studies undertaken at the Stanford Research Institute and
at our office in Athens show that for a city like Detroit it
will soon be much cheaper to use this kind of technique than
to build conventional highways. Research is now being done
at MIT on the use of lasers in opening up underground
routes quickly and economically.

Another commonly stated view is that town planning is
only possible under an authoritarian regime. Yet democratic
societies have given birth to many remarkable cities. Athens

and Florence are two outstanding examples. When Michelangelo placed his statue of David on the Piazza della Signoria, the Florentines came to pass their opinion on it. Recently our office won the competition to develop a new town in Philadelphia. It took three years to finalize the plans, with dozens of committees whose agreement was necessary before the work could be started. But today I know that the project is their own and they are even more dedicated to it than I am. If I had had to deal with a dictator the task might have been easier, but my project would certainly have been subject to severe reappraisal when he died or was deposed. A town is not built like a palace: one depends on the goodwill of the prince, the other is the work of the whole community.

Decisions must be taken democratically, but it is equally important that they should be executed inflexibly. This is an administrative problem. Under Napoleon III, the development of Paris bore little relation to the new needs of the inhabitants until Haussmann was put in charge. The Emperor was astonished at the quality of the work and congratulated Haussmann. "Have you changed the chief architect?" he asked him. "No," replied Haussmann. "You changed the prefect."

Toward Oecumenopolis

We must concede that the extension of urban civilization is inescapable. But we must deal with this growth by building small units linked by the rapid underground transport systems that modern techniques have made possible, develop green spaces—woods, fields and gardens—right in the heart of our cities and, within this framework, enable the inhabitants to choose their own neighborhood and their own way of life. These are the ground rules that should inspire the concept of *oecumenopolis*.

A few generations from now, *oecumenopolis,* in all its ramifications, will cover the entire globe, forming a single worldwide urban system. In practice, steps have already been taken in this direction: in Islamabad, the new capital of Pakistan, and in the renovation of areas of Detroit and Cleveland, for example. It presents a solution through synthesis, by combining the advantages of the old small town with those of megalopolis. It is equivalent to the transformation of a primitive monocellular organism into a pluricellular evolved being. Until now our cities have been like the former, spreading uncontrollably in the manner of malignant growths. We know from biology that only the second model will permit the emergence of a better degree of organization.

TOWARDS A NEW URBAN ERA [6]

In recent times, magazines, newspapers, television, and radio have been full of news about "ecology." We can all remember the old textbook pictures the word *ecology* conjures up: a leafy environment . . . trees . . . ferns . . . moss . . . animals crawling around. But modern man knows—or soon must learn—that ecology is not just a pastoral word. Our mountains and our forests do not stand alone in needing the conservationists' touch. . . .

The nature of contemporary events has made it quite clear that urban life too is dangerously vulnerable to the distortions of man's ingenuity. As a focal point for man's happenings, the urban scene is often subjected to the brunt of man's mistakes and the horrors of his shortsightedness. The "ecology" that governs the city, therefore, is as frail as that of nature itself; and at times, it is more mysterious. . . .

Improving urban life is not an unreasonable task. Cities are not evil; cities are not unmanageable; cities will not respond glowingly to violence or to ineptitude.

They will react, however, to rational and forceful direction, to creative design, to sensitive and practical planning, to humane and relevant programs. Spasmodic responses to immediate crises provide none of these. Therefore, the first

[6] From the Foreword by Senator Edmund S. Muskie (Democrat, Maine) to the book *Up Against the Urban Wall*, edited by Ted Venetoulis and Ward Eisenhauer. Prentice-Hall '71. p vii-xiv. © 1971 by Prentice-Hall, Inc. Reprinted by permission of Prentice-Hall, Inc., Englewood Cliffs, N.J.

and most urgent requirement to improve urban life is a total and unrelenting national pledge to do just that. The "new national commitment" to the city must be a profound, radical, and penetrating effort to marshal the country's ingenuity and resources against urban decay.

Despite all the volumes of literature and the barrels of rhetoric, the nation to this day has not established a comprehensive urban policy outlining what we want our cities to be. It has not assumed a national commitment to make American cities the best in the world. A nation that has landed on the dark side of the moon seems incapable of coping with garbage collection in the dark side of a ghetto alley....

An Outline for Government Policies

Until the nation is willing to make this vital commitment to its cities, they can have no real future. Making the commitment will be difficult; fulfilling it may be even more so. It will require daring experimentation, hard-headed realism and exceptional national political leadership. That leadership must choose its priorities wisely and its alternatives prudently.

At the very minimum, it must:

1. Establish a "tax sharing" program that gives urban areas a definite priority in the distribution of shared revenues. As economist Walter Heller pointed out: "Economic growth creates a glaring fiscal gap; it bestows its revenue bounties on the Federal Government, whose progressive income tax is particularly responsive to growth, and imposes the major part of its burdens on state and local governments." A national program that will distribute monies back to the states and urban communities through a formula that offers fairness and incentive will permit a more flexible and more effective use of tax dollars to cope with urban problems.

2. Reform the national welfare program to provide a guaranteed minimum income for all citizens, eliminating

the stigma and paternalism so degradingly associated with the current system. It is difficult to comprehend how the nation has remained so attached to a welfare system that is detested both by those who rely on it for sustenance and by those who foot the bill. The most sensible alternative deals with establishing a minimum income for all citizens. That income should permit a family head to seek meaningful employment without fear of losing payments he can receive by mere idleness—perhaps the most sinful fault of the present system.

3. Undertake a massive employment program for the inner-city area. Along with housing and education, employment is probably the single most critical issue facing the ghettos. Unemployment in the ghettos ranges seven and eight times higher than in the nation as a whole. Unskilled black workers are the last to be hired; the first to be dismissed; the lowest on the apprenticeship list; and the most difficult to train. But a man without a job . . . can demand no respect from his family and maintain no confidence in himself. The nation must find jobs for the ghetto residents.

The most immediate way is to initiate a vast urban physical renewal program geared to hiring local ghetto residents to work on projects designed to provide the ghetto with needed facilities. These include medical clinics, community day care centers and neighborhood recreational facilities. In order to coordinate the employment program with improving education standards, schools would work intimately with the workers offering courses in the various trades and arranging for incentives to be based on school promotion.

Under such a plan employment would be meaningful and effective. It would not provide an isolated individual with an isolated job that may or may not exist tomorrow. It would offer a full range of employment opportunities, highly visible to local residents, on projects that would improve local conditions. It would have academic incentives to encourage dropouts to stay in school.

4. Undertake a vast inner-city low- and middle-income housing program to make some headway in the estimated 600,000 new dwelling units the country needs every year. This project will require creative and efficient prefabricated housing techniques already used to great advantage in a number of European countries. America can and must do the same.

5. Vigorously enforce open-housing regulations and school-desegregation guidelines that have stifled balanced urban expansion beyond arbitrary geographical city lines.

6. Encourage the development of "new towns," which can be an important ingredient in alleviating the pressures of increased population and mobility. By offering appropriate features of a progressive urban environment, "new towns" promise cities that will remain new and dynamic for succeeding generations. Many of our contemporary urban ills can be laid directly to the period of heavy industrialization and urban migration that caught the city flat-footed. Today these conditions have caught up with us.

New-town planners, blessed with insight on what makes a city decay and what makes a city thrive, can eliminate many of those factors that distort urban life. To do this they will require government help to assemble land and secure the tremendous financing required for such undertakings. Building "new towns," however, cannot be confined to rural or suburban areas. The same imagination and creativity must be applied to building "new neighborhoods" within existing urban settings.

7. Improve the educational opportunities of slum children by undertaking an "impacted-aid" program for ghetto schools similar to the impacted-aid programs for Federal installations. We must also expand the opportunity for community colleges and other local institutions of higher learning to identify with and focus on neighborhood needs.

8. Demand a more enlightened view by industrial leaders of the environment in general and the urban environment specifically. A major industry located in a suburban com-

munity has a great deal of leverage in improving the attitude of that community toward open housing and toward an inner-city resident who must find a reasonable relationship between his employment and his home.

> Manufacturers [said Jeanne Lowe, urban affairs consultant for the *Saturday Review*] are uniquely capable of . . . severing the suburban "white noose" around our core cities, making the metropolitan-housing real estate market work the same for the Negro as for the white, and forcing exclusionist suburbs, exurbs, and smaller cities to accept nonwhites and lower-income families in significant volume and in a harmonious manner.

9. Increase the level of cooperation between local, state and Federal agencies, between suburban and urban officials, between private and public citizens. This cooperation involves concepts such as metropolitan councils of government, special authorities, and local control of special community functions including education, welfare, and housing.

10. Seek new government units that are more visible, more responsive and more alert to the intimacies of local conditions and community patterns.

11. Secure surplus food programs to feed the hungry, medical aid to comfort the impoverished, day care centers to aid working mothers, and community health centers to care for ghetto as well as suburban neighborhoods. When it comes to health, there is no doubt that ghetto Americans are victims of national indifference. The Urban Coalition's Task Force on health revealed the startling facts that the poor have four to eight times the incidence of such chronic conditions as heart disease, arthritis, hyptertension and visual impairment as the nonpoor. It also showed that the ratio of doctors in the ghettos is from one fifth to one half that of the city as a whole.

12. Improve the sophistication of contemporary urban police forces, vastly overhaul and streamline local judicial systems to provide speedy and equitable justice.

13. Provide for a more orderly migration of work forces from one community to another through aggressive planning

relating to growth and demands. "Most of the present urban crisis," the Violence Commission reported, "derives from the almost total absence of positive policies to cope with the large-scale migration of southern Negroes into northern and western cities over the past century, when the number of Negroes living in cities rose from 2.7 to 14.8 million.

14. Overhaul archaic zoning laws, building codes, and urban land-use policies. Presently these are based on principles that are at best outmoded and at worse discriminatory.

15. Improve the quantity and quality of research into urban-oriented problems such as the effectiveness of contemporary educational programs and the realities of drug use and abuse.

16. Provide for a national urban-growth report to summarize annually for the Congress and the public the basic trends of urbanization, an evaluation of these trends, and an assessment of the public and private progress in meeting these trends.

17. Demand that the Federal Government reform its own practices so that it no longer is guilty of illicit behavior we condemn in others—including mediocre architectural design; environmental pollution; insensitive planning; favoritism and corruption in the distribution of funds; and shortsightedness and hardheadedness concerning legitimate citizen views and complaints.

18. Initiate a more healthy and positive dialogue between inner-city blacks and suburban whites. We need this dialogue to lessen antagonism, to prove that continued hostility is disastrous and to show that the good American is ultimately neither silent nor militant but one who cherishes his neighbor whatever his color or ethnic background.

Let's be frank. A large part of the urban issue today is race. Blacks and whites stare at each other from across irrational geographic lines and irrational personal barriers. Blacks resent white institutions reflecting white attitudes and promoting white culture. Whites resent black militancy advocating black power and reflecting a new sense of black identity. The nation must reconcile these differences, must create institutions that are free of racism, and must find ways of sharing the abundance of our society.

A New National Urban Commitment

Once the nation has committed itself to undertaking a healthy and invigorating national program to transform contemporary American cities, then it must face the second and equally essential part of the task.

A commitment to improve urban life is useless if that commitment is made in a vacuum. The city cannot be considered in isolation. It is a vital part of an overall environment that will rise or fall according to remote, often obscure, forces. The American city can prosper only if American society is prospering. And, conversely, society can advance only if the city is advancing.

Again, it is a matter of "ecology." The city cannot improve if suburban attitudes remain rigid, inflexible, and hostile. Inner-city citizens cannot increase their opportunities if white Americans move their plants and their homes beyond the temporary friction. Nor can the city hope to prosper if it continues to be the dumping ground for rural poor, who seek a refuge from the destitution of the countryside and merely add their grief to the city's existing woes. This inbound migration aggravates the urban crisis, further stimulates the outbound migration of whites, which in turn stimulates the urban crises. It is a vicious "ecological" circle that escalates the crisis as each separate element seeks its own separate salvation.

In December 1969, on behalf of the Advisory Commission on Intergovernmental Relations, I introduced in the Senate the balanced urbanization policy and planning act. The bill authorizes a full analysis of urban and rural growth for the development of a national urban policy. It provides additional assistance to state and local governments for developing comprehensive program planning and coordination.

And by placing the power to coordinate urban affairs directly within the executive office of the President the bill would initiate a process at the national level of government to hammer out a balanced urban policy that could ultimately resolve the nightmarish spread of rural decay, central-city deterioration, suburban sprawl, and metropolitan fragmentation.

There is room in this nation for central cities and for suburbs—compact or sprawling; and for rural areas—remote and insulated, but not if each views its condition as separate and isolated from its neighbor. There is but one America and that America is a complex interaction of forces and people.

This leads directly to the next phase of that national commitment we have been discussing. The nation must be equally prepared to invest in its future by investing in the improvement of its total environment. It will mean cleaning rivers and eliminating smog; it will mean resurrecting rural areas and improving rural education; it will mean balanced economic growth and altered social attitudes.

It will mean an excruciating reappraisal of national policies that have encouraged violence, militancy, crime, confrontation, and alienation. It will mean creative, at times radical, institutional adjustments to meet these issues.

This will require not only great moral leadership but also a great amount of money, probably it may take billions of dollars. That money must come from local and state governments, but especially from the Federal Government which has wider and fairer sources of revenue.

It must come from a nation that has reassessed its priorities, diminished its military investments and increased its social obligations.

It must also come from citizens and institutions in the private sphere. One of the greatest needs in this nation today is to direct the latent talents of American industrial and business ingenuity toward social problems. Mr. David

Rockefeller, of Chase Manhattan, addressing a Senate committee, suggested that businessmen often feel that "government officials tend to look upon them as rivals in competition rather than as partners in progress." This impression must be wiped away and a new spirit of unity between the private and public sector must emerge.

The Challenge for the Young

I would like to direct a special word to the students . . . who will be wrestling with the urban problems of the future. You did not make the city what it is, nor are you directly responsible for the conditions of society in general. But you will share the responsibility for saving it.

The society of the future will be even more urban than the society of the past. The streets of the next decade will be more crowded than the streets of today. More schools and more medical facilities will be necessary. Citizens will be crying for better homes and additional recreational space. The gap between the poor and the affluent may be even more severe and, what is worse, it may be more visually apparent.

That's why your generation will have no alternative but to fathom the mysteries of the urban environment, plunge willingly into the morass of relationships that direct and govern its growth and commit yourself to reshaping and redirecting those forces. If the rift between black and white continues . . . if urban education is no more meaningful and urban housing conditions no more tolerable . . . if the suburbs do not open more windows . . . if business does not show more courage and government more flexibility . . . if hunger and poverty are not eradicated in urban slums as well as rural shacks . . . then the next generation of Americans will suffer the horrible consequences of an urban society that could not sustain an important and decent way of life.

You have challenged your elders to seek a new and better way of life; you have demanded reason and tolerance; you have picketed for new priorities and marched to stop hunger and erase poverty and prejudice; you have clamored for commitment and involvement.

The cities will not survive without any of these ingredients. And so we ask whether you will be able to do for us what we could not do for you. Balance the nation's power with the nation's conscience so that the urban citizen is the benefactor, not the victim, of man's victory over nature.

I think you can.

WILL AMERICA MEET ITS HOUSING CRISIS? [7]

There is no question that the United States possesses the financial and total resources to provide a decent home and a suitable living environment for every American family. There is certainly no question that it has the ingenuity to do so. But there is grave doubt, at least in my mind, that it has the *determination of spirit* to do so. For in the end the housing ills of present-day America are largely ills of the national spirit, and all the resources and ingenuity in the world cannot effect a cure for housing—if, indeed, they can even be sufficiently applied—while this illness of spirit persists. And it is persisting, ever more strongly, in the virus of indifference combined with the cancer of racial hostility and fear.

Indifference to the plight of the miserably housed predominates among comfortable Americans. "The plight of the urban poor, the anger of the rebellious, and the bankruptcy of the municipal treasury have not yet hurt or even seriously inconvenienced the vast majority of Americans," the sociologist Herbert Gans has observed. Jason Nathan, New York City's former housing and development admin-

[7] From "The Future and the Crisis," Chapter 9 of *Housing Crisis U.S.A.*, by Joseph P. Fried, reporter on housing and urban affairs for the New York *Times*. Praeger. '71. p 229-32. Copyright © 1971 by Joseph P. Fried. Excerpted and reprinted by permission of Praeger Publishers, Inc., New York.

istrator, declared in late 1969, shortly after a hurricane had
smashed its way into the headlines:

> When a Hurricane Camille strikes and leaves 4,000 or 5,000
> families without homes, the nation's attention is galvanized. The
> Federal Government responds with crisis aid, declarations of emer-
> gency are issued, the National Guard is thrown into action. The
> calamity calls forth emergency responses of all sorts. Yet in our
> cities a thousand times that number of families are ill-housed,
> virtually homeless. But because they are the victims of a slow,
> creeping process rather than a sudden catastrophe, we as a nation
> are neither excited nor galvanized into action, even though the
> emergency, the crisis, the disaster is more real than ten Camilles.

Except for the omission of the plight of rural slum dwellers—just as fully neglected, if not more so, because the slums
of the countryside have been quieter than those of the cities
—these statements sum up the predominant attitude of
America's majority today.

As a result of this attitude, there is a widespread reluctance in Middle America to spend the money that must be
spent, and to invest the national resources that must be in-
vested, if a truly full-scale assault is to be mounted against
the squalor that blights the nation's great cities and its
countryside. Part of this reluctance is certainly understandable. A sizable portion of America's middle class, and especially its lower-middle class, is caught in a vicious squeeze
between spiraling inflation and soaring taxes, which most
emphatically do take a heavy toll of the paycheck brought
home from factory and office. But programs to feed the
poverty-stricken and provide decent shelter for the miserably housed are not responsible for this squeeze, for these
programs are, and always have been, but a minuscule part
of national expenditures.

The villains, if we are to think in terms of villains, are
elsewhere—in the budget-bloated Pentagon; in the headquarters of the wealthy agricultural enterprises . . . ; in the
ranks of the lobbyists for such extravagant ventures as a
supersonic airplane that, had Congress not finally come to

its senses in 1971, already nearly a billion dollars too late, would have soaked up additional billions of public funds so that a small minority of Americans could get to foreign cities a few hours sooner.

But part of the reluctance to spend meaningfully for such needs as low-rent housing and slum clearance extends beyond the squeeze of inflation and taxes. Many middle-class and affluent Americans simply regard such spending as an undeserved handout.

There is more than a little irony in this attitude. Although their members are usually the last to acknowledge it, America's middle and affluent classes have themselves, over all, been the beneficiaries of a vast amount of subsidies from the public treasury, which have played an incalculable role in developing and strengthening much of Middle American society. What, after all, but public subsidies built the roads and highways that made possible the post-World War II suburban explosion—kindled also . . . by the Federal Government's mortgage-backing policies? And what if not a subsidy, are we to call the very sizable income tax deduction that homeowners are permitted for their mortgage interest and property tax payments—a subsidy whose main beneficiaries are the middle class and the well-to-do, and which, again, has been a major factor in the development of suburbia?

Once, in a moment of especially keen frustration, [former Secretary of Housing and Urban Development] George Romney threw out the thought that

maybe we ought to repeal part of the right to deduct the interest rate from the income tax return to bring home to middle-income and affluent families that they are getting a housing subsidy. Maybe that [money] ought to be earmarked to meet the problems of the slums.

(Romney's public relations man hastened to explain that "he just tossed this out as an idea—it is not an Administration position.")

Maybe indeed, but not likely. For the predominant thoughts of middle-class and affluent America today are reflected in the predominant thinking of public officials at all levels. And, whatever the sense of urgency felt by some office-holders over such shortcomings of American life as slums and miserable housing, this sense still remains the exception rather than the rule. One need not be a left-wing malcontent to perceive this. Louis Barba, then president of the very Middle-America-respectable National Association of Home Builders, observed as 1970 was drawing to a close:

> The nation's involvement in the achievement of the housing goals established by the Congress in 1968 is less than total. . . . Establishment of these goals by the Congress and the acceptance of them by two Administrations is insufficiently felt at all levels of government.

And, of course, whether the Nixon Administration has *really* accepted these goals as being of topmost priority is itself uncertain, inasmuch as the commitment of its housing agency [formerly] under George Romney and the commitment of its White House brain trust are not necessarily identical.

Complicating all of these elements is the race issue. Perhaps one of the most tragic contributions of the poison of racial antagonism and fear is its distorting effect on the perception of what a truly adequate campaign to wipe out the nation's housing deficiencies would signify. For many middle-class white Americans, slum-clearance and low-cost-housing programs are largely programs for blacks, and any expansion of these programs means giving "them" more. But . . . there are more whites in substandard housing than blacks, and more whites unable to afford decent housing on their own than blacks, and any program truly mounted to provide a decent home and a suitable living environment for every American family cannot possibly be referred to with justification as a "black" program.

But so the matter is perceived among a large segment of Middle America, and so it will continue to be perceived for a long time to come. And this fact, if no other, makes it difficult to hope for a national effort vast enough not only to make a reality of the goals of the 1968 Housing Act, but also to wipe out the much greater deficits in American housing that these goals . . . severely understate.

One would like to be proved wrong in this discouragement. But from the vantage point of the early 1970s, the vision of an America acting to provide a decent home and a suitable living environment for all its citizens, or even making significant strides toward redeeming this already two-decades-old pledge, seems at times as realistic as the hope of a palace-studded Camelot suddenly arising out of the squalor and decay of Brownsville in Brooklyn.

BIBLIOGRAPHY

An asterisk (*) preceding a reference indicates that the article or a part of it has been reprinted in this book.

BOOKS AND PAMPHLETS

Aaron, H. J. Shelter and subsidies; who benefits from federal housing policies? Brookings. '72.

Abrams, Charles. The city is the frontier. Harper. '65

Alexander, Theron. Human development in an urban age. Prentice-Hall. '73.

Banfield, E. C. The unheavenly city; the nature and future of our urban crisis. Little. '70.

Bell, Gwen and Tyrwhitt, Jaqueline, eds. Human identity in the urban environment. Penguin. '72.

Bent, A. E. Escape from anarchy: a strategy for urban survival. new ed. Memphis State University Press. '72.

Boyce, B. N. and Turoff, Sidney. Minority groups and housing; a bibliography, 1950-1970. General Learning Press. Morristown, N.J. 07960. '72.

Breckenfeld, V. G. Columbia and the new cities. Washburn. '71.

Burghardt, Stephen, ed. Tenants and the urban housing crisis. New Press. '72.

Canty, Donald, ed. The new city. Praeger (for Urban America, Inc.). '69.
    Papers selected from conferences held in 1969 by the National Committee on Urban Growth Policy.

Clapp, J. A. New towns & urban policy: planning metropolitan growth. Dunellen. '71.

Commission on the Cities in the '70's. The state of the cities: report; Senator Fred R. Harris and Mayor John V. Lindsay, cochairmen. Praeger. '72.

Committee for Economic Development. Research and Policy Committee. Financing the nation's housing needs; a statement on national policy. The Committee. 477 Madison Ave. New York 10022. '73.

Drury, M. J. Mobile homes; the unrecognized revolution in American housing. Cornell University. New York State College of Home Economics. Department of Housing & Design. Ithaca, N.Y. 14850.

Faltermayer, E. K. Redoing America; a nationwide report on how to make our cities and suburbs livable. Harper. '68.

*Fried, J. P. Housing crisis U.S.A. Praeger. '71; paper ed. Penguin Books. '72.

Greer, S. A. The urbane view; life and politics in metropolitan America. Oxford University Press. '72.

Haar, C. M. ed. The end of innocence; a suburban reader. Scott, Foresman. '72.

Haar, C. M. Land-use planning; a casebook on the use, misuse, and re-use of urban land. 2d ed. Little. '71.

Hecht, J. L. Because it is right: integration in housing. Little. '70.

Jacobs, Jane. The death and life of great American cities. Random House. '61.

Kramer, John, ed. North American suburbs; politics, diversity, and change. Glendessary. '72.

Long, N. E. The unwalled city; rebuilding the urban community. Basic Books. '72.

Lowe, J. R. Cities in a race with time; progress and poverty in America's renewing cities. Random House. '67.

McClellan, G. S. ed. Land use in the United States. (Reference Shelf. v 43, no 2) Wilson. '71.

McClellan, G. S. ed. Protecting our environment. (Reference Shelf. v 42, no 1) Wilson. '70

McQuade, Walter, ed. Cities fit to live in and how we can make them happen; recent articles on the urban environment. (Urban environment no 1) Macmillan '71.

Masotti, L. H. and Hadden, J. K. eds. (Urban affairs annual reviews, v 7) The urbanization of the suburbs. Sage. '73.

Mumford, Lewis. The culture of cities. Harcourt. '70.

Newman, Oscar. Defensible space; crime prevention through urban design. Macmillan. '72.

Perloff, H. S. ed. The quality of the urban environment; essays on new resources in an urban age. Resources for the Future, Inc. 1755 Massachusetts Ave. N.W. Washington, D.C. 20036. '69. (Distributed by Johns Hopkins Press)

Perloff, H. S. and Sandberg, N. C. New towns: why and for whom? Praeger. '73.

Perloff, H. S. and Wingo, Lowdon, Jr., eds. Issues in urban economics; based on papers presented at a conference sponsored by the Committee on Urban Economics of Resources for the Future, Inc. Resources for the Future, Inc. 1755 Massachusetts Ave. N.W. Washington, D.C. 20036. '68.

Pynoos, Jan and others. (Social Research & Public Policy Ser.) Housing urban America. Aldine. '73.

Reeb, D. J. and Kirk, J. T. Housing the poor. Praeger. '73.

Smith, Fred. Man and his urban environment; a manual of specific considerations for the seventies and beyond. Man and His Urban Environment Project. Room 5600, 30 Rockefeller Plaza. New York 10020. '73.

Sternlieb, G. S. and Indik, B. P. The ecology of welfare: housing and the welfare crisis in New York City. Transaction. '73. (Distributed by Dutton)

Stewart, Murray. The city: problems of planning. Penguin. '72.

Stewart, M. S. Housing: a nationwide crisis. (Pamphlet no 495) Public Affairs Committee. 381 Park Ave. S. New York 10016.

Task Force on Environmental Problems of the Inner City. Our urban environment and our most endangered people: a report to the administrator of the Environmental Protection Agency. U.S. Gov. Ptg. Office. Washington, D.C. 20401. '72.

United States. Advisory Commission on Intergovernmental Relations. Urban and rural America: policies for future growth; report. Supt. of Docs. Washington, D.C. 20402. '68.

United States. Commission on Population Growth and the American Future. Population and the American future; report. Supt. of Docs. Washington, D.C. 20402. '72.

United States. Congress. Senate. Committee on Interior and Insular Affairs. National land use policy; hearings on S. 3354. 91st Congress, 2d session. U.S. Gov. Ptg. Office. Washington, D.C. 20401. '70.

United States. Council on Environmental Quality. Environmental quality: first annual report, together with President's message to Congress, transmitted to Congress August 1970. Supt. of Docs. Washington, D.C. 20402. '70.

United States. Council on Environmental Quality. Environmental quality: the second annual report. Supt. of Docs. Washington, D.C. 20402. '71.

United States. Executive Office of the President. Domestic Council. Report on national growth, 1972- . Supt. of Docs. Washington, D.C. 20402. '72.

United States. Federal Housing Authority. Fourth annual report on national housing goals. (House document no. 92-319) 92d Congress, 2d session. U.S. Gov. Ptg. Office. Washington, D.C. 20401. '72.

United States. National Commission on Urban Problems. Building the American city; report to the Congress and to the President of the United States. Supt. of Docs. Washington, D.C. 20402. '69.

United States. National Commission on Urban Problems. Housing conditions in urban poverty areas. (Research report no 9) U.S. Gov. Ptg. Office. Washington, D.C. 20401. '68.

United States. National Goals Research Staff. Toward balanced growth: quantity with quality; report. Supt. of Docs. Washington, D.C. 20402. '70.

United States. President's Committee on Urban Housing. A decent home; report. Supt. of Docs. Washington, D.C. 20402. '69.

*Venetoulis, T. G. and Eisenhauer, Ward, eds. Up against the urban wall. Prentice-Hall. '71.
    Reprinted in this book: Excerpts from the Foreword by Senator Edmund S. Muskie, p vii-xiv.

*Whyte, W. H. The last landscape. Doubleday. '68.

Yin, R. K. ed. The city in the seventies. Peacock Publishers. '72.

PERIODICALS

America. 128:112-14. F. 10, '73. A Catholic challenge: open housing. J. L. Hecht.

*American Federationist. 79:1-8. Ag. '72. Housing: clear needs, dim prospects. Joyce Pazianos.

Architectural Forum. 132:62-5. My. '70. Zoning; the new battleground; excerpts. Clarence Funnye.

Architectural Forum. 138:66-70. Mr. '73. Dreary deadlock revisited: public housing programs are being reappraised and redirected. But to what end? Al Hirshen and Richard LeGates.

Center Magazine. 6:67-73. N./D. '73. The future of cities. R. H. Wittcoff.

*Challenge. 16:8-15. S.-O. '73. The once and future city. Bennett Harrison.

*Christian Science Monitor. p 14. O. 5, '72. Condominiums booming all over. Martin Skala.

*Christian Science Monitor. p 16. O. 25, '72. Urbs, slurbs, suburbs—and regional government. Martin Gallent.

Christian Science Monitor. p 11. Ag. 6, '73. Labor study finds U.S. housing near crisis. Ed Townsend.

*Christian Science Monitor. p 1+. S. 20, '73. A boost for home mortgages. H. B. Ellis.

Christian Science Monitor. p 18. O. 18, '73. Housing: a public trust? [editorial]

Christianity and Crisis. 33:99-103. My. 28, '73. Housing the poor: a displaced program. L. S. Jung.

City. 5:12-95. Ja.-F. '71. The suburbs: frontier of the '70s [special issue that examines the phenomenon of suburban America from many viewpoints].

*City. 6:64-5+. Ja.-F. '72. Reshaping metropolitan America. S. M. Linowitz.

City. 6:29-44. Mr.-Ap. '72. Metropolity. Donald Canty.

*City. 6.31-4. Winter '72. Unlearned lessons in the history of federal housing aid. M. C. McFarland.

Commentary. 56:74-7. O. '73. Thinking about the city. Walter Berns.

Commonweal. 97:292-3. Ja. 5, '73. No room for the poor. Sally Thran.

*Commonweal. 98:474-8. S. 7, '73. Survival kit for public housing. J. S. Fuerst.

Dissent. 22:455-63. Fall '73. Caliban's abode. Murray Hausknecht.

Ebony. 27:60-4+. S. '72. Countdown in housing. Alex Poinsett.

*Focus/Midwest. v9, no 58:7-9. '73. The wasting of Chicago. Pierre De Vise.

Futurist. October 1970 issue. Special report on population distribution.
    Includes: Is megalopolis inevitable? J. P. Pickard; Toward a rural-urban balance. O. L. Freeman; Growth centers and new communities. I. P. Halpern; The U.S. plan for curbing megalopolis. Maurice Stans.

Futurist. 6:5-12. F. '72. The American city—a forecast. Edgardo Contini.

*Futurist. 6:238-9. D. '72. By the year 2000: half of U.S. people may live in two urban regions.

*Horizon. 14:36-41. Autumn '72. An urban civilization without cities? Irving Kristol.

*Horizon. 15:14-15. Autumn '73. Our floating suburbs. Elaine Kendall.

HUD Challenge. 4:2-5. Mr. '73. Rehabilitation, conservation, preservation. J. E. Armstrong.

*HUD Challenge. 4:5-9. My. '73. Housing design for elderly needs. M. C. McGuire.

*HUD Challenge. 4:24-5. Je '73. Cincinnati's Better Housing League. C. G. Stocker.

HUD Challenge. 4.6-11. S. '73. Defensible space. Oscar Newman.

HUD Challenge. 4:2-15. N. '73. President Nixon's message on federal housing policy, Sept. 19, 1973.

Journal of Housing. 27:527-9. N. 23, '70. Cemeteries becoming critical factor in land-use planning as urban areas grow. Martha Fisher.

Journal of Housing. 29:335-8. Ag. '72. Cooperative housing. Beth Van Houten.

Journal of Housing. 30:165-9. Ap. '73. A policy statement by the board of governors of the National Association of Housing and Redevelopment Officials, March 1973.

Journal of the American Institute of Planners. 39:229-42. Jl. '73. National urban growth policy: 1972 congressional and executive action. Norman Beckman and Susan Harding.

*Los Angeles Times. p 1+. Jl 15, '73. Urban wastelands—isles of hopelessness.

Los Angeles Times. p I 7. Ag. 20, '73. Need for a modern homestead act. P. R. Porter.

Minnesota Law Review. 53:1163-78. Je. '69. Towards a national policy on balanced communities. O. L. Freeman.

Nation. 214:617-21. My. 15, '72. The New-Town mirage. Leonard Downie, jr.

Nation. 214:814-16. Je. 26, '72. Homes for the poor: the well-insured swindle. G. C. Thelen, jr.

*Nation. 216:304-8. Mr. 5, '73. The latest panacea. J. P. Fried.

Nation. 217:493-6. N. 12, '73. Hidden successes of public housing. J. S. Fuerst.

Nation's Cities. 8:15+. D. '70. The New Town idea is vastly overrated. A. L. Otten.

*New Leader. 50:27-32. Ap. 17, '72. Housing. R. J. Margolis.

New Republic. 166:11. My. 27, '72. Falling-apart houses. Ralph Nader.

*New Republic. 169:19-21. S. 25, '73. A fresh approach to integrated housing: racially changing neighborhoods. Charles Hammer.

New Republic. 169:19-21. O. 20, '73. Don't plan a home of your own. David Sanford.

*New York Times. p 41. O. 26, '72. Housing study: high rise—high crime. Jack Rosenthal.

New York Times. p 1+. Ap. 20, '73. Authority over land use is termed a public right. Gladwin Hill.

New York Times. p 1+. Je. 11, '73. Home costs rise 91.7% in 20 years, outstripped only by service industry. Bill Kovach.

New York Times. p 1+. S. 3, '73. Public control growing in a land use revolution. Gladwin Hill.

New York Times. p 23. S. 4, '73. New land ethic: its spread raises political and legal issues to be resolved by public. Gladwin Hill.

New York Times. p 1+. S. 20, '73. Federal housing reform unlikely despite scandal. John Herbers.

New York Times. p 1+. S. 20. '73. President urges U.S. allowances to spur housing. John Herbers.

*New York Times. p 44. S. 20. '73. Housing or facade? [editorial]

New York Times. p 1+. S 28, '73. $10.6-billion housing bill killed by House Rules unit. John Hebers.

New York Times. p R1+. O. 7, '73. For a co-op owner, the lessons are painful. Arthur Unger.

New York Times. p 10. O. 10. '73. Urban planners' seminar puts emphasis on housing.

Newsweek. 80:31-4+. D. 18, '72. Living with crime, U.S.A.

*Public Interest. No 32:34-42. Summer '73. The cost of housing. B. Bruce-Briggs.

*Réalités (English ed.). No. 263:20-1. O. '72. What to do with the cities. Constantinos Doxiadis.

*Ripon Forum. 9:6-7. S. '73. Unrenewed urban renewal. Ralph Thayer.

Ripon Forum. 9:19-23. O. '73. The fate of new towns. W. K. Woods.

Saturday Review. 54:80-6+. D. 4, '71. Cities on the sea? John Lear.

Social Action. 39:14-23. N. '72. Current trends in housing rehabilitation. Clara Fox.

Social Policy. 3:28-32. My./Je. '72. Too poor for public housing: Roger Starr's poverty preferences. Al Hirshen and Vivian Brown.

Social Problems. 16:219-26. Fall '68. Mobile homes: instant suburbia or transportable slums? R. M. French and J. K. Hadden.

*Society. 9:38-42. F. '72. Death of the American dream house. G. S. Sternlieb.

Society. 9:31-7. Jl. '72. The politics of housing; mortgage bankers. M. E. Stone.

Society. 9:19-32+. S. '72. The nation of Newark; symposium [special issue]
        Bibliography p 95.

U.S. News & World Report. 73:30-4. D. 18, '72. Did riots kill these neighborhoods?
        Special report on the aftermath of violence.

*U.S. News & World Report. 74:51-4. Je. 18, '73. What can be done to save the big cities; interview with James T. Lynn, secretary of housing and urban development.

U.S. News & World Report. 75:48-9. Ag. 6, '73. Why rush to condominiums is picking up speed.

Urban Affairs Quarterly. 8:161-79. D. '72. Private investment and public housing: a review of recent exploitation. M. A. Stegman.

Urban and Social Change Review. 5:16-19. Fall '71. New towns as "self-sufficient" growth centers—dream or feasible reality? R. W. Scott.

Vital Speeches of the Day. 39:297-300. Mr. 1, '73. Our housing and our cities; address, November 1972. Perry Prentice.

Wall Street Journal. p 26. D. 6, '72. The changing aspirations of cities. M. W. Karmin.

*Wall Street Journal. p 1. S. 21, '73. Abandoned houses are given free to people willing to restore them. Gail Bronson.

Washington Post. p C 3. D. 10, '72. Public housing: evicting the poor. E. L. Meyer.

Weekly Compilation of Presidential Documents. 7:1132-5. Ag. 9, '71. Environmental quality: the President's message to the Congress [August 6, 1971], transmitting the second annual report of the Council on environmental quality.

World. 1:40-1. D 19, '72. Floating cities. R. B. Fuller.